Siegel's
CRIMINAL PROCEDURE

Essay and Multiple-Choice Questions and Answers

Brian N. Siegel
J.D., Columbia Law School

and

Lazar Emanuel
J.D., Harvard Law School

Aspen Law & Business
Legal Education Division
New York   Gaithersburg

Printed in the United States of America.

ISBN 0-7355-2733-4

1 2 3 4 5 6 7 8 9 0

This book is intended as a general review of a legal subject. It is not intended as a source of advice for the solution of legal matters or problems. For advice on legal matters, the reader should consult an attorney.

About Aspen Law & Business
Legal Education Division

Aspen Law & Business is proud to welcome Emanuel Publishing Corporation's highly successful study aids to its list of law school publications. As part of the Aspen family, Steve and Lazar Emanuel will continue their work on these popular titles, widely purchased by students for more than a quarter century. With the addition of the Emanuel titles, Aspen now offers the most comprehensive selection of outstanding publications for the discerning law student.

ASPEN LAW & BUSINESS
A Division of Aspen Publishers, Inc.
A Wolters Kluwer Company
www.aspenpublishers.com

About the Authors

Professor Brian N. Siegel received his *Juris Doctorate* from Columbia Law School, where he was designated a Harlan Fiske Stone Scholar for academic excellence. He is the author of *How to Succeed in Law School* and numerous works pertaining to preparation for the California Bar examination. Professor Siegel has taught as a member of the adjunct faculty at Pepperdine School of Law and Whittier College School of Law, as well as for the UCLA Extension Program.

Lazar Emanuel is a graduate of Harvard Law School. In 1950, he became a founding partner of the New York law firm now known as Cowan, Liebowitz & Latman. From 1960 through 1971, he was president of Communications Industries Corp., multiple licensee of radio and television stations in the Northeast. He has edited many of the publications in the Professor Series of study aids and in the Siegel's Series. He is publisher of The New York Professional Responsibility Report and author of *Latin For Lawyers*.

Acknowledgment

The authors gratefully acknowledge the assistance of the California Committee of Bar Examiners, which provided access to questions upon which many of the questions in this book are based.

Introduction

Although your grades are a significant factor in obtaining a summer internship or permanent position at a law firm, no formalized preparation for finals is offered at most law schools. Students, for the most part, are expected to fend for themselves in learning the exam-taking process. Ironically, law school exams ordinarily bear little correspondence to the teaching methods used by professors during the school year. They require you to spend most of your time briefing cases. Although many claim this is "great preparation" for issue-spotting on exams, it really isn't. Because you focus on one principle of law at a time, you don't get practice in relating one issue to another or in developing a picture of the entire course. When exams finally come, you're forced to make an abrupt 180-degree turn. Suddenly, you are asked to recognize, define and discuss a variety of issues buried within a single multi-issue fact pattern. In most schools, you are then asked to select among a number of possible answers, all of which look inviting but only one of which is right.

The comprehensive course outline you've created so diligently and with such pain means little if you're unable to apply its contents on your final exams. There is a vast difference between reading opinions in which the legal principles are clearly stated, and applying those same principles to hypothetical exams and multiple choice questions.

The purpose of this book is to help you bridge the gap between memorizing a rule of law and **_understanding how to use it_** in the context of an exam. After an initial overview describing the exam writing process, you will be presented with a large number of hypotheticals which test your ability to write analytical essays and to pick the right answers to multiple-choice questions. **_Do them — all of them!_** Then review the suggested answers which follow. You'll find that the key to superior grades lies in applying your knowledge through questions and answers, not rote memory.

In the sample answers (both to the essays and to the multiple choice), you will notice references to *Emanuel* on *Criminal Procedure,* part of the Emanuel Law Outline (ELO) Series. Each reference tells you where in the outline to find the relevant discussion. Thus, a reference to "ELO Ch. 4–III(C)(1)(d)" means *Emanuel* on *Criminal Procedure*, Chapter 4, section (Roman numeral) III, capital letter C within that section, number 1, paragraph d. This notation is perhaps less convenient than page numbers, but it helps us keep the reference constant from one edition of a book to the next.

GOOD LUCK !

Table of Contents

Preparing Effectively for Essay Examinations

Essay Questions

Essay Answers

Multiple-Choice Questions

Multiple-Choice Answers

Table and Index

Preparing Effectively for Essay Examinations*

To achieve superior scores on essay exams, a student must (i) learn and understand "blackletter" principles and rules of law for each subject, and (ii) analyze how those principles of law arise within a test fact pattern. One of the most common misconceptions about law school is that you must memorize each word on every page of your casebooks or outlines to do well on exams. The reality is that you can commit an entire casebook to memory and still do poorly on an exam. Reviewing hundreds of student answers has shown us that most students can recite the rules. The ones who do *best* on exams understand how problems (issues) stem from the rules which they have memorized and how to communicate their analysis of these issues to the grader. The following pages cover what you need to know to achieve superior scores on your law school essay exams.

The "ERC" Process

To study effectively for law school exams you must be able to *"ERC"* (*E*lementize, *R*ecognize, and *C*onceptualize) each legal principle listed in the table of contents of your casebooks and course outlines. *Elementizing* means reducing the legal theories and rules you learn, down to a concise, straightforward statement of their essential elements. Without a knowledge of these precise elements, it is not possible to anticipate all of the potential issues which can arise under them.

For example, if you are asked, "what is self-defense?", it is *not* sufficient to say, "self-defense is permitted when, if someone is about to hit you, you can prevent him from doing it." This layperson description would leave a grader wondering if you had actually attended law school. An accurate elementization of the self-defense principle would be something like this: "Where one reasonably believes she is in imminent danger of an offensive touching, she may assert whatever force she reasonably believes necessary under the circumstances to prevent the offensive touching from occurring." This formulation correctly shows that there are four separate, distinct elements which must be satisfied for this defense to be successfully asserted: (i) the actor must have a *reasonable belief* that (ii) the touching which she seeks to prevent is *offensive*, (iii) the offensive touching is *imminent*, and (iv) the actor must use no greater force than she *reasonably*

---

* To illustrate the principles of effective exam preparation, we have used examples from Torts and Constitutional Law. However, these principles apply to all subjects. One of the most difficult tasks faced by law students is learning how to apply principles from one area of the law to another. We leave it to you, the reader, to think of comparable examples for the subject-matter of this book.

believes is necessary under the circumstances to prevent the offensive touching from occurring.

Recognizing means perceiving or anticipating which words within a legal principle are likely to be the source of issues, and how those issues are likely to arise within a hypothetical fact pattern. With respect to the self-defense concept, there are four *potential* issues. Did the actor reasonably believe that the person against whom the defense is being asserted was about to make an offensive contact upon her? Was the contact imminent? Would the contact have been offensive? Did the actor use only such force as she reasonably believed was necessary to prevent the imminent, offensive touching?

Conceptualizing means imagining situations in which the elements of a rule of law have given rise to factual issues. *Unless a student can illustrate to herself an application of each element of a rule of law, she does not truly understand the legal principles behind the rule!* In our opinion, the inability to conjure up hypothetical problems involving particular rules of law foretells a likelihood that issues involving those rules will be missed on an exam. It is therefore *crucial* to (i) *recognize* that issues result from the interaction of facts with the appropriate words defining a rule of law; and ii) develop the ability to *conceptualize* fact patterns involving each of the words contained in the rule.

For example, an illustration of the "reasonable belief" portion of the self-defense principle in tort law might be the following:

> One evening, A and B had an argument at a bar. A screamed at B, "I'm going to get a knife and stab you!" A then ran out of the bar. B, who was armed with a concealed pistol, left the bar about 15 minutes later. As B was walking home, he suddenly heard running footsteps coming up from behind him. B drew his pistol, turned and shot the person advancing toward him (who was only about ten feet away when the shooting occurred). When B walked over to his victim, he recognized that the person he had killed was not A (but was instead another individual who had simply decided to take an evening jog). There would certainly be an issue whether B had a reasonable belief that the person who was running behind him was A. In the subsequent wrongful-death action, the victim's estate would certainly contend that the earlier threat by A was not enough to give B a reasonable belief that the person running behind him was A. B could certainly contend in rebuttal that given the prior altercation at the bar, A's threat, the darkness, and the fact that the incident occurred within a time frame soon after A's threat, his belief that A was about to attack him was "reasonable."

An illustration of how use of the word "imminent" might generate an issue is the following:

> X and Y had been feuding for some time. One afternoon, X suddenly attacked Y with a hunting knife. However, Y was able to wrest the knife away From X.

At that point X retreated about four feet away from Y and screamed: "You were lucky this time, but next time I'll have a gun and you'll be finished." Y, having good reason to believe that X would subsequently carry out his threats (after all, X had just attempted to kill Y), immediately thrust the knife into X's chest, killing him. While Y certainly had a reasonable belief that X would attempt to kill him the *next time* the two met, Y would probably *not* be able to successfully assert the self-defense privilege since the "imminency" element was absent.

A fact pattern illustrating the actor's right to use only that force which is reasonably necessary under the circumstances might be the following:

D rolled up a newspaper and was about to strike E on the shoulder with it. As D pulled back his arm for the purpose of delivering the blow, E drew a knife and plunged it into D's chest. While E had every reason to believe that D was about to deliver an offensive impact on him, E probably could not successfully assert the self-defense privilege because the force he utilized in response was greater than reasonably necessary under the circumstances to prevent the impact. E could simply have deflected D's prospective blow or punched D away. The use of a knife constituted a degree of force by E which was *not* reasonable, given the minor injury which he would have suffered from the newspaper's impact.

"Mental gymnastics" such as these must be played with every element of every rule you learn.

Issue-Spotting

One of the keys to doing well on an essay examination is issue-spotting. In fact, issue spotting is *the* most important skill you will learn in law school. If you recognize all of the legal issues, you can always find an applicable rule of law (if there is any) by researching the issues. However, if you fail to perceive an issue, you may very well misadvise your client about the likelihood of success or failure. It is important to remember that (1) an issue is a question to be decided by the judge or jury; and (2) a question is "in issue" when it can be disputed or argued about at trial. The bottom line is that *if you don't spot an issue, you can't discuss it.*

The key to issue-spotting is to approach a problem in the same way as an attorney would. Let's assume you're a lawyer and someone enters your office with a legal problem. He will recite the facts to you and give you any documents that may be pertinent. He will then want to know if he can sue (or be sued, if your client seeks to avoid liability). To answer your client's question intelligently, you will have to decide the following: (1) what theories can possibly be asserted by your client; (2) what defense or defenses can possibly be raised to these theories; (3) what issues may arise if these theories and defenses are asserted; (4) what arguments can each side make to persuade the factfinder to resolve the issue in his favor; and (5) finally, what will the *likely* outcome of each issue be. *All the issues which can possibly arise at trial should be discussed in your answer.*

How to Discuss an Issue

Keep in mind that *rules of law are the guides to issues* (*i.e.*, an issue arises where there is a question whether the facts do, or do not, satisfy an element of a rule); a rule of law *cannot dispose of an issue* unless the rule can reasonably be *applied to the facts.*

A good way to learn how to discuss an issue is to start with the following mini-hypothetical and the two student responses which follow it.

Mini-Hypothetical

A and B were involved in making a movie which was being filmed at a bar. The script called for A to appear to throw a bottle (which was actually a rubber prop) at B. The fluorescent lighting at the bar had been altered, the subdued blue lights being replaced with rather bright white lights. The cameraperson had stationed herself just to the left of the swinging doors which served as the main entrance to the bar. As the scene was unfolding, C, a regular patron of the bar, unwittingly walked into it. The guard who was stationed immediately out-side the bar, had momentarily left his post to visit the restroom. As C pushed the barroom doors inward, the left door panel knocked the camera to the ground with a resounding crash. The first (and only) thing which C saw, how-ever, was A (who was about 5 feet from C) getting ready to throw the bottle at B, who was at the other end of the bar (about 15 feet from A). Without hesita-tion, C pushed A to the ground and punched him in the face. Plastic surgery was required to restore A's profile to its Hollywood-handsome pre-altercation form.

Discuss A's right against C.

Pertinent Principles of Law:

1. Under the rule defining the prevention-of-crime privilege, if one sees that someone is about to commit what she reasonably believes to be a felony or misdemeanor involving a breach of the peace, she may exercise whatever degree of force is reasonably necessary under the circumstances to prevent that person from committing the crime.

2. Under the defense-of-others privilege, where one reasonably believes that someone is about to cause an offensive contact upon a third party, she may use whatever force is reasonably necessary under the circumstances to prevent the contact. Some jurisdictions, however, limit this privilege to situations in which

the actor and the third party are related.

First Student Answer

"Did C commit an assault and battery upon A?

"An assault occurs where the defendant intentionally causes the plaintiff to be reasonably in apprehension of an imminent, offensive touching. The facts state that C punched A to the ground. Thus, a battery would have occurred at this point. We are also told that C punched A in the face. It is reasonable to assume that A saw the punch being thrown at him, and therefore A felt in imminent danger of an offensive touching. Based upon the facts, C is liable for an assault and battery upon A.

"Were C's actions justifiable under the defense-of-others privilege?

"C could successfully assert the defense of others and prevention of crime privileges. When C opened the bar doors, A appeared to be throwing the bottle at B. Although the "bottle" was actually a prop, C had no way of knowing this fact. Also, it was necessary for C to punch A in the face to assure that A could not get back up, retrieve the bottle, and again throw it at B. While the plastic surgery required by A is unfortunate, C could not be successfully charged with assault and battery."

Second Student Answer

"Assault and Battery:

"C committed an assault (causing A to be reasonably in apprehension of an imminent, offensive contact) when A saw C's punch about to hit him, and battery (causing an offensive contact upon A) when he (i) C knocked A to the ground, and (ii) C punched A.

"Defense-of-Others/Prevention-of-Crime Defenses:

"C would undoubtedly assert the privileges of defense-of-others (where defendant reasonably believed the plaintiff was about to make an offensive contact upon a third party, he was entitled to use whatever force was reasonably necessary to prevent the contact); and prevention-of-crime defense (where one reasonably believes another is about to commit a felony or misdemeanor involving a breach of the peace, he may exercise whatever force is reasonably necessary to prevent that person from committing a crime).

"A could contend that C was not reasonable in believing that A was about to cause harm to B because the enhanced lighting at the bar and camera crash should have indicated to C, a regular customer, that a movie was being filmed. However, C could probably successfully contend in rebuttal that his belief was reasonable in light of the facts that (i) he had not seen the camera when he attacked A, and (ii) instantaneous action was required (he did not have time to notice the enhanced lighting around the bar).

"A might also contend that the justification was forfeited because the degree of force used by C was not reasonable, since C did not have to punch A in the face after A had already been pushed to the ground (*i.e.*, the danger to B was no longer present). However, C could argue in rebuttal that it was necessary to knock out A (an individual with apparently violent propensities) while the opportunity existed, rather than risk a drawn-out scuffle in which A might prevail. The facts do not indicate how big A and C were; but assuming C was not significantly larger than A, C's contention will probably be successful. If, however, C was significantly larger than A, the punch may have been excessive (since C could presumably have simply held A down)."

Critique

Let's examine the First Student Answer first. It mistakenly phrases as an "issue" the assault and battery committed by C upon A. While the actions creating these torts must be mentioned in the facts to provide a foundation for a discussion of the applicable privileges, there was no need to discuss them further because they were not the issue the examiners were testing for.

The structure of the initial paragraph of First Student Answer is also incorrect. After an assault is defined in the first sentence, the second sentence abruptly describes the facts necessary to constitute the commission of a battery. The third sentence then sets forth the elements of a battery. The fourth sentence completes the discussion of assault by describing the facts pertaining to that tort. The two-sentence break between the original mention of assault and the facts which constitute this tort is confusing; the facts which call for the application of a rule should be mentioned *immediately* after the rule is stated.

A more serious error, however, occurs in the second paragraph of the First Student Answer. While there is an allusion to the correct principle of law (prevention of crime), the *rule is not defined*. As a consequence, the grader can only guess why the student thinks the facts set forth in the subsequent sentences are significant. A grader reading this answer could not be certain that the student recognized that the issues revolved around the *reasonable belief* and *necessary force* elements of the prevention-of-crime privilege. Superior exam-writing requires that the pertinent facts be *tied* directly and clearly to the operative rule.

The Second Student Answer is very much better than the First Answer. It disposes of C's assault and battery upon A in a few words (yet tells the grader that the writer knows these torts are present). More importantly, the grader can easily see the issues which would arise if the prevention-of crime-privilege were asserted (*i.e.*, "whether C's belief that A was about to commit a crime against B was reasonable" and "whether C used unnecessary force in punching A after A had been knocked to the ground"). Finally, it also utilizes all the facts by indicating how each attorney would assert those facts which are most advantageous to her client.

Structuring Your Answer

Graders will give high marks to a clearly-written, well-structured answer. Each issue you discuss should follow a specific and consistent structure which a grader can easily follow.

The Second Student Answer above basically utilizes the *I-R-A-A-O format* with respect to each issue. In this format, the *"I"* stands for the word *"Issue;"* the *"R"* for *"Rule of law"*; the initial *"A"* for the words *"one side's Argument"*; the second *"A"* for *"the other party's rebuttal Argument"*; and the *"O"* for your *"Opinion as to how the issue would be resolved."* The *I-R-A-A-O* format emphasizes the importance of (1) discussing **both** sides of an issue, and (2) communicating to the grader that when an issue arises, an attorney can only advise her client as to the **probable** decision on that issue.

A somewhat different format for analyzing each issue is the *I-R-A-C format*. Here, the *"I"* stands for *"Issue";* the *"R"* for *"Rule of law";* the *"A"* for *"Application of the facts to the rule of law";* and the *"C"* for *"Conclusion."* *I-R-A-C* is a legitimate approach to the discussion of a particular issue, within the time constraints imposed by the question. The *I-R-A-C format* must be applied to each issue; it is not the solution to an entire exam answer. If there are six issues in a question, for example, you should offer six separate, independent *I-R-A-C* analyses.

We believe that the *I-R-A-C* approach is preferable to the *I-R-A-A-O* formula. However, either can be used to analyze and organize essay exam answers. Whatever format you choose, however, you should be consistent throughout the exam and remember the following rules:

First, *analyze all of the relevant facts*. Facts have significance in a particular case *only as they come under the applicable rules of law*. The facts presented must be analyzed and examined to see if they do or do not satisfy one element or another of the applicable rules, and the essential facts and rules must be stated and argued in your analysis.

Second, you must communicate to the grader the **precise rule of law** controlling the facts. In their eagerness to commence their arguments, students sometimes fail to state the applicable rule of law first. Remember, the **"R"** in either format stands for "Rule of Law." Defining the rule of law **before** an analysis of the facts is essential in order to allow the grader to follow your reasoning.

Third, it is important to treat **each side of an issue with equal detail.** If a hypothetical describes how an elderly man was killed when he ventured upon the land of a huge power company to obtain a better view of a nuclear reactor, your sympathies might understandably fall on the side of the old man. The grader will nevertheless expect you to see and make every possible argument for the other side. Don't permit your personal viewpoint to affect your answer! A good lawyer never does! When discussing an issue, always state the arguments for each side.

Finally, don't forget to **state your opinion or conclusion** on each issue. Keep in mind, however, that your opinion or conclusion is probably the **least** important part of an exam answer. Why? Because your professor knows that no attorney can tell her client exactly how a judge or jury will decide a particular issue. By definition, an issue is a legal dispute which can go either way. An attorney, therefore, can offer her client only her best opinion about the likelihood of victory or defeat on an issue. Since the decision on any issue lies with the judge or jury, no attorney can ever be absolutely certain of the resolution.

Discuss All Possible Issues

As we've noted, a student should draw **some** type of conclusion or opinion for each issue raised. Whatever your conclusion on a particular issue, it is essential to anticipate and discuss **all of the issues** which would arise if the question were actually tried in court.

Let's assume that a negligence hypothetical involves issues pertaining to duty, breach of duty, proximate causation, and contributory negligence. If the defendant prevails on any one of these issues, he will avoid liability. Nevertheless, even if you feel strongly that the defendant owed no duty to the plaintiff, you **must** go on to discuss all of the other potential issues as well (breach of duty, proximate causation, and contributory negligence). If you were to terminate your answer after a discussion of the duty problem only, you'd receive an inferior grade.

Why should you have to discuss every possible potential issue if you are relatively certain that the outcome of a particular issue would be dispositive of the entire case? Because at the commencement of litigation, neither party can be **absolutely positive** about which issues he will win at trial. We can state with confidence that every attorney with some degree of experience has won issues he thought he would lose, and has lost issues on which he thought victory was assured. Since one can never be absolutely certain how a factual issue will be resolved by the factfinder, a good attorney (and exam-writer) will consider *all* possible issues.

To understand the importance of discussing all of the potential issues, you should reflect on what you will do during the actual practice of law. If you represent the defendant, for example, it is your job to raise every possible defense. If there are five potential defenses, and your pleadings only rely on three of them (because you're sure you will win on all three), and the plaintiff is somehow successful on all three issues, your client may well sue you for malpractice. Your client's contention would be that you should be liable because if you had only raised the two additional issues, you might have prevailed on at least one of them, and therefore liability would have been avoided. It is an attorney's duty to raise *all* legitimate issues. A similar philosophy should be followed when taking essay exams.

What exactly do you say when you've resolved the initial issue in favor of the defendant, and discussion of any additional issues would seem to be moot? The answer is simple. You simply begin the discussion of the next potential issue with something like, "Assuming, however, the plaintiff prevailed on the foregoing issue, the next issue would be…" The grader will understand and appreciate what you have done.

The corollary to the importance of raising all potential issues is that you should avoid discussion of obvious non-issues. Raising non-issues is detrimental in three ways: first, you waste a lot of precious time; second, you usually receive absolutely no points for discussing a point which the grader deems extraneous; third, it suggests to the grader that you lack the ability to distinguish the significant from the irrelevant. The best guideline for avoiding the discussion of a non-issue is to ask yourself, "would I, as an attorney, feel comfortable about raising that particular issue or objection in front of a judge?"

Delineate the Transition from One Issue to the Next

It's a good idea to make it easy for the grader to see the issues which you've found. One way to accomplish this is to cover no more than one issue per paragraph. Another way is to underline each issue statement. Provided time permits, both techniques are recommended.

One frequent student error is to write a two-paragraph answer in which all of the arguments for one side are made in the initial paragraph, and all of the rebuttal arguments by the other side are made in the next paragraph. This is *a bad idea*. It obliges the grader to reconstruct the exam answer in his mind several times to determine whether all possible issues have been discussed by both sides. It will also cause you to state the same rule of law more than once. A better-organized answer presents a given argument by one side and follows that immediately in the same paragraph with the other side's rebuttal to that argument.

Understanding the "Call" of a Question

The statements *at the end of* an essay question or of the fact pattern in a multiple-choice question are sometimes referred to as the "call" of the question. It usually asks you to do something specific like "discuss..." "discuss the rights of the parties..." "what are X's rights?..." "advise X..." "the best grounds on which to find the statute unconstitutional are..." "D can be convicted of..." "how should the estate be distributed?...", etc. The call of the question should be read carefully because it tells you exactly what you're expected to do. If a question asks, "what are X's rights against Y?" or "X is liable to Y for..." you don't have to spend a lot time discussing Y's rights against Z. You will usually receive absolutely no credit for discussing facts that are not required by the question. On the other hand, if the call of an essay question is simply "discuss" or "discuss the rights of the parties" then *all* foreseeable issues must be covered by your answer.

Students are often led astray by an essay question's call. For example, if you are asked for "X's rights against Y..." or to "advise X...", you may think you should discuss only X's viewpoint on the issues. This is *not correct*! You cannot resolve one party's rights against another party without considering the issues which might arise (and the arguments which the other side would assert) if litigation occurred. In short, although the call of the question may appear to focus on one of the parties to the litigation, a superior answer will cover all the issues and arguments which that person might *encounter* (not just the arguments she would *make*) in attempting to pursue her rights against the other side.

The Importance of Analyzing the Question Carefully before Writing

The overriding *time pressure* of an essay exam is probably a major reason why many students fail to analyze a question carefully before writing. Five minutes into the allocated time for a particular question, you may notice that the person next to you is writing furiously. This thought then flashes through your mind, "Oh, my goodness, he's putting down more words on the paper than I am, and therefore he's bound to get a better grade." It can be stated *unequivocally* that there is no necessary correlation between the number of words on your exam paper and the grade you'll receive. Students who begin their answer after only five minutes of analysis have probably seen only the most obvious issues, and missed many, if not most, of the subtle ones. They are also likely to be less well organized.

Opinions differ as to how much time you should spend analyzing and outlining a question before you actually write the answer. We believe that you should spend at least 12-18 minutes analyzing, organizing, and outlining a one-hour question before writing your answer. This will usually provide sufficient time to analyze and organize the question thoroughly **and** enough time to write a relatively complete answer. Remember that each word of the question must be scrutinized to determine if it (i) suggests an issue under the operative rules of law, or (ii) can be used in making an argument for the resolution of an issue. Since you can't receive points for an issue you don't spot, it is usually wise to read a question *twice* before starting your outline.

When to Make an Assumption

The instructions on an exam may tell you to *"assume"* facts which are necessary to the answer. Even where these instructions are **not** specifically given, you may be obliged to make certain assumptions with respect to missing facts in order to write a thorough answer. Assumptions should be made when you, as the attorney for one of the parties described in the question, would be obliged to solicit additional information from your client. On the other hand, assumptions should **never be used to change or alter the question**. Don't ever write something like "if the facts in the question were …, instead of …, then … would result." If you do this, you are wasting time on facts which are extraneous to the problem before you. Professors want you to deal with **their** fact patterns, not your own.

Don't assume that your professor has inadvertently or accidentally omitted some fact that you think essential to the correct answer. Actually, your professor may have omitted the facts deliberately to see if you **can figure out what to do** under the circumstances. (True, in some instances, your professor may have omitted the facts inadvertently. Even law professors are sometimes human).

The way to deal with the omission of essential information is to describe (i) what fact (or facts) are missing, and (ii) why that information is important. As an example, go back to the "movie shoot" hypothetical we discussed above. In that fact pattern, there was no mention of the relative strength of A and C. This fact could be extremely important. If C weighed 240 pounds and was built like a professional football linebacker, while A tipped the scales at a mere 160 pounds, punching A in the face after he had been pushed to the ground would probably constitute unnecessary force (thereby causing C to forfeit the prevention-of-crime privilege). If the physiques of the parties were reversed, however, C's punch to A's face would probably constitute reasonable behavior. Under the facts, C had to deal the ***"knockout"*** blow while the opportunity presented itself. The last sentences of the Second Student Answer above show that the student understood these subtleties and correctly stated the essential missing facts and assumptions.

Assumptions should be made in a manner which keeps the other issues open (*i.e.*, necessitates discussion of all other possible issues). Don't assume facts which would virtually dispose of the entire hypothetical in a few sentences. For example, suppose that A called B a "convicted felon" (a statement which is inherently defamatory, *i.e.,* a defamatory statement is one which tends to subject the plaintiff to hatred, contempt or ridicule). If A's statement is true, he has a complete defense to B's action for defamation. If the facts don't tell whether A's statement was true or not, it would ***not*** be wise to write something like, "We'll assume that A's statement about B is accurate, and therefore B cannot successfully sue A for defamation." So facile an approach would rarely be appreciated by the grader. The proper way to handle this situation would be to state, "if we assume that A's statement about B is not correct, A can not raise the defense of truth." You've communicated to the grader that you recognize the need to assume an essential fact and that you've assumed it in such a way as to enable you to proceed to discuss all other potential issues.

Case Names

A law student is ordinarily ***not*** expected to recall case names on an exam. The professor knows that you have read several hundred cases for each course, and that you would have to be a memory expert to have all of the names at your fingertips. If you confront a fact pattern which seems similar to a case which you have reviewed (but you cannot recall the name of it), just write something like, "One case held that …" or "It has been held that …" In this manner, you have informed the grader that you are relying on a case which contained a fact pattern similar to the question at issue.

The only exception to this rule is in the case of a landmark decision. Landmark opinions are usually those which change or alter established law.[**] These cases are usually easy to identify, because you will probably have spent an entire class period discussing each of them. *Palsgraf v. Long Island Rail Road* is a prime example of a landmark case in Tort law. In these special cases, you may be expected to remember the case by name, as well as the proposition of law it stands for. However, this represents a very limited exception to the general rule which counsels against wasting precious time trying to memorize case names.

[**] The only subject to which this does not apply is Constitutional Law, since here virtually every case you study satisfies this definition. Students studying Constitutional Law should try to associate case names with holdings and reproduce them in their exam answers.

How to Handle Time Pressures

What do you do when there are five minutes left in the exam and you have only written down two-thirds of your answer? One thing *not* to do is write something like, "No time left!" or "Not enough time!" This gets you nothing but the satisfaction of knowing you have communicated your personal frustrations to the grader. Another thing *not* to do is insert the outline you may have made on scrap paper into the exam booklet. Professors rarely will look at these items.

First of all, it is not necessarily a bad thing to be pressed for time. The person who finishes five minutes early has very possibly missed some important issues. The more proficient you become in knowing what is expected of you on an exam, the greater the difficulty you may experience in staying within the time limits. Second, remember that (at least to some extent) you're graded against your classmates' answers and they're under exactly the same time pressure as you. In short, don't panic if you can't write the "perfect" answer in the allotted time. Nobody does!

The best hedge against misuse of time is to *review as many old exams as possible*. These exercises will give you a familiarity with the process of organizing and writing an exam answer, which, in turn, should result in an enhanced ability to stay within the time boundaries. If you nevertheless find that you have about 15 minutes of writing to do and five minutes to do it in, write a paragraph which summarizes the remaining issues or arguments you would discuss if time permitted. As long as you've indicated that you're aware of the remaining legal issues, you'll probably receive some credit for them. Your analytical and argumentative skills will already be apparent to the grader by virtue of the issues that you have previously discussed.

Write Legibly

Make sure your answer is legible. Students should *not* assume that their professors will be willing to take their papers to the local pharmacist to have them deciphered. Remember, your professor may have 75-150 separate exam answers to grade. If your answer is difficult to read, you will rarely be given the benefit of the doubt. On the other hand, a legible, well-organized paper creates a very positive mental impact upon the grader.

Many schools allow students to type their exams. There are, however, a few disadvantages to typing. For one thing, all the typists are usually in a single room. If the clatter of other typewriters will make it difficult for you to concentrate, typing is probably *not* wise. To offset this problem, some students wear earplugs during the exam. Secondly, typing sometimes makes it difficult to change or add to an earlier portion of your answer. You may have to withdraw your paper from the carriage and insert another. Try typing out a few practice exams before you decide to type your exam. If you do type, be sure to leave at least one blank line between typewritten lines, so that handwritten changes and insertions in your answers can be made easily.

If you decide against typing, your answer will probably be written in a "bluebook" (a booklet of plain, lined, white paper which has a light blue cover and back). It is usually a good idea to write only on the odd numbered pages (*i.e.*, 1, 3, 5, etc.). You may also want to leave a blank line between each written line. Doing these things will usually make the answer easier to read. If you discover that you have left out a word or phrase, you can insert it into the proper place by means of a caret sign ("^"). If you feel that you've omitted an entire issue, you can write it on the facing blank page. A symbol reference can be used to indicate where the additional portion of the answer should be inserted. While it's not ideal to have your answer take on the appearance of a road map, a symbol reference to an adjoining page is much better than trying to squeeze six lines into one, and will help the grader to discover where the same symbol appears in another part of your answer.

The Importance of Reviewing Prior Exams

As we've mentioned, it is ***extremely important to review old exams***. The transition from blackletter law to essay exam can be a difficult experience if the process has not been practiced. Although this book provides a large number of essay and multiple-choice questions, ***don't stop here***! Most law schools have recent tests on file in the library, by course. We strongly suggest that you make a copy of every old exam you can obtain (especially those given by your professors) at the beginning of each semester. The demand for these documents usually increases dramatically as "finals time" draws closer.

The exams for each course should be scrutinized ***throughout the semester.*** They should be reviewed as you complete each chapter in your casebook. Generally, the order of exam questions follows the sequence of the materials in your casebook. Thus, the first question on a law school test may involve the initial three chapters of the casebook; the second question may pertain to the fourth and fifth chapters, etc. In any event, ***don't wait*** until the semester is nearly over to begin reviewing old exams.

Keep in mind that no one is born with the ability to analyze questions and write superior answers to law school exams. Like any skill, it is developed and perfected only through application. If you don't take the time to analyze numerous examinations from prior years, this evolutionary process just won't occur. Don't just ***think about*** the answers to past exam questions; take the time to ***write the answers down***. It's also wise to look back at an answer a day or two after you've written it. You will invariably see (i) ways in which the organization could have been improved, and (ii) arguments you missed.

As you practice spotting issues on past exams, you will see how rules of law become the sources of issues on finals. As we've already noted, if you don't **understand** how rules of law translate into issues, you won't be able to achieve superior grades on your exams. Reviewing exams from prior years should also reveal that certain issues tend to be lumped together in the same question. For instance, where a fact pattern involves a false statement made by one person about another, three potential theories of liability are often present — defamation, invasion of privacy, and intentional infliction of severe emotional distress. You will need to see if any or all of these apply to the facts.

Finally, one of the best means of evaluating if you understand a course (or a particular area within a subject) is to attempt to create a hypothetical exam for that topic. Your exam should contain as many issues as possible. If you can write an issue-packed exam, you probably know that particular area of law. If you can't, then you probably haven't yet acquired an adequate understanding of how the principles of law in that subject can spawn issues.

As Always, a Caveat

The suggestions and advice offered in this book represent the product of many years of experience in the field of legal education. We are confident that the techniques and concepts described in these pages will help you prepare for, and succeed, at your exams. Nevertheless, particular professors sometimes have a preference for exam-writing techniques which are not stressed in this work. Some instructors expect at least a nominal reference to the ***prima facie*** elements of all pertinent legal theories (even though one or more of those principles is ***not*** placed into issue). Other professors want their students to emphasize public policy considerations in the arguments they make on a particular issue. Because this book is intended for nationwide consumption, these individualized preferences have *not* been stressed. The best way to find out whether your professor has a penchant for a particular writing approach is to ask her to provide you with a model answer to a previous exam. If an item is not available, speak to upperclass students who received a superior grade in that professor's class.

One more point. While the rules of law stated in the answers to the questions in this book have been drawn from commonly used sources (*i.e.*, casebooks, hornbooks, etc.), it is still conceivable that they may be slightly at odds with those taught by your professor. In instances where a conflict exists between our formulation of a legal principle and the one which is taught by your professor, *follow the latter!* Since your grades are determined by your professors, their views should always supersede the views contained in this book.

Essay Questions

Question 1

Ace and Bert needed cash quickly. They offered to sell a watch to Chuck. Bert told Chuck, "This watch is really worth $125. But it's hot, so you can have it cheap – $25." Chuck believed Bert, gave him the $25, and took the watch. Both Ace and Bert knew that the watch was not stolen and that its retail value was $25.

Chuck, discovering that the watch was worth only $25, reported the incident to the police. The police arrested Ace and Bert. At the time of the arrests, a police officer told each, "Anything you say can and will be used against you in court; you have the right to consult with counsel prior to questioning; and if you are unable to afford counsel, a lawyer will be appointed for you." Neither made any statements when they were arrested.

Later at the police station, the booking officer, who was one of Ace's neighbors, asked Ace why he was there. Ace stated that he and Bert had "conned" Chuck into buying a watch by telling Chuck that because the watch was stolen, Ace and Bert were selling it to him "cheap."

Ace and Bert were charged with theft. The two were tried together after the court denied motions by each for severance. Ace's statement to the booking officer was admitted at trial over the objections of each defendant, and both were convicted as charged.

Did the court err in admitting Ace's statement:

1. Against Ace? Discuss.

2. Against Bert? Discuss.

Question 2

Detective Trace received a telephone call from an informant who had given reliable information to Trace on several prior occasions. The informant truthfully told Trace, "Doris is planning to sell stolen silicon chips to Vic and probably will deliver the chips to Vic within the next two weeks. Doris usually rents a room at the Savoy Hotel to use when she makes her sales." Trace immediately prepared an affidavit detailing the informant's past reliability and quoting the informant's statement. On the basis of the affidavit, a magistrate issued a warrant authorizing a search for silicon chips in any Savoy Hotel room rented by Doris in the two weeks following the date of the affidavit.

One week after the warrant was issued, Trace learned from the hotel manager that Doris had rented a room at the Savoy Hotel. Armed with the warrant, Trace went to the hotel intending to search the room in Doris' absence. As he listened at the door to determine whether the room was occupied, however, he overheard Doris offering to sell silicon chips to Vic. He then heard the two arguing, the sounds of a struggle, a crash, and silence. Trace knocked on the door and announced, "Police with a search warrant — open the door." He entered when Doris opened the door. Seeing Vic on the floor unconscious and apparently injured, Trace drew his gun and asked Doris, "What did you do to him?" Doris replied, "I pushed him and he hit his head against a table." Trace summoned an ambulance, but Vic died of head injuries before it arrived.

Doris has been charged with murder and attempting to sell stolen property, both of which are felonies. She moved to exclude testimony by Trace regarding his observations in the hotel room, all silicon chips found in the hotel room, Doris' statement to Vic which Trace had overheard, and Doris' statement to Trace after he entered the room, all on the ground that the evidence had been obtained in violation of Doris' Fourth and Fifth Amendment rights. The trial court denied the motion.

Was the trial court correct in denying the motion? Discuss.

Question 3

Fred, a federal customs inspector, saw Dan speaking to Anon as Dan and Anon walked across the international border into the United States. Fred recognized Anon as someone who had previously been convicted of smuggling narcotics. Over Dan's protests, Fred searched Dan's and Anon's luggage. Fred found a packet of glassine envelopes and some dextrose powder in Dan's suitcase, and a large quantity of heroin in the lining of Anon's suitcase.

Fred knew that dextrose powder is used to dilute heroin, and that heroin is sold in envelopes like those carried by Dan. Fred, therefore, ordered that Dan be searched in private by a male physician, who found a small quantity of heroin in a body cavity. Dan was then arrested on a federal charge of importing illegal narcotics.

Fred notified state narcotics agents of the arrest. Olson, a state agent, located Dan's car parked legally on a street in the United States near the border crossing. Olson impounded the car and, during a search of the car on the following day, discovered a large quantity of heroin. Dan was then charged with violation of a state statute prohibiting possession of narcotics for sale.

At a pre-trial bail hearing, Dan now argues that he is entitled to have bail fixed, or because he is indigent, to be released on his own recognizance. A state statute permits denial of pre-trial bail when a defendant poses too great a risk to society to remain free pending trial.

1. How should the federal court rule on Dan's motion to exclude the envelopes and powder discovered in Dan's suitcase? Discuss.

2. How should the federal court rule on Dan's motion to exclude the heroin found on his person from evidence at the federal trial? Discuss.

3. How should the state court rule on Dan's motion to exclude the heroin found in his car from evidence at the state trial? Discuss.

4. How should the state court rule on Dan's claim that he is entitled to have bail fixed or to be released pending trial on the state charge? Discuss.

Question 4

State Officer Abby, an undercover agent, told her superior, Officer Sue, that Deer, a suspected dealer in stolen property, had (three hours earlier) shown Abby 12 stolen U.S. Army pistols that were stored in Deer's car trunk. Sue immediately prepared an arrest warrant affidavit alleging that "a reliable informant has reported that Deer possesses stolen property." The affidavit was presented to a magistrate who then issued an arrest warrant. After the warrant was issued, a police bulletin was issued for Deer's arrest.

One hour later, Sue observed Deer on the public walkway outside Deer's home, watering his front lawn with a garden hose. After Sue informed Deer of the outstanding warrant, she arrested Deer, searched him and found one of the stolen pistols in a pocket of Deer's jacket.

Concurrently with the arrest, Sue read Deer his *Miranda* warnings and then demanded that Deer reveal the location of the remaining weapons. Deer refused to say anything until he spoke with an attorney. Sue then told Deer that Deer was subject to both federal and state prosecutions, but that only the state charge would be prosecuted if he "talked immediately." Deer then told Sue that the other 11 pistols were in the trunk of his car parked across the street.

Sue had the car towed to a police parking lot, where the trunk was pried open and the remaining 11 pistols removed. A thorough search of the trunk also turned up a notebook, which listed the serial numbers of all the pistols, including the one Sue had taken from Deer's pocket.

Deer has been charged with receiving stolen property. He has made a motion to exclude from evidence, on federal constitutional grounds, the 12 pistols, Deer's statement to Sue, and the notebook. What results on Deer's motion to exclude? Discuss.

Question 5

The Rural Fire Department extinguished a small hay fire in a barn at 11:00 p.m. At 11:15 p.m., Deputy Carr, a member of the Rural Sheriff's Department, walked through the barn and detected the odor of gasoline.

Carr stopped a truck on a nearby road at 11:45 p.m. to ask the driver if she had seen anything suspicious that evening. While the truck was stopped, Denise, the driver of the truck, bent down to the floor twice. Carr approached the truck and ordered Denise to get out. Denise complied and closed the vehicle door behind her. Carr then asked Denise if she had seen any vehicles speeding past her or anything else "out of the ordinary." When Denise answered in the negative, Carr told Denise she could leave.

As Denise reopened the truck door, Carr saw a red gasoline can on the floor. He advised Denise to "Stay right there, please." Carr then commented, "I guess some people don't know how to set a good fire." Denise retorted, "I didn't burn the barn." Carr then seized the can, told Denise she was a suspect in an arson investigation, and took her to the sheriff's office. At the sheriff's office, Denise, after receiving proper *Miranda* warnings, admitted that she had "torched" the barn.

Later, authorities learned that Denise owned the barn and a nearby farmhouse, and had leased the house and barn to Tenant (who had fallen behind in rent payments).

Denise was charged with arson. Evidence of these facts was admitted at trial over appropriate objections. Denise was convicted.

As Denise's attorney, what issues should you raise on appeal with respect to the evidence admitted against her, and how should the appellate court rule on each? Discuss.

Question 6

Detective, a knowledgeable and experienced narcotics law enforcement officer of State X, received information from a proven and reliable informer that Addict was using heroin from a supply which Addict maintained in his apartment at a particular address. Detective had previously arrested Addict on two occasions for possession of heroin, and the arrests had led to convictions. He conducted surveillance of Addict's apartment house from a position in the building's lobby.

When Addict stepped into the lobby, Detective briefly observed Addict's physical appearance and immediately concluded that he was then under the influence of a narcotic. Detective arrested Addict in the lobby and searched his person, finding a key to Addict's apartment. Detective entered the apartment and found and seized a large quantity of heroin. Detective had neither a search nor an arrest warrant.

At the police station, over Addict's violent objection, a physician removed a sample of blood from Addict's finger for the purpose of testing for narcotics. Addict was charged with "possession of heroin" and with being "addicted to the use of a narcotic" in violation of State X statutes.

State X criminal procedure provides for a preliminary hearing for the sole purpose of testing the sufficiency of the state's evidence for holding an accused to answer charges. Addict, claiming that he was an indigent, moved for, but was denied, the right to be represented by counsel at the hearing. He was held to answer by the magistrate.

At the trial, Addict, as an indigent, was represented by appointed counsel. The narcotics and the narcotic content of the blood sample were introduced as evidence. Addict was convicted on both counts. On appeal to the highest State X court, appointed counsel stated in his brief only that he had made a thorough examination of the record and, in his considered opinion, there were no meritorious contentions which could be raised on appeal.

Assume that Addict has preserved all objections and claims he might have made at trial or on appeal, and that all such objections and claims are now before the United States Supreme Court for decision. What would be the likely result of each? Discuss.

Question 7

Dan planned to rob the XYZ bank. He entered through the open doors of the bank during business hours, pointed a loaded revolver at a teller and demanded money. A bank guard ordered Dan to drop his gun. When Dan hesitated, the guard fired a warning shot in Dan's direction. Acting purely on reflex, Dan fired his revolver at the guard, killing him instantly. He then fled.

Two days later, after Dan had been identified to the police as the probable killer, Norm, a plainclothes police detective, went to Dan's house. Pretending to be a door-to-door salesperson, Norm led Dan into a lengthy conversation concerning the killing. Dan made incriminating statements which, although unknown to him, were recorded by a device concealed in Norm's clothing. The following day the police arrested Dan, who blurted out, "I didn't mean to kill him."

At the police station, Dan was advised for the first time that he had a right to an attorney, that he had a right not to make any statements, and that any statement he might make could be used against him at the trial. Dan made no further statement and retained an attorney. At the trial, Dan exercised his right not to testify. Norm and the arresting officers testified for the state about the statements made by Dan before and at his arrest. In closing arguments, the prosecutor commented, over objections by Dan's counsel, on Dan's failure to testify, and urged that the jurors draw an adverse inference of Dan's guilt. Dan was convicted of murder and sentenced to death.

On appeal to the state's highest court, Dan urged that the judgment must be reversed because the evidence by the police officers was improperly admitted against him, and because the prosecution's comments at trial were improper.

What are the merits of each of Dan's arguments? Discuss.

Question 8

Jones, a police officer in a small town in State X near an interstate freeway, was told by the police chief that, according to a report she had received, a lone male driving in a car with an out-of-state license plate would be coming through town within a few days, traveling in an easterly direction, and carrying an illegal shipment of heroin. Shortly thereafter, while on a routine patrol, Jones saw a car with an out-of-state license plate traveling east. The car was being driven by a lone male, Don. Jones pulled Don over and asked him for his driver's license. Don's license had expired, so Jones placed Don under arrest for violation of a State X law requiring a valid license for anyone operating a vehicle in the state. The maximum penalty for violation of the law is a $100 fine and 10 days in the county jail.

Under State X law, an arresting officer had the discretion to issue a citation for violation of the license statute, but it was normal practice in this town to take a license violator who was from out-of-town into custody, and to require bail to be posted before the person could be released.

Jones removed Don from the vehicle, placed him under arrest, and patted him down. While doing so, Jones felt something small and round; Jones thrust his hand into Don's coat pocket to retrieve the object. The object turned out to be a small clear plastic vial containing 10 pills. Jones asked Don if he had a doctor's prescription for the pills, and Don replied that he did not. Jones then asked Don for permission to search the car, and Don replied, "Go ahead, why not?"

During his search of the car, Jones found a plastic bag taped behind the glove compartment; the bag contained a substance that looked and smelled like marijuana. After laboratory analysis, the pills found in Don's possession were determined to be a drug the possession of which is illegal under State X law without a prescription, and the substance in the plastic bag was determined to be marijuana.

Don was charged with: (1) illegal possession of marijuana and other dangerous drugs (the pills); and (2) violation of the State X vehicle license statute. Don's attorney filed a motion to suppress the evidence, seeking to exclude Don's statement to Jones, as well as the pills and marijuana, from introduction at trial.

The constitution of State X has a clause identical to Amendment IV of the United States Constitution.

What rights, if any, under the federal and state constitutions could be asserted for Don in support of the motion to suppress evidence, and how should the State X court rule on the motion? Discuss.

Question 9

Mike and Donna entered the Shorecliff Pharmacy just before closing time to steal money and narcotics. While Mike ransacked the store, Donna took the proprietor, Fred, outside. Donna pointed a gun at Fred to persuade him to reveal the location of valuables, but the gun accidentally discharged, wounding Fred. Donna dropped the gun and fled the scene on foot, but she was arrested the next day. Mike ran outside, saw Fred bleeding profusely, and picked up Donna's gun. As he drove away at high speed, Mike accidentally struck and ran over Fred. Fred's gunshot wound was not serious, but he died from the injuries sustained from being run over by Mike.

A neighbor called the police and reported that he had heard a gunshot. He also reported that he had seen a dark blue car speed away from the pharmacy. Police immediately set up roadblocks around the area. At one of these roadblocks, Mike's car was stopped. When an officer asked Mike where he had been that afternoon, Mike hesitated. The officer ordered Mike out of the car. As Mike got out, the officer noticed a bulge in Mike's pocket. The officer reached into the pocket and pulled out Donna's gun. Mike was immediately arrested.

The next day Mike's car was towed to the station and searched. Under the front seat, police found a "Shorecliff" envelope filled with drugs taken from the robbery at the pharmacy. When Officer Bill showed the envelope to Mike (who was then in a "holding" cell), Mike blurted out, "Donna was the one who did the shooting."

Donna was interrogated and asked for a lawyer. Before a lawyer arrived, Donna was interrogated further and admitted her part in the events.

Mike and Donna were indicted for the murder of Fred. Separate trials were ordered at the request of each defendant. Mike testified against Donna at her trial.

On appropriate motion, which (if any) of the following items of evidence should be suppressed at Donna's trial:

1. The gun taken from Mike's pocket.

2. The Shorecliff envelope and contents taken from Mike's car.

3. Mike's statement.

4. Donna's admission.

Question 10

Dan asked Art, an undercover police agent posing as a hit man, to assist him in murdering Carl. When Art pretended to agree, Dan showed Art a bomb he had made. Art advised Dan that it needed a few improvements, but secretly rigged it not to explode. Dan took the bomb to Carl's house and attached it to the bottom of Carl's car. Tipped off by Art, the police arrived (without a search or arrest warrant) just as Dan finished. They immediately arrested Dan, removed the bomb, and took Dan to the nearest police station. The police then returned to Carl's house, where they conducted a thorough search of both Carl's and Dan's cars (Dan's car was still parked across the street from Carl's house). In Dan's car they found a sales receipt for the type of explosive used in the bomb attached to Carl's car.

Dan was charged with attempted murder. After he was indicted and while he was in jail awaiting trial, Dan was visited by Art. Dan still did not suspect that Art was an undercover agent. Art said to Dan, "Gee, I was surprised to hear they nabbed you." Dan responded by stating, "Carl is a no-good louse. If I don't get him, someone will."

At trial, the prosecution introduced the bomb and the sales receipt into evidence. Art testified to Dan's original request that Art help him murder Carl. Art also testified to the conversation he had with Dan during his visit to Dan in jail.

Assuming that all Dan's rights were properly preserved, what constitutional problems are presented on appeal to the highest court of the state? Discuss.

Question 11

During an afternoon at the bar, Dave pulled a gun on Babs, the bartender, and demanded money. Babs took a gun from under the bar and shot at Dave. Dave shot back, killing Babs. John, a customer in the bar, then attacked Dave with a broken bottle, whereupon Dave shot and killed John. Wounded by John's attack, Dave dropped his gun and slumped to the floor. Officer Leslie heard the gunfire and entered the bar with her gun drawn. Seeing the three wounded people, Officer Leslie cried, "What the devil happened here?" Dave replied, "I killed them both in self-defense."

Dave was charged by State X with the first degree murder of Babs. Under State X law, first degree murder includes murder committed during an "attempt to perpetrate a robbery." Any other non-premeditated murder is second degree murder.

At Dave's trial, the prosecution presented Officer Leslie's testimony that Dave had admitted to the shooting. Dave then testified that he had been in a drunken stupor and was only "joking with Babs," that he never intended to take any money from Babs or to harm her, and that he shot her only in self-defense. Defense counsel offered no supporting testimony because he was told by the prosecutor that there was only one eyewitness to the shooting (Witt), and that Witt had said Dave was sober when he demanded money from Babs.

The only defense objection at trial was to the following jury instruction: "Whether Dave was drunk or intended to frighten Babs into giving him money is irrelevant; the crucial issue, for first degree murder, is whether Babs reasonably was put in fear of being harmed unless she gave up her money."

Dave was convicted of the first degree murder of Babs.

After the verdict, Dave's attorney discovered that the eyewitness (Witt), had, in fact, told the prosecutor that while he had not witnessed the shooting, he had seen Dave in the bar and that Dave was quite drunk shortly before the shooting.

1. What issues might be raised by Dave on appeal and how should they be decided? Discuss.

2. If Dave's conviction is reversed on appeal and he is acquitted of the charge of murdering Babs on retrial, can he thereafter constitutionally be convicted of the first degree murder of John? Discuss.

Question 12

Ashley entered a small federally-chartered bank located in State X and, armed with a revolver, robbed the three tellers. As Ashley was leaving the bank, she shot Fred who was then entering it. Fred was a federal bank examiner who was about to conduct an audit.

The state charged Ashley with three separate counts of armed robbery (a separate count for each teller). At the state's trial on the first charge, Ashley's sole defense was an alibi, that she was out of the city at the time of the robbery. The jury, apparently believing the alibi, returned a verdict of not guilty. Ashley was then tried on the second state charge. The evidence was substantially the same as at the first trial. The jury, apparently disbelieving the alibi, returned a verdict of guilty.

Ashley was also indicted by the federal government on three joined counts of armed robbery of a federal bank. After the jury was selected and sworn in for the trial of all three counts, the U.S. Attorney asked that the case be adjourned for 48 hours because a key witness was unable to appear. The judge, however, discharged the jury over Ashley's attorney's objection.

The U.S. Attorney and Ashley's attorney then agreed that, if Ashley pleaded guilty to one of the indictments, the other two charges would be dismissed. This would make it much more likely that Ashley would receive a more lenient sentence than if she were convicted after trial on all three charges. Ashley's attorney fully explained this to Ashley and she agreed to plead guilty after admitting to her attorney that she had robbed the tellers,.

The next morning, Ashley, her lawyer, and the U.S. Attorney appeared before the judge. Ashley's attorney announced that Ashley wished to change her plea to guilty to one of the indictments. The judge asked Ashley, "Do you wish to change your plea to guilty?" Ashley replied, "Yes, I wish to plead guilty to the one charge." The judge stated, "The guilty plea will be recorded." The other charges were dismissed and Ashley was sentenced to federal prison.

There is a federal statute (the "Statute") which provides: "Whoever assaults, with a deadly weapon, any federal officer engaged in the performance of her duties is guilty of a felony."

In proper proceedings, Ashley appealed her state conviction and sought to vacate her federal sentence. Both cases are now properly before the United States Supreme Court.

1. How will the Court decide

    a. on the state conviction? Discuss.

    b. on the federal sentence? Discuss.

2. If Ashley succeeded in vacating the federal sentence, could she then be successfully prosecuted by federal authorities under the Statute? Discuss.

Question 13

Police Detective Smart set up an officially authorized "fencing" operation, which purported to buy and sell stolen goods under the cover of an import-export business. He quickly filled a warehouse with stolen property which he purchased from thieves.

Dan, who had prior convictions for burglary and larceny, posed as a customer and looked over the operation, intending to burglarize the warehouse. Smart recognized Dan and hoped to arrest him for receiving stolen property. Smart told Dan that he was working for Thug, and that the "merchandise" was stolen property. He said that the two of them could make some money if Dan would break into the warehouse, make it appear that a burglary had occurred, take the merchandise, sell it elsewhere, and divide the receipts between them. Dan agreed.

Late that night, Dan entered the warehouse through a skylight which Smart had left unlocked. After Dan loaded his truck with items from the warehouse, he noticed that uniformed police officers were approaching him. Dan fled, dropping a gun (which he was not legally authorized to carry). Dan was soon captured and taken back to the warehouse, where investigating officers truthfully told him the gun had been identified as belonging to him. Dan then blurted out a confession, was given "*Miranda* warnings," and confessed again.

Dan has been charged with possession of stolen property and an illegal firearm.

In an attempt to lessen any sentence he might receive, Dan told officers that he had recently delivered a large quantity of forged stamps to Betty.

A federal officer visited Betty's stamp shop, purchased four stamps from her and delivered them to experts for examination. Upon receipt of a report that they were forgeries, the officer returned to Betty's shop without a warrant and arrested Betty for the federal felony of knowingly possessing forged stamps. Over Betty's objections, the officer searched the display cabinet in front of her and seized 200 stamps, later found to be forgeries.

After her release on bail, Betty offered a hotel detective $500 to let her into a hotel room occupied by her Aunt Emma to retrieve a suitcase which Aunt Emma was keeping for her. Emma was away on a trip. The detective told Betty to return later and, curious as to why Betty wanted the suitcase so badly, entered the room with a passkey, searched it, and found Betty's suitcase under the bed. The hotel detective opened the suitcase and saw that it contained bonds in Betty's name and a gun. The hotel detective then called the police and showed them the suitcase and its contents. Upon her return, Betty was arrested under a statute for felonious possession of a weapon.

1. What objections based on the United States Constitution should Dan make to the admission of his confessions at his trial?

2. Should Dan prevail on an entrapment defense to the charge of receipt of stolen property?

3. What objections should Betty make to the admission of the stamps at her trial?

4. What objections should Betty make to the admission of the gun?

Question 14

Two plainclothes police officers, Able and Baker, were walking to their cars after attending a mutual friend's birthday party. They saw Cain and Doe, two reputed gamblers, leave Eddy's home. Eddy had been arrested on two previous occasions by Able. These arrests had resulted in convictions for running a "bookmaking operation."

Suspecting that Eddy might be taking bets in his home, Able and Baker walked over to the front of Eddy's house. They noticed several windows, about nine feet above the ground, along the side of the dwelling. There were no curtains or drapes over the windows. They knocked on the door of the home next to Eddy's. When no one answered, they went to the back of that house. They found a ladder, which they then used to climb to the roof of the neighbor's house. They were then able to peer into a side window of Eddy's home. The room they looked into contained several telephones, charts and other electronic equipment often used in bookmaking operations.

Able and Baker decided they had enough information to question Eddy. Before they could get down from the neighbor's roof, they saw Eddy leave his house, shouting to someone who was apparently just inside his front door, "I'm going to get a paper and a cup of coffee, I'll be back soon." Eddy did not see Able and Baker.

After Eddy got into his car and drove away, Able and Baker knocked on the front door of his house. A little girl's voice answered, "Who is it?" Able replied, "It's Miss Able, I know your father, I need to ask him some questions." Cathy, Eddy's 14-year-old daughter opened the door and said, "My Daddy's not home." Able responded, "Well, could we wait for him?" Cathy replied, as she opened the door wide, "O.K., you can sit in the living room." After Able and Baker were seated, Cathy excused herself, saying that she had lots of homework to do.

About one minute after Cathy left, through a door down the hallway (about 20 feet from the living room), the officers heard a telephone ring and someone say, "All right, that's $50 on Mountain Man in the third in Santa Anita. Got it." Able and Baker then went to that room, and slowly nudged the door open. Inside, they saw that a bookmaking operation was obviously in progress. They immediately arrested the two people inside the room. They also confiscated the books, records and charts found in the room.

Suddenly, there was a knock on the door. Able said she would answer the door while Baker instructed the two prisoners to remain silent and stay inside the room. When Able opened the door, she saw Joe, an underworld kingpin. Able asked Joe, "Can I help you?" Joe replied, "I want to put $1,500 on Citation in the Sixth at Santa Anita." Able then informed Joe that he was under arrest for attempted illegal gambling.

At Joe's trial, the prosecution introduced into evidence the books and records which had been seized at Eddy's house. These items contained numerous references to Joe. Officer Able also testified as to what Joe had said in response to her inquiry.

Assuming that all appropriate objections were made in a timely manner, what constitutional issues are presented and what result is likely to occur? Discuss.

Question 15

Debbie, 17, was a student at City High, a public high school in the State of Central. One evening, a water pipe leak caused water to seep onto a row of student lockers. The school principal was summoned to the school by the janitor. The principal immediately opened all the lockers in the row with a master key to determine what damage had been done. When he reached Debbie's locker, he picked up a water-soaked paper bag which fell apart in his hands, revealing among other things, three marijuana cigarettes.

When she arrived at school the next day, Debbie was called into the principal's office. The principal told her what he had found, advised her that her possession of marijuana violated a school regulation against bringing contraband upon campus, and immediately expelled her from school. The principal also notified the State Youth Authority, which instituted proceedings in Juvenile Court to have Debbie declared a "delinquent." Delinquency in the State of Central is defined as "violation of any Penal Code provision which is punishable by at least six months imprisonment." Possession of marijuana falls within this definition.

At the hearing in Juvenile Court, Debbie was represented by counsel of her own choosing. The only evidence presented by the State Youth Authority was testimony of the principal concerning his search, the three cigarettes (which were determined to be marijuana), and a written form previously signed by Debbie, which authorized "any member of the faculty or staff of the school I am attending to inspect my locker at any time." A rule adopted by the local school board required each student renting a locker to sign an authorization at the beginning of the school year.

Debbie testified that the bag and its contents did not belong to her, but to another student who had used Debbie's locker when she lost the key to her own locker. Debbie refused to name or identify the other student, although she was ordered to do so by the judge.

Following the hearing, Debbie was adjudged a juvenile delinquent on two independent grounds: (1) possession of marijuana, and (2) refusing to answer questions when ordered to do so by the court. She was committed to the custody of the State Youth Authority for three months.

Debbie, through her attorney, has now instituted proceedings in the state superior court for her release, claiming that the Juvenile Court proceedings (*i.e.*, the lack of a jury trial and adjudication) violated her Fourteenth Amendment rights. Assuming that all such rights were properly asserted and preserved in the prior proceeding, how should the superior court rule? Discuss.

Question 16

Cindy was a wealthy stockbroker. Allen was one of her customers. After Allen slapped Cindy in the face during a violent argument over money at Allen's apartment, Cindy stabbed Allen with a metal letter opener. Her clothes spotted with blood from Allen's wound, Cindy ran from the apartment screaming, "What will I ever do? What will the Stock Exchange do with me?" Sylvia, Allen's friend, arrived at the front door of the apartment just as Cindy fled. Sylvia saw the blood on Cindy's clothes and heard her screams.

After Sylvia had entered the apartment and found Allen wounded and unconscious, she called the police. When the police arrived, Sylvia described the woman who had fled the apartment. Allen's dining room table was covered with documents and records dealing with Allen's recent stock transactions. The police concluded that the assailant might well be someone who had participated in these transactions, perhaps Allen's broker.

Finding Cindy's address among the documents on his dining room table and relying on the description provided by Sylvia, the police arrested Cindy within 10 minutes after she arrived home. Cindy was immediately taken to Allen's hospital room. Allen, who was on the critical list and was not expected to live through the night, identified Cindy as his assailant. Allen died the next day.

After the hospital visit, Cindy was taken to police headquarters and placed in a lineup. At the demand of the police and over her objection, Cindy was forced to repeat the words, "What will I ever do? What will the Stock Exchange do with me?" At the lineup, Sylvia identified Cindy both by sight and by voice as the woman she had seen leaving Allen's apartment. Later, over Cindy's objection, a police officer confiscated all the clothing in her closets. Subsequent laboratory analysis matched Allen's blood type with the blood on the cloths Cindy was wearing. Cindy was charged with murder and placed in detention.

The police told Paula, another prisoner, that they were going to put her in the same cell with Cindy. They told Paula that they were interested in obtaining incriminating statements from Cindy. The police further advised Paula not to initiate any conversations or elicit information from Cindy. She was told to listen if Cindy wanted to speak.

Unable to restrain herself, Cindy confided in Paula that she felt "very guilty about stabbing Allen."

Cindy has moved to prevent the introduction into evidence at her trial of:

1. Any testimony relating to Allen's identification of her.

2. Any testimony relating to Sylvia's visual identification at the lineup.

3. Any testimony relating to Sylvia's voice identification at the lineup.

4. Cindy's clothing and the result of the laboratory analysis of the blood found on it.

5. Cindy's statement to Paula while awaiting trial.

How should the court rule on each of the five motions? Discuss.

Was Cindy's arrest valid? Discuss.

Question 17

Doug was driving home from a party with his friend, Thompson. They were both very drunk. Thompson began to make insulting remarks about Doug's girlfriend. Doug warned him to stop but Thompson persisted. Unable to take it any longer, Doug reached into the glove compartment of his car, took out a gun, and shot Thompson. Doug then pulled over to an unlighted part of the roadway and pushed Thompson's body out of the car.

The next morning, Doug started out for work carrying the same gun in his pocket. He was stopped at one of the boarding gates of the local public inter-city bus terminal when the gun activated a metal detector. The bus company, which was privately owned, had instituted the boarding procedure in response to several bomb threats in the preceding weeks.

A security guard of the bus company stopped Doug, reached into Doug's pocket, and found the gun. The morning newspapers had been full of the story of Thompson's death, and the guard knew that the gun Doug was carrying fit the description of the gun used on Thompson. Doug saw an opening and ran. Later that morning, the security guard took the gun to the police and told the police why he had taken it from Doug.

The day after the bus terminal incident, Officer West spotted Doug driving his car with the hazard lights on. Officer West pulled Doug over, intending to ask Doug about his hazard lights. When Officer West came alongside Doug's car he noticed that Doug appeared to be very nervous. Officer West asked, "Everything all right?" Doug shot back in a sarcastic voice, "Oh yes, I'm just getting out of town because there's way too much acid rain." Perplexed and troubled by this reply, Officer West decided to look into Doug's car and saw blood stains on the front seat. Taking a closer look at Doug, Officer West realized that he resembled the description of Thompson's assailant. Officer West then arrested Doug. He told Doug that ballistics tests had proved that his gun had fired the bullet which killed Thompson. Doug then blurted out, "I shot him because he provoked me and I was drunk."

Doug has been charged with murder.

What objections based on the United States Constitution should Doug make to the admission into evidence of the gun, the blood stains and his statement to Officer West? Discuss.

Question 18

Tony was glad his law school exams were finally over. He partied long and hard after his last final, consuming alcoholic beverages, marijuana, cocaine, and five dozen twinkies. He started to drive home, but was soon pulled over by Officer Meane who had observed Tony driving his sports car (1) lawfully, but 20 m.p.h. under the speed limit, and (2) with a weird smile on his face.

Meane asked Tony to step out of the car and gave Tony a field sobriety test, which Tony flunked. Before arresting Tony, Meane said, "What in the world have you been drinking?" Meane patted Tony on the back good-naturedly, and laughed in a friendly way.

Tony replied, also with a laugh, "Twinkies, many twinkies."

Meane replied, "But you can't *drink* twinkies. Have you been drinking anything?"

Tony answered, "A six-pack of Genny Cream Ale, and about 20 Jello shooters, give or take five or six."

Meane placed Tony under arrest on a charge of "willful drunken driving." Meane then took out a little notecard from her jacket and read Tony his *Miranda* rights. After listening to them, Tony replied, "I waive my rights."

Meane then proceeded to interrogate Tony. Tony admitted the use of marijuana and that he knew he should not have been driving while intoxicated. As a gesture of friendship, Tony reached into the breast pocket of his shirt and handed Meane his last marijuana cigarette.

Tony was taken back to the station house and placed in a holding cell. About two hours later, after again receiving proper *Miranda* warnings, he was questioned about the incident by Officer Phil. Tony confessed to being drunk and having marijuana in his possession.

Tony was charged with "willful drunken driving" and "possession of an ounce or less of marijuana." Prior to trial, Tony told the judge that he wanted to represent himself. The judge said, "Absolutely not, young man!" The judge then appointed an excellent public defender to be Tony's attorney.

1. Which of the preceding pieces of evidence will be admissible in the criminal prosecution against Tony? Discuss.

2. Assuming Tony loses at trial, what other issues are available on appeal?

Question 19

Dot was one of 50 women employed by Store. Nine months ago, on a day when Dot was on duty at Store, a man dressed as a delivery clerk stole several radios from Store during the lunch hour. Grace, a customer, told Marsh, the store manager, that at the time of the theft and from a distance of about 30 feet, she had observed a clerk, whom she described as a young woman of average build and wearing a Store smock, speaking to a delivery man. In the presence of Police Officer Brown, Marsh showed Grace a photograph of Dot. Grace stated, "She could be the one." A few minutes later, Marsh asked Dot in Brown's presence if she had been in the store during the lunch hour. Dot answered that she had been, but had seen nothing unusual.

Recently, Officer Brown validly arrested Dot's ex-husband, Hal, on another matter. After being advised of his rights, Hal confessed to the Store theft, stating that Dot had helped him and that the stolen radios were in her apartment. Brown immediately obtained both a search warrant for Dot's apartment and an arrest warrant for Dot, after submitting an affidavit which stated in part:

> "I have information from a reliable source who knows Dot that the radios stolen from Store nine months ago are now in the apartment of Dot. . . ."

The affidavit also stated that Dot had previously been convicted of grand larceny and has been known to associate with other convicted felons.

Dot was arrested the next afternoon as she was returning home from work. After she was shown the search warrant, Dot asked if she could telephone her sister to come over, so that someone would be in the apartment when Dot's daughter (Ann) returned home from school. Officer Brown agreed, but accompanied Dot as she entered her apartment and walked to the telephone. They had to walk through the living room to enter the kitchen where Dot's telephone is located. While walking through the living room, Officer Brown noticed two rows of small boxes, stacked one on top of the other in a corner. Officer Brown walked over to the boxes and inspected them. Inside each box was a radio of the type stolen from Store. Officer Brown seized these items. Later, it was established that they were the radios taken from Store.

Dot and Hal were indicted. Hal pleaded guilty and Dot not guilty. At Dot's trial, Grace identified Dot as the Store clerk she had seen speaking to the delivery man. Hal did not testify on behalf of the prosecution. However, Officer Brown testified as to Hal's statements to him. Dot testified in her own defense and denied being in Store during the lunch hour. The prosecution called Marsh as a rebuttal witness, and he testified that Dot had told him she was in Store during the lunch hour on the day of the theft.

As counsel for Dot, what motions or objections would you have made before or during the trial? How should the court have ruled on each motion or objection? Discuss.

Question 20

Dunn worked as a computer programmer at Arcon Enterprises. Dunn had been seeing Sally, who was only 17.

Buck was jealous of Dunn. He wanted to win Sally's affections, but realized he could never do so with Dunn around. Buck knew that Sally was only 17. He decided that the best way to get rid of Dunn was to get him prosecuted for violation of a state law which provides that anyone who has sex with a person under the age of 18 has committed statutory rape. Buck began to follow Dunn and Sally around on their dates. Buck noted that on two occasions, Dunn and Sally entered Dunn's apartment at about 11:00 p.m. and did not come out until 10:00 the next morning. Buck reported his observations to the police, suggesting that they prosecute Dunn for statutory rape.

The next evening, the police began a surveillance of Dunn's apartment. Watching with the aid of high-powered binoculars from a nearby apartment building, they saw Dunn and Sally kissing. Dunn suddenly picked Sally up and carried her into what was presumably his bedroom.

The next day, after Dunn left his office to have lunch, the police were given permission by his employer to search his work area. The officers found a letter (which apparently Dunn had decided not to send) in a trash can which Dunn shared with another employee. The letter was addressed to Sally. It said that he hoped they would have another "hot night next weekend."

The next morning, the police arrested Dunn in his carport as he was getting into his car to drive to work. The charge was statutory rape; the police had no arrest warrant. The arresting officers searched the vehicle and found two marijuana cigarettes under the front seat. A charge of possession of an illegal substance was then added to the charge of statutory rape.

What arguments can Dunn make to suppress the marijuana cigarettes, and what arguments is the prosecution likely to make in rebuttal?

Question 21

On Wednesday, Police Officer was told by an informer that Smith was dealing in marijuana and would be receiving a large shipment on the following Friday. Because this informer had often given reliable information to Officer in the past, Officer presented the information (but no additional facts) to a magistrate, who issued a search warrant covering both Smith's apartment and a house owned by Smith but occupied by his estranged wife.

In executing the warrant on the following Saturday, the police (led by Officer) knocked on the front of the house owned by Smith, and announced their authority and purpose. Wanda, Smith's estranged wife, told the police, "Search everywhere. That S.O.B. has ruined my life. I hate his guts." The police located and seized large quantities of marijuana in the garage of Smith's house. To enter this area, the police had to break a small lock on the garage door. They later found Smith and arrested him, under a state statute making it unlawful to possess marijuana.

Immediately after the arrest, Officer asked Smith, "What do you keep in your garage?" Smith blurted out, "That's Wanda's marijuana." Smith was then searched, and more marijuana was found in his pocket.

At the police station, Smith was properly and fully advised of his rights, after which he demanded an attorney.

Assume that you are appointed to represent Smith. What issues would you raise in an attempt to win his acquittal on the charge of possession of marijuana? Discuss.

Essay Answers

Answer to Question 1

1. Did the court err in admitting Ace's statement against him?

Ace's lawyer would argue that Ace's statement to his neighbor, the booking officer, was inadmissible as a violation of his Fifth Amendment rights, because it was in response to a custodial interrogation and the warnings given to Ace by the arresting officers were incomplete in that Ace was not told that he had the right to remain silent. (See ELO Ch.5-IV(C).)

The prosecution would make two arguments in rebuttal. First, it would contend that the failure to advise Ace that he could remain silent was not critical under the circumstances because (1) Ace was advised that anything he said could be used against him, and (2) he apparently understood that he could remain silent as shown by the fact that he had remained silent in the presence of the arresting officers. Ace failed to request an attorney although he was advised that he could have one, so the police had the right to interrogate him. Second, the prosecution would argue that the booking officer's inquiry was not an "interrogation;" he was simply expressing his surprise at seeing a neighbor at the police station. His intent was not to elicit an incriminating statement.

The prosecution's second argument would probably fail. Whatever his intent, the booking officer should have realized that his question to Ace (if answered) was reasonably likely to elicit incriminating information. (*See* ELO Ch.5-VII(A)(3).) It's a close call whether the prosecution's first argument (that it wasn't critical to advise Ace that he could remain silent) will prevail. Many courts insist on strict observance of the Miranda requirements, including a specific reference to the option to remain silent. ELO Ch.5-IX(A)(2).

Considering the arguments on both sides, it's unlikely that an appellate court would overrule the court's exercise of its discretion in admitting Ace's statement against him.

2. Did the court err in admitting Ace's statement against Bert?

The facts do not tell us whether Ace testified in his own defense. If he did, then Bert had the ability to confront and cross-examine him on the issues raised by Ace's statement to his neighbor, the booking officer. On the other hand, if Ace asserted his Fifth Amendment privilege against testifying, Bert could argue that Ace's statement was inadmissible against him because the statement would violate Bert's Sixth Amendment *confrontation* right (*i.e.*, Bert was denied the opportunity to cross-examine Ace).

The prosecution would respond that Ace's statement was admissible even against Bert because it was made under circumstances which proved that it was reliable (*i.e.*, the statement was spontaneous; it was against the declarant's penal interest;

and it was voluntary and not coerced). The Sixth Amendment right of confrontation was therefore inapplicable.

Bert is likely to prevail on the issue of confrontation. The Supreme Court has held that if two co-defendants are tried simultaneously, the rights of one are violated if the other refuses to testify but his confession is introduced against both. This is true even if the jury is instructed to use the confession only against the defendant who made it. *Bruton v. U.S.*, 391 U.S. 123 (1968). ELO Ch.9-VII(C)(3). The prosecution had the option of trying Ace and Bert separately or of asking for two separate juries, both of which would hear all the testimony except Ace's statement, which would be heard by only one of the juries. The prosecutor's failure to exercise either of these options should result in a new trial for Bert.

Answer to Question 2

Was the warrant validly issued?

Evidence obtained with an invalid search warrant may be inadmissible against the defendant at trial. The validity of a search warrant is one of the elements guaranteed by the Constitution. Therefore, the admissibility of all the evidence Trace obtained in the hotel room rests on the validity of his warrant. (*See* ELO Ch.7-I(A).)

Doris should have contended that the warrant was not validly issued because (1) there was no probable cause (*i.e.*, the warrant rested primarily upon the hearsay statement of the informant, without any corroboration that the information was accurate), (2) a search warrant ordinarily must be executed (*i.e.*, acted upon) within a reasonable time from the date it was issued, (3) a specific location was not designated (*any* Savoy Hotel room could be searched). (*See* ELO Ch.2-III(B), V(D)(1), V(G)(1).)

The prosecution should have argued in rebuttal that, under the "totality of the circumstances" test for informants (*Illinois v. Gates*, 462 U.S. 213 (1983)), probable cause did exist in light of the declarant's prior history of furnishing correct information and the specificity of his information (*i.e.*, the exact building and the time frame within which the transaction would occur). Furthermore, 14 days was a reasonable period of time in the light of the informant's data. In any event, the search was actually made within one week of the warrant's issuance. Also, the location was as precise as possible under the circumstances. (*See* ELO Ch.2-IV(B).)

The trial court was probably correct in determining that the search warrant was validly issued.

Even if the warrant was *not* validly issued, the court was probably correct in admitting the evidence because: (1) there was a reasonable basis for issuing the warrant, and (2) Trace acted reasonably in believing that the warrant was valid; *U.S. v. Leon*, 468 U.S. 897 (1984). (*See* ELO Ch.2-V(H).)

Was the evidence obtained as a result of the eavesdropping admissible?

Doris could contend that Trace's eavesdropping at her door constituted a search within the meaning of the Fourth Amendment (applicable to the states via the Fourteenth Amendment). Since this search was beyond the scope of the search warrant, its fruits (hearing Doris' offer to sell silicon chips to Vic and the subsequent scuffle) would be inadmissible. However, Trace paused outside the door to the room for a reasonable and legitimate purpose — to ascertain whether someone was inside before announcing his presence. Doris' offer to sell and the ensuing scuffle were voluntary acts by Doris which were not induced by anything Trace did or didn't do.

Because Trace's actions in executing the warrant were proper, and the warrant is probably valid, the evidence obtained by Trace's eavesdropping would be admissible. (*See* ELO Ch.2-II(D)(6), V(G).)

Assume the warrant was not properly issued and that Trace did not have an objective, good faith belief that it was valid. Would Trace's observations and the evidence seized in Doris' hotel room nevertheless be admissible?

Evidence obtained by lawful means **independent** of any illegal taint is admissible. If the argument between Vic and Doris was of such volume that persons walking through the hallway would hear it, Doris would have lost all expectation of privacy in the consequences of her words. (*See* ELO Ch.2-II(B),C)). The sounds of a violent argument and of an ensuing crash would probably constitute exigent circumstances, justifying a warrantless entry by Trace into Doris' hotel room. It would be reasonable for a police officer to verify whether a violent felony had occurred and to ascertain the cause and the persons involved. (*See* ELO Ch.3-IV(C)(2).)

Once inside, Trace had probable cause to arrest Doris, since Vic was unconscious and Doris was the only other person in the room. Trace's resulting observations (*i.e.*, those items that were in plain view) within the room would be admissible. (*See* ELO Ch.3-V(B).) Under this theory, Trace probably would not have the right to search anything not in the area within Doris' immediate control without obtaining a warrant. But evidence (i) within Trace's view upon entering the hotel room, (ii) upon Doris' person, and (iii) within Doris' immediate control, would be admissible, even if the warrant was invalid. (*See* ELO Ch.3-III(B).)

Assuming Trace's entrance into Doris' hotel room was valid, is Doris' statement admissible?

Statements made to police officers during a custodial interrogation are not admissible in the prosecution's case-in-chief, unless (1) *Miranda* warnings preceded the questioning, and (2) there was a waiver of *Miranda* rights. (*See* ELO Ch.5-IV(C),(F).) Doris should have contended that (1) since Trace had drawn his gun, a custodial situation ensued, and (2) Trace's question ("What did you do to him?") was interrogation (*i.e.*, reasonably calculated to elicit an incriminating response). The prosecution should have argued in rebuttal that Trace's statement was a spontaneous, on-the-scene *oyb* inquiry made to determine Vic's physical condition so that the proper medical attention could be given; in that case, *Miranda* would not apply under the "public safety" exception. See *New York v. Quarles*, 467 U.S. 649 (1984). (*See* ELO Ch.5-VIII(B).) However, because Trace's question ("What did you do to him?") seems to have been addressed more to eliciting Doris' statements about her own actions rather than to finding out whether Vic needed medical help, the court could reasonably have concluded that the "public safety" exception did not apply, and that Doris' statement should have been excluded.

Summary

Of the evidence presented against Doris, her offer to sell silicon chips to Vic, her scuffle with Vic (both of which Trace heard through the door), and Trace's observations of Vic's physical condition and of any physical evidence found in the immediate vicinity, are all admissible against Doris. The court was correct in denying her suppression motion as to these items. Only Doris' statement to Vic is inadmissible and the court should have granted the motion as to that item alone.

Answer to Question 3

The question assumes that Dan will be tried separately in the federal and state courts.

1. Dan's motion to exclude the evidence found in his suitcase

Under the Fourth Amendment, a federal governmental agent must, in order to search a person's suitcases, ordinarily obtain a warrant based on probable cause. However, an exception to this rule exists with respect to "border" searches of a person's belongings when he enters this country from abroad. Border searches are generally limited to vehicles, suitcases and personal searches that are not excessively intrusive. These objects may be searched without probable cause (or even reasonable suspicion) that they contain indicia of criminal activity. Therefore, the search of the suitcases was valid. (*See* ELO Ch.3-X(C)(1).)

2. Dan's motion to exclude the evidence found on his person

Dan would next contend in his federal trial that Fred did *not* have sufficient probable cause to order a search of Dan's body cavity. However, the need to safeguard the nation's borders means that customs agents may conduct even reasonably intrusive body searches based on less than probable cause. In one case, the Supreme Court held that an incoming traveler's body cavities may be searched as long as the agents have "a particularized and objective basis for suspecting [the traveler] of alimentary canal smuggling." *U.S. v. Montoya de Hernandez*, 473 U.S. 531 (1985). (*See* ELO Ch.3-IX(F)(5).)

True, all that Fred had seen in Dan's suitcase were two items of heroin-related paraphernalia. But the government could probably argue successfully that Fred had sufficient suspicion to detain and body-search Dan on the following basis: (1) the items found in Dan's suitcase; (2) the items found in Anon's suitcase (Dan probably had no standing to object to the search of Anon's suitcase); (3) Anon's prior criminal record; and (4) Fred's probable experience that persons smuggling heroin frequently utilize body cavities to conceal as much as they can. Taken together, these facts would appear to meet the "particularized and objective basis" test of *Montoya*. (*See* ELO Ch.3-IX(F)(5)(c).)

There is nothing in the facts to indicate that the search was performed in other than a reasonable manner (*i.e.*, it was carried out by a male physician who presumably made no greater intrusion upon Dan than necessary under the circumstances to determine if he had placed illegal drugs in his body cavity). Nor is there any indication that Dan was detained for longer than necessary before the exam was completed.

The federal court should deny Dan's motion to exclude the heroin found in his person.

3. Dan's motion to exclude the evidence found in his car

In the state court action, Dan will assert that since the search of his car and seizure of the heroin found within it were conducted without a warrant, evidence of the heroin in the car is not admissible.

When the police have probable cause to believe that a vehicle on a public road contains evidence of a crime, the vehicle may be searched without a warrant. The State could contend that given Dan's earlier federal arrest and the close proximity of the car to the border, there was probable cause to believe that the vehicle contained evidence of criminal activity. However, it is doubtful that there was probable cause on these facts alone. The State should lose on the issue of probable cause to search, in the absence of other factors. (*See* ELO Ch.3-VI(A)(3).)

However, when a car is in police possession pursuant to an arrest, a warrantless "inventory" search of the vehicle may be made (without probable cause) provided that there is a standard police procedure allowing inventory searches. *Colorado v. Bertine*, 479 U.S. 367 (1987). (*See* ELO Ch.3-VI(J)(3).) The facts are silent as to whether the state agents here adhered to a standard procedure for impounding the car of a suspect while its owner was in custody. Also, it can be argued that the car was seized illegally because there was no accompanying arrest. Fred was arrested by a federal customs agent, not by Olson, the state agent. But this argument is not likely to have much weight in the light of recent Supreme Court decisions on auto searches. See, *Bertine, supra.* If the search of the vehicle satisfied the standard-procedure test, then the search might be valid under the "inevitable discovery" exception to the exclusionary rule; i.e., the heroin would inevitably have been discovered under the impoundment-search procedure. Therefore, the exclusionary rule wouldn't be applied even if the actual search was made without the required probable cause. (*See* ELO Ch.7-III(C)(2).)

We have been assuming that the heroin in Dan's car could not be seen from outside the car. If the heroin could be seen — and reasonably identified as heroin — from the sidewalk or street, then the sighting would itself supply probable cause for the search. (This would be an application of the "plain view" doctrine.) (*See* ELO Ch.3-V(B).)

In summary, there is good reason for the state court to decide that the heroin found in Dan's car should be admitted against him.

4. Is Dan entitled to have bail fixed or to be released pending trial?

Under the Eighth Amendment, "excessive bail" (*i.e.*, an amount exceeding the sum reasonably calculated to assure the defendant's presence at trial) is impermissible. The Supreme Court has never decided whether this provision is binding on the states via the Fourteenth Amendment. Even if the Eighth Amendment were binding on the states, the courts have held that when a suspect poses a danger to society, bail is *not* constitutionally required. Preventive state detention statutes like the one under scrutiny here have generally been upheld, provided the defendant is afforded the right to a *hearing*, and to individualized consideration of his circumstances, on the bail issue. See *Stack v. Boyle*, 342 U.S. 1 (1951). (*See* ELO Ch.9-II(C).)

The State will probably contend that all heroin distributors (a large quantity of the drug was found in Dan's car) pose a great risk to society. But given the facts that (1) drug dealing is usually a victimless crime, and (2) there is no indication that Dan was a habitual trafficker in heroin, a complete denial of pre-trial bail might be unwarranted in this instance.

Dan might also claim that the Due Process and Equal Protection Clauses of the Fourteenth Amendment require that he should be released on his own recognizance if he cannot afford even reasonable bail. The clauses probably require that the bail scheme of a state not work an invidious discrimination upon the poor. However, a suspect is not entitled to release simply because he is indigent. (That theory would discriminate against persons who are *not* poor.) Thus, it does not appear that Dan would be entitled to be released upon his own recognizance solely because of his indigency. (*See* ELO Ch.9-II(B).)

On these facts, the state court is likely to fix bail at an amount that makes it reasonably certain Dan will not attempt to leave the jurisdiction.

Answer to Question 4

Is the pistol found in Deer's jacket admissible?

Deer can be expected to contend that the pistol found in his jacket is inadmissible because the arrest warrant was invalid. He would argue that the gun was found as a consequence of the illegal arrest. Under *Illinois v. Gates*, 462 U.S. 213 (1983), a warrant based on an informant's information is measured, on the issue of probable cause, in the same way as warrants based on other sources (*e.g.*, direct observation by a police officer). (*See* ELO Ch.2-IV(B)(1).) Deer would argue that even this broad standard was *not* satisfied: Sue's affidavit did not describe: (1) the basis for her statement that the informant was reliable (*i.e.*, Had the informant given accurate information to the police in the past? Had he personally been witness to Deer's conduct?); (2) how the stolen property came into Deer's possession (Did Deer "knowingly" have possession?); or (3) what items comprised the stolen property (guns, jewels, etc.).

The prosecution would make several arguments in reply. First, no arrest warrant is necessary when (1) the defendant is not taken into custody within his home, and (2) there is probable cause to believe that the defendant has committed a felony. (*See* ELO Ch.3-II(A)(B).) Since the possession of stolen firearms constitutes a felony, the prosecution would argue that the arrest was proper in that (1) the probable cause element was satisfied by Abby's statement to Sue that she had actually seen the stolen pistols only a few hours earlier, and (2) the arrest occurred **on the sidewalk,** not in Deer's home. Deer could respond that, since he was just outside his residence and performing a function related to the home, he should be considered to have been within his house. The prosecution would probably prevail. And, because the police may search a suspect's outer clothing incident to a valid arrest, the pistol found in Deer's jacket would be admissible; *Chimel v. California*, 395 U.S. 752 (1969). Thus, even in the absence of a valid warrant, Deer's arrest was proper. (*See* ELO Ch.3-III(B)(2).)

Second, (assuming that Deer prevailed on the invalid-warrant issue), the prosecution could argue that Sue acted reasonably and in good faith in relying on the warrant (even if probable cause did not exist); *U.S. v. Leon*, 468 U.S. 897 (1984). (*See* ELO Ch.2-V(H).) However, Deer would probably respond that the basis for Sue's affidavit (*i.e.*, a "reliable" informant's report that Deer had possession of stolen property) was so obviously conclusory that no reasonable police officer would have relied on it. However, because Abby, a police officer, was Sue's "informant" and because Sue herself had prepared the affidavit, Sue probably was justified in relying on the warrant despite any possible deficiency in its form.

Therefore, under either prosecution argument, (*i.e.*, no warrant was necessary under the circumstances, or there was reasonable reliance on the warrant), the gun seized from Deer's jacket pocket is probably admissible.

The guns in Deer's trunk

Even if Deer's arrest was valid, he would contend that the pistols found in his trunk were unlawfully seized: (1) Sue did not have a warrant to search the car; and (2) the location of the pistols was obtained as a consequence of an illegal interrogation (*i.e.*, Sue induced Deer to disclose the location by offering to drop the federal charges; this pressure to talk caused Deer to abandon his request for an attorney and was a violation of his *Miranda* rights.).

However, the prosecution could offer several arguments in rebuttal. First, it will argue that the search was incident to a valid arrest. *New York v. Belton,* 453 U.S. 454 (1981). Although the *Belton* case authorized warrantless searches limited to the passenger compartment, later cases have arguably extended the incident-to-arrest principle to other sections of the car. (See, *Ross, infra*.) Second, where probable cause exists to believe that contraband or evidence of crime will be found in a vehicle which is temporarily at rest on a public highway (Deer's car was parked *across the street* from his home) the police may make a warrantless search that is co-extensive with the search that might have been authorized by a judicial magistrate; *United States v. Ross,* 456 U.S. 798 (1982). Based upon Abby's statement to Sue that she had actually seen the stolen army pistols in the trunk of Deer's car, probable cause to search that area would appear to have existed. Thus, the warrantless search of that area was proper. The fact that the trunk was not opened until the day after Deer's car was towed back to the station house is insignificant. (*See* ELO Ch.3-VI(G)(6).)

Third, the prosecution might argue that even if the discovery of the guns was the fruit of an illegal interrogation, the illegality should be ignored under the "inevitable discovery" exception. *Nix v. Williams,* 467 U.S. 431 (1984). (*See* ELO Ch.7-III(C)(2).) Under this exception, the guns would inevitably have been discovered; a valid search warrant (based upon Abby's observation) would ultimately have been issued and executed. Deer will argue, however, that it was not likely that a search warrant for the car would be obtained — four hours had passed since Abby saw the pistols and no warrant had been sought. But the prosecution will probably win on this point by arguing that it was more important for them to focus first on arresting Deer (to prevent him from removing any of the pistols) than to seize the guns.

Finally, the prosecution will assert that the requirement of a search warrant did not apply to the search of the trunk because "exigent circumstances" existed. (*See* ELO Ch.3-IV(C).) That is, if the guns were not seized immediately after the arrest, they would be disposed of and used to take innocent lives. But, given the fact that (1) there was sufficient time to obtain an arrest warrant, and (2) Deer was in custody, this argument would probably *not* be successful.

In sum, because the prosecution would probably prevail on at least one of its arguments, the guns in Deer's trunk would be admissible.

Is Deer's statement admissible?

Deer will contend that his statement to Sue about the location of the guns was inadmissible as a violation of his *Miranda* rights. Once a suspect says he wants a lawyer, the police cannot question him until they provide one, unless the suspect himself initiates further communication. *Edwards v. Arizona*, 451 U.S. 477 (1981). This is a "bright-line" rule which has few, if any, exceptions. (*See* ELO Ch.5-X(C)(9)(b).)

The only possible rebuttal which the prosecution could make is that "exigent circumstances" existed justifying Sue's pressure on Deer: failure to confiscate the weapons immediately might have resulted in their transfer to persons who would utilize them to rob and murder. (*New York v. Quarles*, 467 U.S. 649 (1984)). However, the "exigent circumstances" exception to *Miranda* has generally been limited to situations in which the danger to the public is immediate, which was not the case here. Deer's statement to Sue as to the location of the 11 guns should probably be suppressed. (*See* ELO Ch.5-VIII(B).)

Is the notebook admissible?

Whether the notebook is admissible will probably turn upon whether police were entitled to search the car's trunk without a warrant. (See above). If they were not, the notebook would be inadmissible. If they were, they would be allowed to examine anything that might constitute evidence (or contain evidence) of the crime they were investigating. Since the crime was possession of stolen guns, the police could reasonably have believed that the notebooks might contain evidence relating to the purchase of stolen guns. This possibility justified them in opening the notebook. Once they saw the serial numbers in the notebook, they were justified in impounding the notebook.

Answer to Question 5

Was the walk-through of the barn by Deputy Carr an unreasonable search?

Denise can contend that Carr's walk-through of the barn (presumably for the purpose of detecting evidence pertaining to the source of the fire) was an unreasonable search, since it was done without a warrant. Denise would argue that "but for" this action by Carr, she would not have been stopped, and consequently her admission would not have occurred.

The prosecution can assert in rebuttal that: (1) Denise has no standing (*i.e.*, a reasonable expectation of privacy in the area searched), because she had leased the barn to Tenant; and (2) exigent circumstances to inspect existed (*i.e.*, unless a walk-through was performed relatively quickly, the smell of gasoline, which is often utilized to start fires, might dissipate in the night air). Also, a post-fire inspection was justified as an administrative or regulatory search; in that case, probable cause would not be necessary (though it is not clear whether an administrative search warrant is needed for such a search). Since the prosecution would probably be successful with respect to at least two of these arguments, Carr's conduct (and the evidence derived from it) was proper. (*See* ELO Ch.2-II(C)(2)(b); Ch.3-IV(A), IV(C)(4), X(B)(5); Ch.7-II(C)(2).)

Did Carr have the right to stop Denise and ask her to get out of her vehicle?

Denise can next contend that Carr had no right to stop her, since she was not driving illegally. If Denise had not been pulled over by Carr, none of the evidence implicating Denise would have been discovered; the evidence was therefore the "fruit of a poisonous tree." (*See* ELO Ch.7-III(B)(2).)

But the prosecution will argue in rebuttal that Carr's initial act in pulling Denise over was *not* a detention. She was flagged down in connection with an ongoing criminal investigation — a legitimate police procedure — rather than for questioning with respect to her own culpability.

Denise can also claim that even if Carr had the right to pull her over, he did not have the right to order her out of her car. She will point out that while a person who is stopped for a traffic violation may be requested to leave her car (*Pennsylvania v. Mimms*, 434 U.S. 106 (1977)), she herself had been driving in a lawful manner and, thus, could not be ordered to get out of the car. (*See* ELO Ch.3-IX(C)(4).) If Denise can convince the court on this point, she can probably exclude the evidence of the gas can and perhaps her confession. The gas can would probably never have come to light if Denise had not been ordered out of the car, and the discovery of the can (and the later confession stemming from that discovery) would be illegal fruit resulting from the unlawful order to exit the car.

But the prosecution has a convincing response to these arguments: once Carr saw Denise making two furtive movements towards the floor of the driver's seat, Carr had a reasonable suspicion that Denise was armed or was attempting to conceal some element of criminal activity. At that moment, he had the right to investigate further — by having Denise get out of the car — even though the initial stop was to seek help with his investigation rather than because of Denise's wrongdoing. (*See* ELO Ch.3-IX(B)(2)(c).)

The prosecution would probably prevail on these issues relating to the stopping of Denise's car and Carr's order that she exit the car.

Did Carr lawfully seize the gasoline can?

Next, Denise can claim that Carr's seizure of her gas can was unlawful, in that it occurred without a warrant.

But Denise is unlikely to prevail on this point. Under the ***plain view*** doctrine, when police observe evidence from a vantage point they have a right to occupy, they may seize items which they have probable cause to believe are indicia of criminal activity (*Horton v. California*, 496 U.S. 128 (1990)). (*See* ELO Ch.3-V(B).) Assuming (as discussed above) that Carr lawfully (1) stopped Denise's vehicle, and (2) ordered her out of it, Carr had probable cause to believe that the gasoline can in Denise's vehicle was connected with the fire at the barn (given the gasoline odor he had discovered during this walk-through). On this basis, Carr's seizure of the gasoline can was probably valid.

Is Denise's statement to Carr admissible?

A statement made by a suspect who is in custody in response to interrogation is not admissible unless it is preceded by *Miranda* warnings. Denise can assert: (1) she was in custody (she was ordered to "stay right there"); and (2) Carr's statement was an "interrogation" because it was reasonably likely to elicit an incriminating response by Denise (why else would Carr have made his statement?). (*See* ELO Ch.5-IV(C).)

The prosecution will respond that Denise was not in custody. First, roadside questioning after the operator of a vehicle has been stopped for a minor traffic violation does not constitute "custody" for *Miranda* purposes — a reasonable driver who is stopped under these circumstances is not likely to think that she's being restrained. (*Berkemer v. McCarty*, 468 U.S. 420 (1984)). (*See* ELO Ch.5-V(D)(3).) Second, Carr's direction included the word "please" (a word seeking cooperation, not a demand). While Denise will continue to argue that a reasonable person in her position would have felt constrained by Carr's statement, the prosecution will probably prevail on this issue. (*See* ELO Ch.5-V(C).) Carr had no reason to anticipate that Denise would respond in the way she did to a remark which was not directed against her and did not even require a reply.

The prosecution will probably prevail on these contentions, and Denise's response is probably admissible.

Is Denise's confession at the sheriff's office admissible?

Denise will contend that because her statement to Carr was inadmissible, her subsequent confession at the sheriff's office was also inadmissible. The earlier statement was inculpatory — it indicated that Denise knew that a fire had occurred. This was something she would not be expected to know unless she herself was involved. Having blurted out her reply to Carr--Denise will argue--she assumed that she had already "let the cat out of the bag" and had to respond to questioning by admitting her guilt. Consequently, confession in the sheriff's office was the tainted fruit of her illegally-obtained "I didn't burn the barn" statement.

A similar argument was resolved against the accused in *Oregon v. Elstad*, 470 U.S. 298 (1985). In that case, the Supreme Court refused to treat a later confession as the fruit of an earlier illegal confession. Instead, the Court considered whether the later confession was "voluntary" in light of all the circumstances; if it was, then it is admissible even though it followed an inadmissible confession. Here, the passage of time, change in location, the proper *Miranda* warnings and absence of police trickery, taken together, suggest that the later confession was voluntary and wasn't an outgrowth of the earlier (assumedly illegally-obtained) statement. Therefore, Denise will probably lose on her "cat out of the bag" argument. (*See* ELO Ch.7-III(J)(4).)

Answer to Question 6

Was the surveillance of Addict's apartment house by Detective a "search" within the Fourth Amendment?

Addict will contend that the surveillance constituted a "search" of his home and required a warrant. Because Detective had no warrant, any evidence he obtained would be inadmissible against Addict.

Under the Fourth Amendment (applicable to the states via the Fourteenth Amendment) an individual has no right to object to the search of an area in which he does not have a reasonable expectation of privacy. Addict will contend that the lobby of his apartment house was an extension of his own apartment and that he had a reasonable expectation of privacy while in the apartment house lobby. We may assume that the apartment lobby had no security which prevented access to nonresidents because Detective was apparently able to gain easy access. Addict's argument will probably fail. Even if the lobby was inaccessible to nonresidents, the fact that other residents of the apartment house would have free access to the lobby substantially diminishes Addict's expectation of privacy in the lobby. Thus, the surveillance of Addict in the lobby was lawful. (*See* ELO Ch.2-II(C)(2)(b).)

Was Addict's arrest valid?

An individual may be arrested without a warrant outside his home when the arresting officer has probable cause to believe that the individual is committing or has committed a crime (this is not true in the case of a misdemeanor which was not perpetrated in the officer's presence). (*See* ELO Ch.3-II(A)-(B).)

But because Addict was arrested for possession of heroin and for being a narcotics addict (rather than for being under the influence of a narcotic), he can argue that probable cause did not exist for the arrest which actually occurred. A person under the influence of a particular drug at a particular time is not necessarily either (a) "in possession of heroin", or (b) "addicted" to the use of a narcotic. While the prosecution can reply that one who is under the influence of a particular drug probably has that substance on his person or is addicted to it (especially in light of the informant's finding that Addict had a huge supply of heroin in his possession in the apartment), Addict would probably prevail on this issue. Briefly observing someone who appears to be under the influence (even an individual who has a prior history of drug-related arrests) would probably *not* constitute adequate probable cause to arrest. On this theory, because all the evidence against Addict was derived from an arrest which would be considered illegal, the evidence is inadmissible. (*See* ELO Ch.2-IV(A), (C).)

Because the Court may reject our conclusions, however, we will discuss all of the other issues raised by these facts.

Was the search of Addict's apartment valid?

Pursuant to a *valid* arrest, police officers may search the suspect's outer clothing (whether or not the officers actually fear for their safety or believe that evidence of a crime will be found); *United States v. Robinson*, 414 U.S. 218 (1973). (*See* ELO Ch.3-III(H).) Assuming Addict's arrest was proper, the resulting discovery of a key to his apartment was also valid.

Addict will contend that the search of his apartment was nevertheless improper. Under the Fourth Amendment, a warrantless search and seizure of an individual's premises is generally unlawful (exceptions to the rule do exist). (*See* ELO Ch.2-I(A).) The only exception which would be plausible on these fact is the "exigent circumstances" exception. The prosecution will argue that exigent circumstances were present (*i.e.*, unless Addict's apartment was searched, he would utilize his right to make a telephone call after his arrest to advise others to destroy or move the heroin), but this argument will probably fail. The prosecution would have to show a stronger basis for believing that the evidence would be destroyed or removed. (*See* ELO Ch.3-IV(B).)

Is the blood sample admissible against Addict?

Addict will claim that the forcible extraction of his blood in effect compelled him to furnish evidence against himself, in violation of the Fifth Amendment's prohibition against compulsory self-incrimination. However, the Fifth Amendment (applicable to the states via the Fourteenth Amendment) bars only testimonial communications; blood samples obtained by means of an ***involuntary blood test*** are ***not*** protected. *Schmerber v. California*, 384 U.S. 757 (1966). The facts here are analogous to those of *Schmerber*. Therefore, the fact that the blood test was involuntary will not, in and of itself, be a bar to the use of the results as evidence against Addict. (*See* ELO Ch.6-II(A).)

Addict will also argue that the extraction of his blood violated his Fourth Amendment right to be free of "unreasonable" searches and seizure, because the intrusion was severe, and the government did not have a compelling need for the evidence.

But this assertion will probably fail because (1) the medical procedure involved is well established and can be (and was) accomplished in complete safety, and (2) the intrusion into Addict's body was minimal and relatively painless. See generally *Winston v. Lee*, 470 U.S. 753 (1985), discussing the use of a balancing test to determine the reasonableness of the intrusion. (*See* ELO Ch.2-V(G)(9).)

Addict will also claim that his Sixth Amendment rights were violated in that counsel was not made available to him prior to or during the test. However, no Sixth Amendment right to counsel existed at the time of the blood test, because the test occurred prior to any court appearance and even before Addict was formally charged. (*See* ELO Ch.6-III(A).)

Thus, assuming Addict's arrest was proper, the results of the blood test would probably be admissible against him.

Was Addict entitled to counsel at the preliminary hearing?

Once an individual has been charged with a crime, he is entitled to the assistance of counsel at every "critical stage" (any context in which substantial rights of the accused may be affected) thereafter. Since the purpose of the preliminary hearing was to test the sufficiency of the state's evidence, the hearing was probably a "critical stage" of the proceedings. If so, Addict was entitled to have counsel appointed for him. *Coleman v. Alabama*, 399 U.S. 1 (1970). (*See* ELO Ch.8-IV(D).)

Was Addict deprived of his right to effective counsel?

Under the Sixth Amendment (applicable to the states via the Fourteenth Amendment), a person charged with a crime has a right to "effective" representation. To succeed with an ineffective representation claim, the accused must show that (1) his counsel's performance fell below an objective standard of reasonable representation, and (2) "but for" such unprofessional conduct there is a "reasonable probability" that the result of the proceedings would have been different, *Strickland v. Washington*, 466 U.S. 668 (1984). Since (as discussed above) there are numerous arguments upon which the prosecution's case could reasonably and effectively have been attacked, the failure by Addict's counsel to raise any issues on appeal probably violated Addict's Sixth Amendment right to effective counsel. (*See* ELO Ch.8-VI(A)(1).)

Does Addict's conviction for heroin addiction violate the Eighth Amendment?

Addict will claim that his conviction for addiction to the use of a narcotic violated the Eighth Amendment prohibition on cruel and unusual punishment, applicable to the states via the Fourteenth Amendment. He will claim that the facts show no reasonable basis upon which to conclude that he was addicted.

It is now well established that the imposition of criminal penalties for "status" (rather than for commission of a specific criminal act) violates the Eighth Amendment. *Robinson v. California*, 370 U.S. 660 (1962). Because addiction is a status or condition rather than a specific action, Addict will probably succeed with this claim. As a result, his conviction for addiction will be overturned.

Answer to Question 7

Are Dan's statements to the plainclothes detective admissible?

Dan will argue that the admission of his tape-recorded statement to Norm violated his Fifth Amendment right against self-incrimination (because he received no *Miranda* warnings), his Sixth Amendment right to counsel, and his Fourteenth Amendment right to due process. However, Dan will probably lose on each point.

No Fifth Amendment violation occurred by reason of the detective's failure to give Dan *Miranda* warnings, because Dan was not in custody at the time the questioning took place. A reasonable person in Dan's position would have believed himself to be free to leave at any time during the discussion with the plainclothes officer, especially since Dan didn't even suspect that he was talking to a police officer. On these facts, custody did not exist when Dan's statements were made and recorded. (*See* ELO Ch.5-V(B)(1), V(C).)

The right to counsel is triggered only by the institution of formal proceedings against a defendant. Therefore, no Sixth Amendment violation occurred here, because Dan had not been formally charged with a crime when his statements to the detective were made. (*See* ELO Ch.8-IV(B).)

Finally, enticing Dan into a discussion about his crime did not violate his due process rights. Norm's conduct would not be viewed as the type of governmental overreaching which "shocks the conscience." Dan assumed the risk that the person he was speaking with might spread his statements to others.

Norm's testimony and the tape-recorded conversation between Norm and Dan would be admissible against Dan.

Was Dan's arrest valid?

Dan can claim that his arrest was invalid, and that the statement he blurted out was, therefore, the fruit of the poisonous tree (the arrest). This claim would be supported by the argument that an arrest warrant was required, and that the police lacked probable cause to arrest him.

Assuming the police officers who took Dan into custody did not have an arrest warrant, whether Dan's arrest was valid depends upon where it occurred. The facts are silent here. If Dan was arrested in his home, a warrant was required, unless the officers had reason to believe exigent circumstances existed (*e.g.*, Dan was about to flee the state). If Dan was not arrested in his residence, no warrant was required because bank robbery is a felony. (*See* ELO Ch.3-II(B).)

Whether or not a warrant was required, the police were required to have probable cause at the time they arrested Dan. That is, they were required to be aware of facts which made it more probable than not that Dan had committed the crime at issue. (*See* ELO Ch.2-III(B).) Since Dan had (1) been identified to the police as the likely killer, and (2) made incriminating statements to the detective posing as a door-to-door salesman, the "probable cause" test appears to be satisfied. Therefore, the arrest was probably valid.

If the arrest is found to have been invalid, the "fruit of the poisonous tree" doctrine would probably make the blurted-out confession inadmissible. The connection between the arrest and the confession was close in time and there was no significant intervening event to break the chain of causation (i.e., to "purge the taint.") See *Taylor v. Alabama*, 457 U.S. 687 (1982). (*See* ELO Ch.7-III(J)(2)(e).)

Was the statement Dan blurted out admissible?

Dan will also argue that his statement, "I didn't mean to kill him," should be inadmissible because he had not been given *Miranda* warnings before he made the statement. The prosecution will probably reply successfully that: (1) no interrogation had occurred; and (2) Dan's statement was voluntary. Therefore, the lack of *Miranda* warnings would not be fatal and Dan's statement (assuming the arrest was proper) would be admissible. (*See* ELO Ch.5-VII(A).)

Was the prosecution's comment during his closing statement improper?

The prosecution may not undermine the exercise of an accused's Fifth Amendment privilege (applicable to the states via the Fourteenth Amendment) by commenting upon the accused's refusal to testify; *Griffin v. California*, 380 U.S. 609 (1965). (*See* ELO Ch.9-VII(D)(2).) But the prosecution will argue that the comment should be tested under the "harmless error" standard (*i.e.*, the error was harmless because it did not contribute to Dan's conviction). See *Chapman v. California*, 386 U.S. 18 (1967). Given the volume of direct evidence against Dan and the relative insignificance which the jury probably attached to Dan's refusal to testify, the "harmless error" standard is probably satisfied on these facts. Further, the prosecution can point out that Dan's counsel could have requested an instruction from the judge to the jury that it was not to draw any adverse inference from Dan's failure to testify. *Carter v. Kentucky*, 450 U.S. 288 (1981). Although a close issue, reversal of the verdict against Dan probably is not warranted. (*See* ELO Ch.9-VII(D)(2).)

Answer to Question 8

Was the stop of Don's car proper?

A warrantless vehicle stop is tested by the standard for a "stop and frisk" enunciated in *Terry v. Ohio*, 392 U.S. 1 (1968). Under that standard, the police need have only a reasonable suspicion, based upon objective, articulable facts, that criminal activity may be afoot. In other words, something less than probable cause is required. The prosecution will contend that this standard was satisfied: (1) Don fit the description of the heroin smuggler reported to the police chief, and (2) Don drove through the town within the time frame (the next week) contained in the report. (*See* ELO Ch.3-IX.)

Even if we assume that the information reported to the police chief originated in a reliable source (*i.e.*, one known for accurate information about criminal activities in the past), it's unlikely that the vague description here would constitute a "reasonable suspicion" that Don himself was engaged in criminal activity. Because the town was located near an interstate freeway, numerous out-of-state vehicles would be likely to pass through it. If the "reasonable suspicion" standard was not satisfied--the probable result on these facts--the stop was a violation of Don's Fourth Amendment rights. Therefore, all of the evidence derived from the illegal stop (*i.e.*, Don's driver's license, the illegal pills and marijuana) would be inadmissible as "fruits of the poisonous tree." (*See* ELO Ch.7-III(B)(2).)

On the assumption however, that our conclusions will be rejected by the court, we will discuss the other issues which can arise under these facts.

Was the request to see Don's driver's license proper?

Assuming Jones had a reasonable suspicion to stop Don, Don will contend that Jones had no right to request his driver's license. However, when the police make a valid auto stop, they are always free to verify that the driver is licensed. Therefore, Don will almost certainly lose on this issue, and the resulting arrest of Don for violation of the license statute will not be thrown out.

Was the warrantless arrest of Don valid?

An arrest, even for a misdemeanor (presumably driving without a proper driver's license would be a misdemeanor rather than a felony), may be made without a warrant when: (1) probable cause exists, and (2) the offense was committed in the arresting officer's presence. Since these elements are satisfied here, the lack of an arrest warrant would not invalidate Don's arrest. (*See* ELO Ch.3-II(B)(2).)

Don will contend his equal protection rights were violated. He will argue that Jones' insistence on placing him under arrest (instead of merely issuing a citation) constituted unlawful, selective enforcement. But to assert this theory successfully a defendant must show: (1) the defendant was, in fact, selected for prosecution while others who were similarly situated were not, and (2) the determination to prosecute the defendant was arbitrary or unreasonable. Although Don can apparently show that drivers who lived in the town were merely cited, the decision to imprison (at least until bail could be obtained) out-of-town drivers would probably not be unreasonable. Out-of-town drivers would be less likely to appear for trial or sentencing. Also, presumably, fines would be more difficult to collect (*i.e.*, out-of-state personnel might be needed to pursue collection). If the stop and the request to see Don's driver's license were valid, then Jones' decision to arrest (as opposed to merely cite) Don was probably proper also.

Was the "pat down" of Don proper and the evidence derived therefrom admissible?

When the police make a valid *arrest* (even for a misdemeanor), they may search the suspect's outer garments incident to that arrest; *U.S. v. Robinson*, 414 U.S. 218 (1973). Therefore, if the arrest was valid, the pills taken from Don were properly seized. (*See* ELO Ch.3-III(I).)

Even if the arrest was invalid (*e.g.*, suppose Don won on the "selective enforcement" argument), but the police still had grounds for a *Terry* "stop" of Don's car, the pat down of Don — and the subsequent search of Don's pocket and seizure of the pills — would arguably be justified under the "stop and frisk" doctrine. But when the police conduct a pat down in a stop-and-frisk situation, they are permitted to check only for weapons, not for contraband. *Minnesota v. Dickerson*, 508 U.S. 366 (1993). When Jones conducted the pat down, he discovered something small and round; he could properly conclude that this was (as it, in fact, was) contraband, but it was not reasonable for him to conclude that he had found a weapon. For this reason, Jones probably did not have have the right to reach into Don's pocket, and did not have probable cause to seize the pills. The facts are similar to those in *Dickerson, supra,* where the seizure of the contraband was found to be unlawful. (*See* ELO Ch.3-IX(G).)

Is Don's statement that he did not have a prescription for the pills admissible against him?

Don can argue that he was entitled to *Miranda* warnings before he admitted that he didn't have a prescription for the pills. Don was entitled to *Miranda* warnings if Jones was conducting a *custodial* interrogation. Because Don had already been placed under arrest when Jones asked his question about a prescription, the inquiry would probably be considered custodial. If Jones neglected to give Don his *Miranda* warnings before he asked the question, Don's response would be inadmissible. (*See* ELO Ch.5-V(D)(3)(b).)

Did Don consent to a search of his car's interior?

The prosecution will contend that Don voluntarily gave permission to search the car. The prosecution will argue that in *Schneckloth v. Bustamonte*, 412 U.S. 218 (1973), permission by the occupants of a car to search the vehicle after a stop for a minor traffic violation was deemed to be voluntary. (*See* ELO Ch.3-VII(B).) Don will argue that in *Schneckloth*, the occupants had not been arrested and a congenial atmosphere existed between them and the officer who had detained them. Here, by contrast, Don had already been arrested. But Don will probably lose on this point — most consent searches following arrest have been upheld, as long as the police didn't assert or imply that they had a right to make the search. (*See* ELO Ch.3-VII(E).)

Was the search of the vehicle's interior valid (even if Don did not consent to it)?

If Don was properly arrested, the search of the vehicle's interior was legal as incident to arrest. *New York v. Belton*, 453 U.S. 454 (1981). Therefore, so long as the arrest was valid the search was valid, even if Don's "consent" is found not to have been voluntarily given. (*See* ELO Ch.3-VII.)

What is the effect of the State X constitutional provision?

States may give greater procedural protection to persons accused of a crime than the protection required by the U.S. Constitution. It's possible--as is sometimes the case--that State X's version of the Fourth Amendment has been interpreted by State X courts to require stricter police conduct than the conduct required by the U.S. Constitution as interpreted by the Supreme Court. If so, Don can assert these decisions to preclude evidence which might otherwise be introduced against him. (*See* ELO Ch.1-II(F).)

Answer to Question 9

1. The gun taken from Mike's pocket:

Donna will argue initially that because the police did not have a search warrant for the gun, it is not admissible against her.

The prosecution will reply that Donna *lacks standing* to contest the discovery of her gun (*i.e.*, a suspect must have a reasonable expectation of privacy in the area intruded upon to object to a warrantless search). Because (1) Donna had dropped the gun on a public street, and (2) the gun was obtained from the clothing of another individual, Donna probably has no standing to object to seizure of the gun. *Rakas v. Illinois*, 439 U.S. 128 (1978); *Rawlings v. Kentucky*, 448 U.S. 98 (1980). (*See* ELO Ch.7-II(C).)

It may be, however, that this jurisdiction (under the state constitution or an applicable law) gives an accused standing to object to any unlawful police conduct. In that case, Donna may be able to persuade the court to reject the gun.

Police are ordinarily entitled to establish fixed roadblocks to check for some legitimate police purpose (*e.g.*, driver sobriety), provided their questioning is carried out in a neutral, objectively measurable manner (*e.g.*, every car, or every ninth car, is stopped). Assuming the police here were questioning the occupants of all cars, the stop of Mike's vehicle was proper; *Michigan Dept. of State Police v. Sitz*, 496 U.S. 444 (1990). (*See* ELO Ch.3-X(F).)

Donna will next contend that Mike's hesitation in responding to the officer's question did not reasonably create sufficient suspicion to cause him to order Mike out of the vehicle. Although a driver may be ordered out of a vehicle even for a minor traffic violation, Mike had not committed any vehicular offense. The prosecution will argue in reply that, given the matching color of Mike's car and his hesitation in answering a relatively straightforward question, the police officer was reasonable in his suspicion that Mike was the killer he was looking for. Because (1) the crime had involved the use of a gun, and (2) Mike was in the vicinity, the officer could reasonably order Mike out of the vehicle for additional questioning. In this way, the officer would avoid the possibility that Mike would draw a gun on him. (*See* ELO Ch.3-IX(C)(4).)The prosecution would probably prevail on this issue.

Finally, Donna will contend that since Mike had not yet been arrested, the officer had no right to reach into Mike's pocket and seize the gun. But a warrantless frisk of a suspect's outer clothing may be made when the officer has reason to believe the suspect may be carrying a weapon. The officer had observed the bulge in Mike's pocket. Given the violence with which the crime had been committed (*i.e.*, use of a gun and then of a motor vehicle as homicidal weapons), the officer's actions were lawful if he reasonably believed the bulge was a weapon (as opposed to, say, contraband). Thus, even if Donna had standing to contest the police seizure of her gun from Mike's pocket, the firearm would probably be admissible against Donna. (*See* ELO Ch.3-IX(B)(2)(c).)

2. The Shorecliff envelope and its contents:

As with the gun taken from Mike's pocket, Donna would have to show that she has standing to oppose the admission of the evidence found in Mike's car. Because Donna has no justifiable expectation of privacy with respect to Mike's car or its contents, she probably lacks standing and the evidence will be admitted even if it was seized in violation of Mike's rights. (*See* ELO Ch.7-II(C)(1).)

Even if Donna is found to have standing to contest the search of Mike's car, the prosecution can still assert that the search was proper because the interior of a vehicle may be searched in the course of a valid, full custodial arrest of its occupants. *New York v. Belton*, 453 U.S. 454 (1981). The fact that the vehicle was towed back to the police station before the search actually occurred would be immaterial. *Chambers v. Maroney*, 399 U.S. 42 (1970); *U.S. v. Johns*, 469 U.S. 478 (1985). (*See* ELO Ch.3-III(D),VI(B),(G)(6).)

Thus, the Shorecliff envelope and its contents will probably be admissible against Donna, even though they were obtained without a warrant.

3. Mike's statement:

The statement by Mike was not a confession of his own guilt but an accusation directed only at Donna. It is therefore distinguishable from those cases which hold that only the person making the confession may object to its admission. (ELO Ch.7-II(B).) Donna is objecting here not because Mike made a confession of his own guilt but because he denied his own guilt and attempted to accuse her.

When a suspect has been taken into custody, he may not be interrogated unless the questioning is preceded by *Miranda* warnings. An interrogation takes place when the conduct of police officers is reasonably likely to elicit incriminating evidence from a suspect. (*See* ELO Ch.5-VII(A)(3).) Donna will assert that when the police held the Shorecliff envelope in front of Mike, they were interrogating him: a suspect facing an object held by a police officer would be likely to make some (possibly inculpatory) statement in response. *Rhode Island v. Innis*, 446 U.S. 291 (1980). Although the prosecution will argue that there was no "interrogation" because no specific inquiry was directed at Mike, Donna should, nevertheless prevail on this issue. Additionally, if Mike had been indicted or charged prior to the police conduct in question (the facts are unclear as to this point), Donna could also contend that Mike's Sixth Amendment right to counsel (applicable to the states via the Fourteenth Amendment) had also been violated. The conversation initiated by Officer Bill arguably constituted a "critical stage of the proceeding" at which Mike's counsel was entitled to be present. *Gilbert v. California*, 388 U.S. 263 (1967). Thus, assuming Mike had been charged, Donna's reliance on the Sixth Amendment would probably be sustained. (*See* ELO Ch.8-IV(B).)

Whether or not Mike had already been formally charged, Donna can also argue that Officer Bill's conduct in taunting Mike with the envelope full of drugs constituted governmental overreaching in violation of Mike's Fourteenth Amendment due process rights. However, it is doubtful that Officer Bill's actions "shock the conscience." This argument would probably not be successful.

Assuming Mike refused to testify in Donna's trial (*i.e.*, Mike elected to assert his Fifth Amendment privilege against self-incrimination), Donna will argue that admission of Mike's earlier statement violates her Sixth Amendment right of cross examination (applicable to the states via the Fourteenth Amendment). However, the Supreme Court has held that the right to confront a hostile witness is satisfied if there are other adequate measures of reliability (whether or not the hearsay declarant is available). *Ohio v. Roberts*, 448 U.S. 56 (1980). An out-of-court declaration which falls within a "firmly rooted hearsay exception" is enough to constitute adequate indicia of reliability. *Roberts, supra.* The prosecution will argue that since Mike's statement was an excited utterance (one of the classic exceptions to the hearsay rule), the *Roberts* standard is satisfied. The prosecution should prevail on this issue. (*See* ELO Ch.9-VII(C)(2).)

4. Donna's admission:

Once an accused requests counsel, all questioning must cease until she is provided with an attorney; *Edwards v. Arizona*, 451 U.S. 477 (1981). Questioning may proceed only if the suspect: (1) *initiates conversations* with the officers interrogating her, and (2) makes a "knowing and intelligent *waiver* of the right to counsel." See ELO Ch. 5–X(C)(9)(b); *Oregon v. Bradshaw*, 462 U.S. 1039 (1983). There is no indication that these conditions were satisfied here. Thus, Donna's statement is inadmissible.

Answer to Question 10

Is the bomb attached to Carl's car admissible?

Dan can argue that because the police did not have a search warrant, their seizure of the bomb violated his Fourth Amendment rights (applicable to the states via the Fourteenth Amendment). (*See* ELO Ch.2-I.) The prosecution will respond with several arguments.

First, Dan has no standing (*i.e.*, reasonable expectation of privacy) with respect to Carl's car. The prosecution will probably win on this point, because no one has an expectation of privacy with respect to an object attached to the exterior of another person's vehicle, especially when the object may be a bomb attached by the suspect himself. (*See* ELO Ch.7-II(C)(1); Ch.3-VI(A)(3)(b).)

Alternatively, the prosecution will assert that the bomb was recovered pursuant to a search incident to a lawful arrest. Because (1) Dan had asked Art to assist him in murdering Carl, (2) the device was known to be a bomb (although disarmed) and (3) Dan himself had installed the device on Carl's automobile, probable cause to arrest Dan existed. In a valid arrest, the area within the suspect's immediate control may be searched, and any incriminating evidence seized. The bomb was apparently within Dan's reach, because the facts tell us that he had "just finished" attaching it to Carl's car when he was arrested by the police. (*See* ELO Ch.3-III(B)(2)(a).)

Finally, the prosecution will contend that exigent circumstances existed (*i.e.*, unless the device was seized at that moment, someone might find it, rearm it and become severely injured). (*See* ELO Ch.3-IV(C).)

The prosecution will probably prevail on at least one of its arguments, and the bomb will be admissible against Dan.

Were the search of Dan's car and the seizure of the receipt valid?

Because the police lacked a warrant to search Dan's car, he will contend that the sales receipt was inadmissible.

Again, the prosecution will make several points in reply.

First they will argue that this case is analogous to a case in which the police have stopped a vehicle with probable cause but without a search warrant and then conducted an immediate search of the vehicle. See *Chambers v. Maroney*, 399 U.S. 42 (1970). Because the police had arrested Dan and Dan's car was stopped at Carl's house, the police had a right to conduct a warrantless search of the vehicle (*See* ELO Ch.3-VI(D).) The prosecution will argue that since Dan had obviously used his car to travel to Carl's house, there was probable cause to believe that the car might contain incriminating evidence.

Also, the prosecution will argue that when probable cause exists to believe that contraband or evidence of a crime will be found in a vehicle which is temporarily at rest upon a public highway, the police may make a warrantless search that is co-extensive with the search that might have authorized by a judicial officer.

Alternatively, the prosecution will ask the court to apply the same reasoning as in *New York v. Belton*, 453 U.S. 454 (1981). (*See* ELO Ch.3-III(D).) The *Belton* case dealt with a situation in which the search of a vehicle followed the arrest of the car's occupants for a traffic violation. In this case, although Dan was taken into custody for a crime totally unrelated to the operation of the vehicle, the prosecution can argue that the vehicle was the instrument which enabled Dan to travel to Carl's car to plant the bomb. Indeed, it was conceivible that Dan had made other bombs which he had not shown to Art and which were still armed. The court will probably be persuaded by this argument and allow the evidence taken from Dan's car.

If (1) it was law or policy in this jurisdiction to impound vehicles on a public highway following the arrest of the owner, and (2) it was the resulting practice to conduct an "inventory" search of these vehicles, the prosecution can successfully argue that the sales slip would inevitably have been discovered (even if probable cause for the search was otherwise lacking). Therefore, under the "inevitable discovery" doctrine, the lack of a warrant should be treated as harmless error. *South Dakota v. Opperman*, 428 U.S. 364 (1976). (*See* ELO Ch.3-VI(J)(3); Ch.7-III(C)(2); *Colorado v. Bertine,* 479 U.S. 367 (1987).)

Were Dan's statements to Art after his indictment admissible?

The statements made by Dan to Art while Dan was in jail following his indictment would probably be inadmissible. The statements may violate Dan's Sixth Amendment right to counsel (applicable to the states via the Fourteenth Amendment). The U.S. Supreme Court has held that the use of "active" informants after the Sixth Amendment right to counsel has attached, violates that clause (*U.S. v. Henry*, 447 U.S. 264 (1980)), but that the use of "passive" or "listening post" informants does not (*Kuhlmann v. Wilson*, 477 U.S. 436 (1986)). (*See* ELO Ch.8-VI(D)(3).) Here, the right to counsel had attached because the jailhouse conversation occurred after Dan's indictment. The issue is whether Art was an "active" agent when he said to Dan, "Gee, I was surprised to hear they nabbed you." Although this was not a direct question, its purpose was almost certainly to elicit a response. This makes Art an "active" informant. Dan's Sixth Amendment rights were probably violated.

Answer to Question 11

1. *Issues Dave can raise on appeal:*

Was Dave's Sixth Amendment right to effective counsel (applicable to the states via the Fourteenth Amendment) violated?

Dave will certainly make an "effective assistance of counsel" claim. This claim is not easy to establish. In order to succeed, the accused must show: (1) his attorney's performance fell below the reasonable norm of competence for attorneys in the area generally; and (2) "but for" the lawyer's lack of professionalism, there is a reasonable possibility the results of the proceedings would have been different; *Strickland v. Washington*, 466 U.S. 668 (1984). (*See* ELO Ch.8-VI(A)(1).)

Dave will argue that his lawyer did not meet this standard: (1) the lawyer failed to conduct his own investigation to determine whether there were other witnesses than Witt; (2) he failed to question Witt to determine the extent of Witt's knowledge (if he had done this, he would have learned that Witt was not a witness to the shootings, but only to Dave's presence in the bar and to his drunkenness; (3) he apparently failed to make a formal request to the prosecution for *any* evidence which might be helpful to his client's case; and (4) he failed to argue the *Miranda* issue raised by the introduction of Officer Leslie's testimony (discussed below).

The prosecution will reply that Dave's attorney did not act unreasonably in accepting its statement that Witt was the only witness to the shooting and that Witt would testify that Dave was sober at the time. It will also argue that Dave's attorney could reasonably have concluded that the court was not likely to accept any arguments based on the *Miranda* rule on these facts.

Dave is likely to succeed on the issue of lawyer incompetence. Most significantly, his lawyer failed to direct a *Brady* request for exculpatory evidence to the prosecution. Under the decision in *Brady v. Maryland*, 373 U.S. 83 (1963), the prosecution is required under the Due Process Clause to disclose any exculpatory evidence in its possession. If Dave's lawyer had made his request, he would have learned that Witt was not a witness to the shooting and that Witt would testify that Dave was in fact quite drunk.

Were Dave's due process rights violated by the prosecution's failure to advise Dave's attorney of Witt?

As we have seen, an accused's attorney has the right under *Brady* to request and obtain from the prosecution any evidence which is material and favorable to his client. Dave will contend that because the prosecution failed to inform

Dave's attorney of the true substance of Witt's testimony, reversal is required. *U.S. v. Bagley*, 473 U.S. 667 (1985). (*See* ELO Ch.9-VI(A)(1).)

Although the prosecution did disclose that Witt was a witness, it had the affirmative duty to disclose not only the names of witnesses but also the *substance* of their testimony, if exculpatory. The prosecution failed to do that here. Thus, the *Brady* claim has a good chance of success.

Was the jury properly instructed with respect to whether Dave had attempted to perpetrate a robbery?

Under the Due Process Clause of the Fourteenth Amendment, if a jury in a criminal trial is improperly instructed on a material issue of law, the conviction must be reversed. Dave's conviction for first-degree murder required one of two critical premises: either (1) he intended to kill or seriously injure Babs, or (2) the killing occurred in the commission of a robbery. Dave's *mens rea* would be critical in determining whether either premise was satisfied. The prosecution would have to show a specific intent either (1) to kill (or seriously injure) Babs, or (2) to commit a robbery (*i.e.*, permanently deprive Babs of property by force, or the threat of force). In light of these factors, the court's instruction was incorrect because (1) Dave may have been so intoxicated as to make it impossible for him to form the requisite specific intent for first degree murder, and (2) Babs' state of mind was irrelevant on the issue of Dave's intent.

Because the court's instruction probably influenced the jury improperly, Dave's conviction should be reversed.

Was Dave's statement to Officer Leslie admissible?

Dave can argue that Officer Leslie's testimony about his confession to her should not have been admitted. Statements made to police officers during a custodial interrogation are ordinarily inadmissible, unless preceded by *Miranda* warnings. (*See* ELO Ch.5-IV(C).) Because Officer Leslie entered the bar with her revolver drawn, her question arguably constituted a custodial interrogation (*i.e.*, was reasonably calculated to elicit an incriminating response). The prosecution will reply, however, that: (1) Dave was not in custody; Officer Leslie drew her gun only because she had previously heard shots; and (2) Officer Leslie's question was more in the nature of a general and spontaneous inquiry directed at no one in particular, rather than an attempt to obtain a response from Dave which might implicate him in a crime. The prosecution should prevail on this issue. (*See* ELO Ch.5-VII.)

Summary

Because Dave's right to due process (including his right to effective assistance of counsel) were probably violated, reversal of his conviction on appeal would be proper.

2. *Can Dave be constitutionally convicted for the murder of John?*

The double jeopardy clause of the Fifth Amendment (applicable to the states via the Fourteenth Amendment) prohibits a person from being retried for the same crime after jeopardy has attached. But Dave's conduct with respect to John constitutes a separate and distinct offense from his conduct against Babs, and the mere fact that John was killed in the same incident would not bar retrial. (*See* ELO Ch.9-VIII(A).)

However, the double jeopardy doctrine also encompasses the doctrine of *collateral estoppel.* But this doctrine applies only when acquittal on one charge *necessarily* demonstrates that the suspect cannot be guilty on the other charge. *Ashe v. Swenson*, 397 U.S. 436 (1970). Thus, if Dave were retried for Babs' murder and the jury acquitted Dave after finding that he had become so intoxicated as to be incapable of forming the specific intent to (1) kill, (2) cause serious bodily injury, or (3) perpetrate a robbery, the prosecution would be bound by these findings in a subsequent prosecution of Dave for John's murder.

However, unless we know for certain that the basis for acquittal on the Babs charge was Dave's lack of the requisite "specific intent" (instead, for example, because the jury found that Dave had acted in self-defense against an attack by Babs), we can't say that a trial for John's murder would be inconsistent with the acquittal on the Babs charge. (The valid self-defense claim with respect to Babs wouldn't necessarily compel a finding of self-defense in the trial for John's killing; the facts might be different.) Consequently, collateral estoppel, and, thus, double jeopardy, may not apply.

Answer to Question 12

1. (a) The State X conviction:

The Fifth Amendment to the Constitution prevents criminal defendants from being tried twice "for the same offense." This is generally called the "double jeopardy" doctrine and is applicable to the states by means of the Fourteenth Amendment. In general, if a defendant has been tried once and acquitted, he may not be tried again, so long as the facts constituting the crime are the same in both trials. *Ashe v. Swenson*, 397 U.S. 436 (1970). Here, the facts establish that the first jury acquitted Ashley because they believed her alibi. Because the facts constituting the alibi would be the same for the first count as for the other two counts, a conviction in the second trial could not logically be sustained. The prosecution is never permitted to appeal a jury acquittal. Similarly, it cannot retry the defendant on the same facts again. Ashley cannot be prosecuted for robbery with respect to the two other tellers. Thus, the State X conviction should be reversed. See ELO Ch. 9-VIII.

(b) The federal sentence:

Under the "dual sovereignty" doctrine, a conviction or acquittal by one jurisdiction does **not** bar prosecution by **another jurisdiction on the same facts.** (*See* ELO Ch.9-VIII(G).) Therefore, the federal government can also indict and try Ashley for armed bank robbery, even though the facts presented by the prosecution will be essentially the same as in the state trial.

In a criminal jury trial, jeopardy attaches when the jury is sworn in. This fact becomes important when a mistrial occurs. Usually, the prosecution is not prevented from retrying the defendant after a mistrial. But there are circumstances in which a mistrial will preclude a new trial. If the defendant moves for mistrial, the prosecution may always retry. But if the prosecution has been guilty of "overreaching" (i.e., "pushing" or "goading" the defendant to move for a mistrial), a new trial may not be permitted. *Downum v. U.S.,* 372 U.S. 734 (1963). (*See* ELO Ch.9-VIII(C)-(D).) Here, the facts don't tell us anything about the reason for the jury discharge. Presumably, the judge was annoyed by the prosecution's request for an adjournment after the jury was sworn. On the other hand, we have the objection to the jury's discharge by the defendant's lawyer. Presumably, he would not have objected if he had believed a mistrial would preclude further prosecution.

Generally, if the prosecution asks for a reasonable delay and there is no evidence that its request is designed to get an unfair tactical advantage, it's unlikely that a mistrial will be a bar to a new trial. *Illinois v. Somerville*, 410 U.S. 458 (1973).

Was Ashley's guilty plea valid?

A defendant cannot change a guilty plea that was made voluntarily and with knowledge of its consequences. In determining whether this standard is satisfied, the judge must be assured that the defendant is competent and that she understands: (1) that she has the right to plead not guilty; (2) she is waiving the right to a trial by jury; (3) the nature of the charge as to which the plea is offered (*i.e.*, the elements which must be proved for the prosecution to be successful), and (4) the maximum possible penalty for the offense; *McCarthy v. United States*, 394 U.S. 459 (1969). In federal cases, the judge's statements and the defendant's responses must be transcribed on the record; FED.R.CRIM.P. 11(f). Because the judge merely asked Ashley whether she wanted to change her plea from guilty to innocent, these requirements were *not* satisfied. Additionally, the facts fail to indicate that Ashley's attorney explained the necessary information to her (*i.e.*, Ashley was advised only of the fact that a more lenient sentence would probably be rendered than if she were convicted of all three charges). (*See* ELO Ch.9-III(D).)

On these facts, the Supreme Court would probably vacate the guilty plea and order that Ashley be retried.

2. Can Ashley be prosecuted under "the Statute"?

Because Ashley was never charged (placed in jeopardy) for shooting and killing Fred, she can be prosecuted under the Statute without invoking double jeopardy.

Ashley can argue that because the robbery of the tellers and the shooting of Fred arose from the same set of actions, they constituted the "same" offense and that prosecution under the Statute is barred by the double jeopardy clause. However, when a second crime can be proved by at least one additional fact which is not present in or common to the first crime, the two crimes are not the "same" for double jeopardy purposes. *Brown v. Ohio*, 432 U.S. 161 (1977). Here, the Statute requires proof that a federal officer was assaulted while in the pursuit of his duties; the robbery charge required proof of the taking of property from the persons of three other people. The "additional fact" test of *Brown* would appear to be satisfied, and the prosecution is not prevented from trying Ashley under the Statute. (*See* ELO Ch.9-VIII(H)(1).)

Answer to Question 13

1. *Constitutional objections to the admission of Dan's confessions:*

A confession obtained during a custodial interrogation before the suspect has received his *Miranda* warnings is ordinarily inadmissible. Dan will argue that the statement by police officers that the gun had been identified as his constituted an "interrogation" (*i.e.*, no statement implicating him in the events should have been made to him before he was given the *Miranda* warnings), and that, therefore, his response was not admissible. Whether the statement constitutes an "interrogation" will depend upon whether the police should have recognized that their conduct was likely to evoke an incriminating response by the defendant. While the prosecution will argue that no direct questioning occurred (that Dan "blurted out" his initial confession after being told the simple facts as the police knew them), Dan will probably prevail on this issue. (*See* ELO Ch.5-VII(A)(3).)

The police will then insist that even if the initial statement is inadmissible on *Miranda* grounds, the second confession was properly preceded by *Miranda* warnings, and was, therefore, valid. Dan would respond that the two confessions cannot be separated from each other because there was not enough of a time gap between them. He would argue that he was influenced by his first pre-*Miranda* response to continue with his admissions, and that the second confession was not truly "voluntary" (*i.e.*, it was tainted by the original confession). But the Supreme Court has held that when a Mirandized second confession follows an un-Mirandized first confession, the second confession will not normally be deemed "tainted fruit" of the first — all that's required is that the second confession be "knowingly and voluntarily made." *Oregon v. Elstad*, 470 U.S. 298 (1985). Under this standard, the second confession will be admissible even if the first is not. (*See* ELO Ch.7-III(J)(4).)

2. *Entrapment defense:*

The defense of entrapment exists when the police have instigated or induced the crime for which the defendant is charged (*i.e.*, the police caused the defendant to perpetrate a crime which he was not otherwise predisposed to commit). Because Dan had several prior convictions for burglary and larceny, his predisposition to commit another similar crime is manifest. It is unlikely that Dan will succeed in asserting this defense. (*See* ELO Ch.4-V.)

A few courts have held that the defense of entrapment will be recognized when a reasonable person (regardless of his previous disposition) would, under the circumstances, be induced to commit the crime in question. If this jurisdiction held this view, Dan would argue that the average person, given the opportunity to obtain merchandise with very little risk of apprehension (*i.e.*, an employee of the place to be burglarized had promised and arranged easy access to it), would be tempted to commit the offense. But this argument would probably not work either. While many people might agree to buy or sell stolen merchandise when an apparently risk-free profit could be made, most people would not be willing to break into a warehouse in the dark of night.

In sum, Dan probably will not prevail on an entrapment defense.

3. *What objections should Betty make to the admission of the stamps?*

Betty will contend that the federal officers were required to obtain a search warrant before seizing the stamps from her.

The prosecution will make two arguments in response. There is no expectation of privacy with respect to items voluntarily delivered by one person to another. Therefore, the stamps which were sold by Betty to the federal officer should be admissible against Betty. (*See* ELO Ch.2-II(E).) Second, the stamps in the cabinet were seized incident to a valid arrest (*i.e.*, they were within Betty's immediate control). Betty will reply that items inside (as opposed to those on top of) the display cabinet were *not* within her immediate control at the time of the arrest. The Supreme Court has continued to hold that a seizure is not incident to arrest unless the suspect has some opportunity at the time of arrest to get control of the item. Betty will probably prevail with respect to the stamps in the cabinet. *U.S. v. Chadwick*, 433 U.S. 1 (1977). (*See* ELO Ch.3-III(C)(1)(a).)

4. *What objections should Betty make to the admission of the gun?*

Because the gun was obtained by the police without a warrant, Betty could contend that it is inadmissible. It is well established that a hotelkeeper cannot consent to the search of a room occupied by a guest. *Stoner v. California*, 376 U.S. 483 (1964). (*See* ELO Ch.3-VIII(G)(1)(a).)

But the prosecution will make two arguments in reply. First, Betty has no standing to complain of an unlawful search of her aunt's hotel room (*i.e.*, she had no expectation of privacy with respect to that room). (*See* ELO Ch.7-II(C)(1).) Secondly, even if we assume that this jurisdiction extends standing to anyone affected by unlawful police conduct, here, a person who was not a police officer--he was a hotel employe--conducted the search (and did so on his own, rather than at the instigation or request of the government). Under these circumstances, the defendant has no constitutional right to object if the civilian employee notifies the government about contraband or other evidence of criminality he may have found. *U.S. v. Jacobsen*, 466 U.S. 109 (1984). By the time the police saw the suitcase, they had probable cause (obtained without police violation of Betty's rights) to seize it and to arrest Betty. (*See* ELO Ch.2-II(E)(4).)

Therefore the gun should be admissible against Betty.

Answer to Question 14

Does Joe have standing to object to the introduction of the incriminating books and records found in Eddy's home?

When a defendant has no expectation of privacy with respect to an area searched by the police, he lacks standing to complain about alleged police misconduct within the area. Because all of the possible police misconduct (the observation of the rooms from the roof, and the subsequent entry into Eddy's home, as well as the seizure of gambling paraphernalia) was a violation of Eddy's rights, not Joe's, the prosecution can contend that Joe has no standing to assert any rights under the Fourth Amendment (applicable to the states via the Fourteenth Amendment). The fact that the books and records of the gambling operation referred to Joe is probably not enough to give him any expectation of privacy with respect to those records. However, a few states grant inherent standing to anyone whose rights are affected by police misconduct, even though the majority view would deny Joe standing. Although it's not clear that Joe will be given standing, we will discuss the other issues on the assumption that he will. (*See* ELO Ch.7-II(C).)

Was the observation into Eddy's home a search?

Joe will point out that Eddy's windows were nine feet above the ground, creating an expectation of privacy and immunity from observation. That expectation of privacy, therefore, dictated that the police obtain a warrant before observing into the building from a place above the ground. Without a warrant for the observation, all of the evidence derived from it would be inadmissible. But the prosecution will respond that no one can have an expectation of privacy in areas which can be observed by the public. Eddy's neighbor was free to climb onto his own roof and peer into Eddy's window. If the neighbor could do it, then a police officer could do it without violating Eddy's right of privacy (and, by extension, Joe's.) Joe will reply that it's unlikely that Eddy's neighbor would climb onto his roof just to look into Eddy's window (and, in fact, unlikely that he would climb onto the roof himself for *any* purpose), and since Able and Baker had to trespass and go through a lot of effort just to look in the window, it's reasonable to conclude that Eddy had an expectation of privacy in his quarters. Joe would appear to have the better of these arguments and is likely to prevail on this issue. (*See* ELO Ch.2-II(C)(2)(b).)

Was the police entry into Eddy's home valid?

The prosecution will argue that the police officers acted reasonably in ringing Eddy's doorbell to ask a few preliminary investigative questions. They will assert that their brief questioning at the door of the residence — which did not involve detaining Cathy or anyone else — did not rise to the level of a Fourth Amendment "stop." The prosecution will probably succeed with this argument. (*See* ELO Ch.3-IX(E).)

Joe will argue that (even if it was proper for the police to attempt to question Eddy) the entry into Eddy's home was unlawful in the absence of a warrant to search the premises. Furthermore, the consent to their entry by Cathy did not constitute effective permission to enter and search: (1) the police had misrepresented themselves and their purpose (instead of identifying herself as a police officer, Officer Able stated that she knew Eddy, thus suggesting that he would be pleased to see her and talk to her), and (2) a 14-year-old lacks authority to consent to entry into premises owned by her parent. Finally, in most states, the police must announce their purpose and authority before entering someone's home. Since the entry into Eddy's house was unlawful, the evidence derived as a result should be inadmissible.

The prosecution will respond as follows: First, no warrant was required, because the police merely wanted to question Eddy about what they had seen from the roof, not to arrest him or search his house (so there was, therefore, no Fourth Amendment stop or search at all). Second, their statements to Cathy were not dishonest (*i.e.*, Officer Able had known Eddy for several years and did desire to question him). Third, a 14-year-old can consent to entry into her own home (especially when, as in this instance, her father apparently permitted her to answer the door, and especially because the visitors were given access only to a common room in the house rather than, say, to a study or a bedroom). Finally, the requirement that the police announce their authority and purpose is negated when the police have reason to believe that evidence may be destroyed (these are called "exigent circumstances"). Had Able and Baker identified themselves as police officers, it is likely that (1) they would not have been permitted entry into Eddy's home, and (2) books and records pertaining to Eddy's gambling operation might have been hidden or shredded.

The prosecution will probably win on the issue of entry — most courts hold that deception by undercover agents as to their identity doesn't nullify consent, and most courts also allow a teenager to consent to entry into at least the common areas of her parent's house. (*See* Ch.3-VII(F), VIII(E).)

If their entry into Eddy's home was valid, Able and Baker were probably (1) entitled to open the door to the room in which the bets were being taken (the words being spoken in the room were in "plain sound" and justified Able and Baker in inspecting the area from which they came), and (2) permitted to seize evidence of Eddy's gambling activities under the "plain view" doctrine. (*See* ELO Ch.3-V(B).)

Is Joe's statement ("I want to bet $1,500 on Citation") admissible?

Joe can contend that his statement is inadmissible because Officer Able's question was not preceded by *Miranda* warnings. But, because Joe was not in custody at the time of Able's inquiry, this contention should fail. (*See* ELO Ch.5-V(C).)

Finally, we should mention that Joe will probably not be able to assert an entrapment defense. The relatively innocent inquiry, "Can I help you?" cannot reasonably be considered a police invitation to engage in illegal activity. Also, because Joe was a reputed mobster and his name was found in the gambling records confiscated at Eddy's home, the prosecution should have no difficulty showing that Joe was predisposed to the crime for which he was charged. (*See* ELO Ch.4-V(A).)

Answer to Question 15

Juvenile delinquency adjudication

The argument by Debbie's attorney that Debbie was entitled to a jury trial will *not* be successful. The Supreme Court has held that this right does not extend to delinquency proceedings; *McKeiver v. Pennsylvania*, 403 U.S. 528 (1971).

Because Debbie was adjudged a juvenile delinquent on two independent grounds---possession of marijuana and refusal to answer the court's questions, each one must be analyzed separately.

The findings based on possession of marijuana

The facts raise important issues surrounding searches of students and their effects in public schools. So long as there are "reasonable grounds for suspecting that the search will turn up evidence that the students has violated or is violating either the law or the rules of the school," a warrantless search is permitted. And the search may be conducted by an authorized agent of the school, *e.g.,* the principal. *New Jersey v. T.L.O.*, 469 U.S. 325 (1985). (*See* ELO Ch.3-X(I)(2).)

It is still an open question, however, whether the warrantless search may extend to lockers, desks or other areas provided by the school for the private use of the student. As to those areas, the Court may ultimately decide that a warrant is necessary before a search. (See ELO Ch.3-X(I)(4). Debbie's best argument is that it wasn't necessary for the principal to open any locker. Even assuming the lockers were waterlogged, the consequence would be damage to student property, not to any interest of the school. In any event, before he opened lockers, the principal was required to obtain a warrant, especially as it might relate to any specific locker. The prosecution will reply that no "search" within the meaning of the Fourth Amendment occurred, because the principal acted with the intent of preserving student property, rather than the intent to seek evidence that might implicate anyone in a crime. The prosecution will also rely on Debbie's signed consent which authorized members of the high school staff to inspect her locker at any time. (*See* ELO Ch.3-VII(A).)

Debbie's signature on the consent form is a difficult fact for Debbie's attorney to overcome. His best argument is that the consent was only intended to apply when circumstances would indicate on some reasonable basis that her individual locker might contain a weapon, or some item of contraband, or another object which would violate the school's rules. On these facts, there was nothing which would justify any suspicion of Debbie by the school authorities.

On the facts, Debbie should prevail and the marijuana should be excluded from evidence.

The finding of juvenile delinquency based upon Debbie's refusal to answer the court's questions

Debbie's attorney will argue that this issue is moot: if Debbie's locker had not been opened unlawfully and the marijuana found, Debbie would not have been accused and tried; and she would not have been subjected to the need to tattle on her friend or to confront the court's questions.

This is a subtle argument and it may not impress the court. The prosecution will argue, of course, that however she got there, Debbie was required to obey the court and answer its questions. But Debbie's attorney will also argue that refusal to answer a judge's questions probably does not constitute delinquency as defined in the laws of Central.

Debbie should win on these arguments, but we will assume for the moment that the court will decide to the contrary.

Debbie's refusal to answer the court's questions will be based in part on her own Fifth Amendment right not to incriminate herself. (A witness has, of course, no right to refuse to answer questions on the grounds that this would incriminate someone else.) The Fifth Amendment is applicable to delinquency proceedings (*In re Gault*, 387 U.S. 1 (1967)), but once an accused takes the stand, this privilege is waived. Thus, even if Debbie had a good faith reason for believing that disclosure of her friend's name might somehow implicate her in a crime, she could no longer rely on on her Fifth Amendment rights. Ordinarily, the court would be justified in insisting on her answer, at least in the absence of the other factors which justify her refusal (see above). (*See* ELO Ch.7-IV(D)(4); Ch.9-VII(D)(1).)

Eighth Amendment

Debbie will also argue that declaring her a delinquent because she refused to answer the court's questions violated her Eighth Amendment right. That is, even though some punishment for contempt may have been reasonable, confinement for three months simply for refusing to answer a question constitutes cruel and unusual punishment in violation of the Eighth Amendment (applicable to the states via the Fourteenth Amendment). The penalty is unreasonably disproportionate to the conduct in question (*i.e.*, refusing to divulge the name of a classmate). Debbie should prevail on this issue.

Summary

Close review of all the issues suggests that the search of Debbie's locker by the principal was unjustified under all the circumstances. There was no reasonable basis for searching Debbie's locker in particular. The discovery of the marijuana was the fruit of an invalid search. Debbie should not have been prosecuted in the first place. Her refusal to answer the judge's questions was the inevitable consequence of the principal's wrongful act. The court should rule for Debbie.

Answer to Question 16

Did the police legally arrest Cindy?

If the police did not have probable cause to arrest Cindy, or if an arrest warrant was required, much of the evidence described below would probably represent "fruits of the poisonous tree." As such, the evidence would be inadmissible. (*See* ELO Ch.7-III(B).)

Cindy will contend that the police lacked probable cause to arrest her based solely upon Sylvia's description and upon the documents and records found on Allen's dining room table. Alternatively, she will argue that even if the police had probable cause to arrest, they were required to obtain an arrest warrant before they would be permitted to arrest Cindy in her home.

On the probable cause issue, the prosecution will rely on the following: (1) the fact that Allen had financial documents pertaining to stock transactions strewn on his dining room table, and (2) the statement concerning the Stock Exchange made by Cindy. These were enough to arouse reasonable suspicion that Allen's stockbroker was responsible for the attack. When they arrived at Cindy's home and she fit the description given by Sylvia, their suspicion ripened into probable cause. As to the lack of a warrant, the prosecution will assert that no warrant was needed because they were in hot pursuit (*i.e.*, they arrived at her house only 10 minutes after her) and exigent circumstances existed (*i.e.*, realizing that the police suspected her, Cindy might flee the jurisdiction if not arrested immediately). (*See* ELO Ch.2-III(B)(1); Ch.3-IV(A), (D).)

The prosecution would probably prevail on these issues.

1. The hospital room identification:

Cindy will argue that Allen's hospital room identification was inadmissible because her due process rights were violated. The appropriate test requires that the procedure used for identification not be "so unnecessarily suggestive and conducive to irreparable mistaken identification" as to deny the suspect her due process. *Stovall v. Denno*, 388 U.S. 293 (1967). (*See* ELO Ch.6-V(A).)

Under the circumstances (the time span involved), we can assume that Cindy was the only person shown to Allen and that she was still wearing her blood-splattered clothing. Cindy has a plausible argument that the procedure under which Allen identified her was indeed "unnecessarily suggestive" and "conducive to irreparable mistake." The prosecution will reply: (1) it was conceivable that Allen would die at any moment (*i.e.*, there was no time to conduct a formal lineup in the hospital room); and (2) because Allen had known Cindy for a long period of time and she was alone with him at the time of the stabbing, there was little likelihood of misidentification. An in-hospital identification by a critically-ill victim was, in fact, upheld in *Stovall* itself. Allen's hospital room identification, therefore, would probably be admissible.

Cindy will argue that her Sixth Amendment right of confrontation (applicable to the states via the Fourteenth Amendment) was violated, because (1) Allen's statement would be proven by the testimony of the police officer who heard it (*i.e.* hearsay), and (2) Allen would not be available for cross-examination. But "dying declarations" (*i.e.*, statements by an individual who sincerely believes that death may be imminent) are deemed to contain sufficient indicia of reliability to overcome an accused's Sixth Amendment objections. (*See* ELO Ch.9-VII(C)(2)(b).)

Lastly, Cindy will assert that she had a Sixth Amendment right to counsel during the hospital-room identification. But this argument will fail — a suspect has no right to the presence of counsel at a show-up or other identification procedure unless formal proceedings have been instituted against her. *Kirby v. Illinois*, 406 U.S. 682 (1972). (*See* ELO Ch.6-IV(A).)

If Cindy does succeed in having the in-hospital ID ruled illegal, she will then argue that many of the other items of evidence (*e.g.*, the blood stains on Cindy's clothing, or Cindy's incriminating statements to Paula) were the fruits of the poisonous identification. That is, the police would never have gotten — or at least, they would not have had probable cause to get — these other pieces of identification without first getting the ID. Cindy has a respectable chance of succeeding on this "poisonous fruits" argument. But the prosecution may be able to show that it would have obtained these pieces of evidence anyway, so that the taint should be deemed "purged." (*See* ELO Ch.7-III(C)(2), (D).) The rest of our discussion assumes that the in-hospital ID will be found valid.

2. *Sylvia's visual identification of Cindy at the lineup:*

We assume that: (1) the lineup was properly conducted (*i.e.*, the other persons taking part in the lineup were of relatively similar size and height as Cindy), and (2) Sylvia will be available to testify as to her identification of Cindy at the lineup. If these assumptions are accurate, then Sylvia's identification at the lineup will be admissible. If the lineup was not properly conducted, Cindy's due process rights may have been violated. If Sylvia will not testify, and, thus, will not be available for cross-examination, a Sixth Amendment right-of-confrontation issue will arise.

Again, Cindy had no Sixth Amendment right to have an attorney present, since she had not yet been formally charged with a crime.

3. Sylvia's voice identification of Cindy at the lineup:

Again, it will be assumed for our discussion that: (1) each person at the lineup was required to state the words, "What will I ever do? What will the Stock Exchange do with me?" and (2) Sylvia will testify at Cindy's trial.

Cindy will argue that her Fifth Amendment rights (applicable to the states via the Fourteenth Amendment) were violated by requiring her to repeat the words which Allen's assailant was heard to scream as she left the apartment. But the prosecution will contend that the Fifth Amendment applies only to "communications" or "testimony" not to real or physical evidence, even evidence taken forcibly from the suspect's body. *Schmerber v. California*, 384 U.S. 757 (1966). (*See* ELO Ch.6-II(A).) Several case have permitted forced statements by the suspect for the purpose of identifying his voice. *U.S. v. Dionisio*, 410 U.S. 1 (1973). The prosecution will prevail on this issue.

4. The results of the laboratory analysis performed on Cindy's clothing:

Cindy will assert that, because they never obtained a search warrant, the police had no right to seize her clothing and do a laboratory analysis on the blood found on the clothing. On the assumption, however, that the prosecution convinces the court that the arrest was lawful, the police search would probably also be permitted as a full inventory search of the suspect's person and clothing. The seizure of Cindy's clothing and the results of the laboratory analysis matching Allen's blood to the blood on her clothing would then be admissible.

If Cindy does establish that her arrest was unlawful, her "fruits of the poisonous tree" argument as it applies to the lab results would be quite powerful — in that event, the seizure would be the direct result of the arrest, and the lab results would be the direct result of the seizure; assuming an unlawful arrest, the court would probably find the lab results inadmissible.

5. Cindy's statement to Paula while awaiting trial:

Cindy will contend that Paula was a police informant who was deliberately put into her cell, thus violating Cindy's Sixth Amendment right to an attorney at all "critical stages" of the proceedings. However, because Paula was strictly instructed to refrain from asking Cindy any questions, and followed these instructions, Cindy's statement to Paula will probably be admissible against her; *Kuhlmann v. Wilson*, 477 U.S. 436 (1986). These circumstances are distinguishable from situations in which a cellmate/informant deliberately solicited statements from the defendant. *U.S. v. Henry*, 447 U.S. 264 (1980). (*See* ELO Ch.8-VI(D).)

Answer to Question 17

1. Is Doug's gun admissible into evidence?

Are Bus Co. personnel considered governmental agents?

The Fourth Amendment proscription against unreasonable searches and seizures (applicable to the states via the Fourteenth Amendment) applies only to *governmental* action. Here, the people who seized Doug's gun worked for a private bus company, and the prosecution will argue that Doug had no right to complain about the search, especially since he had chosen to use the bus instead of some other means of transportation. Doug will reply: (1) the terminal itself was publicly-operated; (2) mass transportation is a quasi-public function; and (3) the security personnel were, in effect, carrying out a police function (*i.e.*, preventing criminal acts which might threaten Bus Co.) For these reasons, the guards who had seized Doug's gun should be viewed as governmental agents.

In dealing with the other issues presented by these facts, we will assume that the court would find that the bus guards should be treated as government agents.

Did use of the metal detector constitute an unreasonable search?

Doug will assert that the metal detector constituted an illegal (*i.e.*, warrantless) search. As a result, the gun would be inadmissible as "fruit of a poisonous tree." The prosecution will reply that a metal detector at a mass transportation facility causes such a minimal intrusion upon a traveler's expectation of privacy, that no "search" within the meaning of the Fourth Amendment occurs. The prosecution will argue that use of a metal detector is like the "sniff-test" by a trained narcotics detection dog, which has been held not to violate the Fourth Amendment. *United States v. Place*, 462 U.S. 696 (1983). Given the impersonal intrusion posed by a metal detector (*i.e.*, there is no physical encroachment upon the individual) and the importance of transportation safety, the prosecution would probably prevail on this issue. (*See* ELO Ch.2-II(C)(2)(b), (D)(6)(c).)

Did Doug consent to the search?

Doug may be deemed to have consented to a search if the presence of the metal detector was or should have been obvious to him. (*See* ELO Ch.3-VII(A).)

If the metal detector constituted a search which was not consented to by Doug, was it valid?

No court today would be likely to question a search of passengers boarding any means of mass transportation, provided the search is carried out in a neutral and non-invasive manner. The public concern for safety in the operation of mass transportation has been deemed to outweigh the relatively minor inconvenience to passengers. This reasoning would be applicable to bus passengers in the same way as airline passengers, especially when bomb threats have already been made.

It has long been the practice to search the clothing and baggage of airline travelers. The searches have traditionally been conducted by private personnel without governmental affiliation. The rationale supporting these searches is that when large groups of people travel in one conveyance, they are entitled to protection against the possible acts of a resolute and violent few. No one would seriously argue any longer that these searches are unjustified or that they raise constitutional issues.

As we become more adjusted to continuing threats of violence in public places, the use of guards to search for guns and knives will grow. Since September 11, 2001, searches have been routinely conducted in many places which would normally be considered inviolate (*e.g.*, searches of briefcases in courthouses, even those carried by lawyers; searches on trains; searches at the entrances of office buildings, sports events, public performances, etc.).

In the present climate, it's unlikely that Doug would get very far in his argument. The court is likely to hold that a search of people entering a bus with 40 or 60 passengers is not essentially different from a search of 200 people boarding an airplane. Here especially, we know that there had been specific bomb threats. The bus company would be considered justified in protecting its passengers, especially in a public terminal. Thus, the gun will almost certainly be admissible against Doug.

Was it proper to detain and search Doug after the metal detector was activated?

When police officers have a reasonable suspicion that someone may be carrying an illegal weapon, they may stop and frisk that individual. Doug will assert that since metal detectors are activated by any number of lawful objects (*i.e.*, keys, belt buckles, etc.), the security personnel did not have sufficient "reasonable suspicion" to search his pockets. However, activation of the metal detector probably justified a search of Doug's pockets (at least if Doug insisted on boarding the bus). Ordinarily, in searches of people in mass facilities (airports, courthouses, etc.) the people are asked to empty their pockets as part of the search. Arguably, reaching into a person's pocket would be no more intrusive. (*See* ELO Ch.3-IX(B).)

Assuming that the search of Doug's pockets was proper, retention of the gun by Bus Co. security personnel was probably also valid — at that point, they had probable cause to believe that the gun was evidence of a crime (the murder of Thompson), especially since the guard had followed the Thompson story in the newspapers and knew that Doug's gun fit the description of the gun used in the killing. The ballistics test and its results would also be admissible, since once an item is validly in police custody, it may ordinarily be subjected to any type of reasonable test or analysis.

2. *The blood stains on the front seat of the car:*

Doug will argue that he was unlawfully stopped and detained--the use of hazard lights does not constitute a traffic violation. The prosecution will reply that no detention occurred — Officer West did not stop Doug for the purpose of questioning him about any criminal activity but to find out if Doug was having car trouble which the officer could help to resolve. Officer West had a right also to be concerned about other motorists (when blinking hazard lights are used, other drivers are uncertain what the driver intends to do--*i.e.,* make a left turn, right turn, or stop). (*See* ELO Ch.3-IX(E).)

Because the initial stop of Doug was probably valid, inspection of the bloodstains on the front seat of Doug's car did not require a warrant. Under the "plain view" doctrine, when a police officer is positioned at a vantage point which he has a right to occupy and sees evidence of criminal activity, she may seize the evidence without a warrant. In the case of evidence attached to or within an automobile, she may seize the auto itself for further investigation. (*See* ELO Ch.3-V(B).)

Thus, the laboratory analysis indicating that the bloodstains matched those of Thompson would be admissible.

3. *Doug's statement to Officer West:*

Assuming the stop of Doug's car is held to be proper, Doug will nevertheless argue that Officer West's comment about Doug's probable guilt was a custodial interrogation (*i.e.*, reasonably calculated to elicit an incriminating response). Since it was not preceded by *Miranda* warnings, it is arguably inadmissible. However, even if the comment was reasonably likely to elicit an incriminating response, the court is likely to hold that Doug was not in "custody." The test is an objective one — would a reasonable person in the suspect's position believe he was free to leave? *Berkemer v. McCarty*, 468 U.S. 420 (1984). While Doug will argue that an individual ordinarily does not feel free to drive away from a police officer who is leaning against his car, the prosecution would probably prevail on this issue too. (*See* ELO Ch.5-V(C).)

Answer to Question 18

1. What evidence is admissible?

Was the initial stop of Tony valid?

If the initial stop was not valid, all of the evidence subsequently obtained would be inadmissible as "fruits of the poisonous tree."

A police officer may stop the driver of a vehicle when she has a reasonable suspicion that he is engaged in criminal activity. To satisfy this standard, the prosecution must show that Officer Meane had an objective, articulable basis for her belief (rather than a mere hunch). Tony will argue that because (1) he was driving legally, and (2) Officer Meane was not in a position to observe the "weird smile" on his face for more than a moment, no "reasonable suspicion" of criminal activity could have been formed. The prosecution will argue, however, that Officer Meane was an experienced Highway Patrol officer and her experience would tell her when weird smile and slow speed combined to raise a reasonable suspicion that the driver was under the influence of an intoxicant. Although this is a close question, the prosecution will probably prevail. (If Tony prevails, the case against him should be dismissed, because all of the evidence against him was derived from the illegal stop.) (*See* ELO Ch.3-IX(D).)

Was the field sobriety test valid?

The field sobriety test constituted an additional search which was not justified without probable cause. The factors (described above) which constituted the basis for stopping Tony, plus the likely odor of beer on Tony's breath, were enough to give Officer Meane probable cause to believe that Tony was drunk, thereby justifying the field sobriety test. If so, the results of that test would also be admissible. Alternatively, the court may reasonably conclude that Tony implicitly consented (by undergoing the test without an objection) to taking the test. If so, probable cause for the test would not be necessary. (*See* ELO Ch.3-VII.)

Is Tony's initial conversation with Officer Meane admissible?

A custodial interrogation must be preceded by *Miranda* warnings. Because these were not given to Tony, he will contend that his statements are inadmissible. However, the prosecution could argue that Tony was not in custody when his conversations with Officer Meane took place. In *Berkemer v. McCarty*, 468 U.S. 420 (1984), the Supreme Court ruled that one who has been stopped on a public road for a minor traffic violation is normally not in "custody" for *Miranda* purposes. Additionally, a cordial atmosphere apparently prevailed at first between Tony and Officer Meane. While Officer Meane could have arrested Tony immediately after Tony failed the sobriety test (in which event Tony would have been in custody), there was no constitutional requirement that she do so. (*See* ELO Ch.5-V(D)(3).)

Tony will then argue that, even if *Miranda* warnings were not required in this context, his statements to Officer Meane were involuntary, and, therefore, violated both his Fifth Amendment privilege against self-incrimination and his Fourteenth Amendment right to due process. This argument will be supported by the fact that Tony was under the influence of intoxicants, and was incapable of understanding the devastating effect which his statements would have in his subsequent trial. In *Colorado v. Connelly*, 479 U.S. 157 (1986), however, the Supreme Court ruled that statements made by a suspect who suffered from an unfounded paranoia that he would be punished if he failed to answer the police's questions were nevertheless admissible. (*See* ELO Ch.5-X(C)(8).) The Court reasoned that as long as no police overreaching had taken place, a suspect's inherent condition did not make his statements involuntary. The theory of *Connelly* would mean that Tony's statement here, even though the product of his drunkenness, was not involuntary.

Thus, Officer Meane can probably testify with respect to her initial conversation with Tony.

Was Tony's statement at the station house admissible?

If the court should rule that Tony's initial conversation with Officer Meane is inadmissible, Tony will argue that his confession at the station house is also inadmissible, (That is, Tony would argue that this confession was tainted by the first; he reasoned that because he had already made one incriminating statement, and another after he had waived his *Miranda* rights (i.e., by admitting his use of marijuana and offering Officer Meane his last marijuana cigarette), he had nothing left to lose by repeating and amplifying his first confession.) But the Supreme Court has rejected this "cat out of the bag" theory and has ruled that an earlier illegal confession does not *per se* invalidate a subsequent one; *Oregon v. Elstad*, 470 U.S. 298 (1985). (*See* ELO Ch.7-III(J)(4).) Because Tony would presumably have "sobered-up" by the time of his station house statements, and because these later verbal statements amplified on the first one (they covered the marijuana, which the first statement did not) the station house statements probably would be ruled untainted and, thus, admissible against Tony. Furthermore, Tony's confession in the station house only confirmed the confession he had already made when he handed Officer Meane a marijuana cigarette and admitted his use of marijuana after waiving his *Miranda* rights.

Is the marijuana cigarette admissible?

Because Tony voluntarily gave this item to Officer Meane after waiving his Miranda rights, he would have no viable argument against its admissibility. In any event, it presumably would inevitably have been discovered by the police anyway, either by Officer Meane as a search incident to a valid arrest or at the station house pursuant to a "booking" (or inventory) search. (*See* ELO Ch.7-III(C)(2).)

2. *What other issues are available on appeal?*

Tony should contend that his Sixth Amendment right to represent himself (applicable to the states via the Fourteenth Amendment) was violated by the court's order to appoint counsel for him; *Faretta v. California*, 422 U.S. 806 (1975). A person has an absolute right to represent himself in a criminal proceeding. This right applies even though the trial judge reasonably believes that the person will do an incompetent job of representing himself. Tony, therefore, will probably have an automatic right to retrial on this basis. (*See* ELO Ch.8-V(C).)

Answer to Question 19

1. Were the arrest and search warrants validly issued? Were the radios admissible?

To arrest an individual or search an area in which that individual had a reasonable expectation of privacy, probable cause must exist. (That is, it must be more probable than not that the defendant committed a crime or that evidence of criminal activity will be located in the area to be searched.) (*See* ELO Ch.2-III(A)-(B).) When tips from an informant are the sole basis for probable cause, the sufficiency of the tips is measured by the "totality of the circumstances." The reputation of the informant as a generally reliable witness, and and the informant's basis for knowing the particular facts at issue, will both be considered in assessing the "totality of the circumstances." *Illinois v. Gates*, 462 U.S. 213 (1983). (*See* ELO Ch.2-IV(B).)

Dot would argue that the affidavit presented to the magistrate was insufficient because: (1) there was no statement telling why the source was reliable (*i.e.*, had he given accurate information in the past; did he actually see the radios?; if so, when and under what circumstances?); (2) the affidavit failed to indicate that Dot had any part in the theft of the radios or knew that they were stolen; and (3) the fact that Dot had previously been convicted of grand larceny and associated with convicted felons was irrelevant to this specific crime. However, the prosecution will reply that (1) implicit in the words "who knows Dot" is that the informant had personal knowledge that Dot was involved in the crime in question, and (2) the affidavit did say that the radios were in Dot's apartment; this supported the charge that she was in possession of stolen property.

Conclusion: the information contained in Officer Brown's affidavit was insufficient to establish probable cause to arrest Dot or search her apartment.

Is the "good faith" exception to the exclusionary rule applicable?

The prosecution will contend that, even if probable cause did not exist, the *"good faith"* exception to the exclusionary rule applied. Under that exception, when police officers reasonably and in good faith rely upon a facially adequate warrant, however deficient, the fruits of that search are admissible; *United States v. Leon*, 468 U.S. 897 (1984). Since Officer Brown was acting in good faith and may be presumed to have believed that his affidavit supporting the warrants was adequate, the radios found at Dot's apartment are arguably admissible. While Dot would assert that Officer Brown should have realized that the warrant was facially insufficient (*i.e.*, he had prepared the warrant himself), the prosecution would probably prevail on this issue. Thus, the radios should be admitted against Dot. (*See* ELO Ch.2-V(H).)

Even if the "good faith" exception is inapplicable, are the radios nevertheless admissible against Dot, under the plain view doctrine?

Even if Dot was successful with respect to the issues discussed above, the prosecution can still argue that the radios are admissible against her.

Its argument would proceed along the following lines: (1) the police may arrest without a warrant and outside her home someone who may have committed a felony (provided probable cause exists); (2) although insufficient information may have been provided to the magistrate, Officer Brown (personally) had enough information to arrest Dot (*i.e.*, a statement by a participant in the crime that he was assisted by Dot); (3) Dot voluntarily let Officer Brown into her apartment (she must have been aware that Officer Brown was accompanying her as she entered the apartment to make a telephone call); and (4) the radios were in *plain view* (*i.e.*, they were observed by Officer Brown from a vantage point he had a right to be in). For these reasons, the radios are admissible.

Dot will reply that (1) probable cause did not exist because the statements of Hal, her ex-husband, might have been prompted by ulterior motives, such as vindictiveness or an effort to get a lighter sentence, and (2) because Officer Brown had to leave Dot's side and walk over to the boxes before he could determine that they contained radios, they were not in plain view from the place where he had a right to be (at Dot's side). But the prosecution should prevail on this issue for the following reasons: (1) Hal's statement probably could be taken as trustworthy, in light of the fact that he had confessed to a crime for which he had not been arrested; (2) an officer is permitted to accompany a suspect who has been lawfully arrested, even in his home. *Washington v. Chrisman*, 455 U.S. 1 (1982); (3) while he's accompanying her, he may continue to observe those areas and inspect those articles that come into view; (4) Officer Brown could see enough as he walked beside Dot to arouse his suspicion that the boxes contained radios, thus justifying his detour; and (5) Officer Brown had a right to inspect the boxes to confirm his suspicions. (*See* ELO Ch.3-III(K), V(B).)

The prosecutor probably gets the better of these arguments. Thus, the radios are probably admissible against Dot.

2. Was the in-court identification of Dot by Grace admissible?

When a witness identifies a suspect through the use of photos under circumstances involving the police, due process requires that the process not be "unnecessarily suggestive." *Simmons v. U.S.*, 390 U.S. 377 (1968). A suggestive identification can undermine the witness' ability to make a fair in-court identification of the suspect during the trial. This will happen when the identification is so suggestive as to create a substantial likelihood of irreparable misidentification. *Simmons*, *supra*. (*See* ELO Ch.6-V(C).)

Dot will argue that it was improper to limit Grace's identification to Dot's photo and not to show the photos of the other women who worked at Store. Fifty women worked at Store. When Marsh showed Grace only Dot's photo, it suggested to Grace that Dot was already a suspect in the robbery. That was enough to cloud Grace's identification. Because a substantial likelihood of misidentification had been created, Dot's due process rights were violated. But the prosecution will reply that (1) no governmental action was involved because it was Marsh (not Officer Brown) who presented the photograph to Grace, and (2) Grace's response to the photograph ("She could be the one") was not a positive identification of Dot. (The significance of the latter point is that witnesses are sometimes reluctant to recant their previous identifications; if the first identification is ambiguous, as here, the witness will be more apt to discount her identification and testify accurately at trial, especially because she will consider her testimony at trial to be more significant to the proceeding than her earlier identification.) Because Grace saw the person talking to the delivery clerk from a distance of only 30 feet, the identification was probably reliable.

On this reasoning, Grace's in-court identification of Dot is admissible. This would be true even if Officer Brown was the one who had asked Grace to look at Dot's photo.

3. Should Officer Brown's testimony with respect to Hal's statement have been admitted?

First, we must assume that any hearsay objection which Dot may have made was properly overruled.

Whether Dot's Sixth Amendment right of confrontation was violated by reason of Officer Brown's testimony about Hal's statements to him would probably depend upon Dot's ability to call Hal as an adverse witness. If Hal could be cross-examined about these statements, Dot's right of confrontation would be satisfied. Hal would apparently be obliged to take the stand if called, because he has already pleaded guilty to the crime of larceny (the Fifth Amendment privilege against self-incrimination could *not* be asserted in that case).

If Hal cannot be cross-examined by Dot, the prosecution will argue that there are sufficient indicia of Hal's reliability as a witness (*i.e.*, he confessed to a crime unrelated to the one for which he was arrested) to overcome an objection based on the right of confrontation. But this argument will probably *fail*. The separation between Dot and Hal may have been less than amicable, and Hal may have wanted to "frame" Dot.

Unless Hal can be cross-examined by Dot, Officer Brown's testimony should *not* be admitted. (*See* ELO Ch.9-VII(C)(2).)

4. Did the court properly admit Marsh's testimony as to Dot 's statement to him?

The court permitted Marsh to testify as to Dot's statement to him at the store on the day of the crime (that she was in the store during the time of the robbery). Dot will argue that Marsh should not be permitted to testify about the statement, because Dot was not given *Miranda* warnings before she made it. But this argument will fail for several reasons. First, the inquiry was made by Marsh (rather than Officer Brown), so no governmental conduct was involved. (*See* ELO Ch.5-VII(D).) Even assuming that the inquiry could somehow be attributed to Officer Brown becauseMarch asked his question in Brown's presence, Dot was not in custody at the time of the interrogation. Finally, statements which do not satisfy a suspect's *Miranda* rights, but which are voluntarily made, may be utilized for purposes of **impeachment** (*Harris v. New York*, 401 U.S. 222 (1971)); Marsh's testimony here was used to impeach Dot's denial of having been in the store at the time of the theft (rather than as part of the prosecution's case in chief). (*See* ELO Ch.5-XII(B).)

Answer to Question 20

Dunn's arrest resulted from a series of police actions prompted by the tips from Buck, an unreliable and prejudiced witness with an ulterior purpose. The court should rule that all the evidence against Dunn was obtained illegally and that both charges against him--statutory rape and possession of marijuana--should be dismissed.

Can the results of the police surveillance of Dunn's apartment be considered in determining whether the police had probable cause to arrest Dunn?

The police surveillance of Dunn's apartment can be regarded as a search. Because no search warrant was obtained, Dunn will argue that the fruits of the search (the observation of Sally's and Dunn's conduct) must be disregarded in determining whether probable cause to arrest Dunn existed. The prosecution will reply that an individual has no expectation of privacy with respect to conduct which can be observed by the general public. Because people from an adjoining apartment were able to see Dunn and Sally, Dunn cannot complain that police officers (rather than his neighbors) were the ones who undertook to observe them. The prosecution will contend the surveillance was simply not a Fourth Amendment search at all. (*See* ELO Ch.2-II(C).)

Dunn will respond that, although he may have surrendered his expectation of privacy with respect to observation by the naked eye, he had not agreed to be observed through high-powered binoculars, especially by the police. The prosecution will contend that binoculars can easily be purchased by the general public and are often used to observe the stars and events around them; if the public can use them. so can the police. (*See* ELO Ch.2-II(D)(3).)

The police will rely on the line of cases permitting observation of suspected areas from airplanes flying overhead. *Dow Chemical v. U.S.*, 476 U.S. 227 (1986). *See*, also, *California v. Ciraolo*, 476 U.S. 227 (1986); *Florida v. Riley*, 488 U.S. 445 (1989). These cases hold that the aerial observations were not searches at all because the areas observed were in plain view from the air.

The distinction here, however, is that the police had no reasonable cause to be observing Dunn and Sally at all. Except for unsubstantiated statements by an informant who is not shown to have demonstrated a history of reliability and who, with the slightest interrogation, would have exposed his animus against Dunn, the police would not have been in the nearby apartment building. The court should rule as inadmissible any evidence resulting from the police observation. [*See, Answer to Question 21,* on the law relating to probable cause as a condition to searches.]

Should Dunn's letter to Sally be considered in determining whether probable cause to arrest him existed?

Dunn will also assert that, because the search of his waste paper basket was made without a warrant, the letter was the fruit of an illegal search and, thus, cannot be relied upon in assessing probable cause to arrest him. The prosecution will make two arguments in reply. First, the search was consented to by Dunn's employer. The employer arguably had equal access and control with Dunn to all non-enclosed areas (*i.e.*, everything but the contents of Dunn's desk drawers) where Dunn worked. Second, Dunn had no reasonable expectation of privacy in the trash can since: (1) the contents were, in effect, "held out" to others (*i.e.*, persons who collected and discarded the office refuse), and (2) Dunn did not have exclusive control over the trash can (it was shared with another employee). The prosecution will probably be successful on either of the foregoing arguments. *California v. Greenwood*, 486 U.S. 35 (1988) (no privacy expectation in trash left outside home). (*See* ELO Ch.2-II(H); Ch.3-VIII(B),(H).)

Assuming for the moment that the police were justified in their surveillance of Dunn and Sally in the first place, the letter probably would be admitted on the issue of probable cause to arrest. Here again, however, it is possible to make a persuasive argument that the letter is not truly relevant on the issue of statutory rape, a crime with a very precise definition. Two people can have a "hot night" without having sexual intercourse.

Was there probable cause to arrest Dunn at all?

Dunn will argue that there was not probable cause to arrest him at all (*i.e.*, it cannot be said that it was more likely than not that Dunn had violated the law defining statutory rape). This is because all evidence leading to the arrest was either unsubstantiated or illegal. What the police saw with their binoculars was only two people kissing and, then, one person being picked up and carried by the other. Neither of these acts confirms the crime of statutory rape, which requires proof of sexual intercourse between an adult and an underage person. There is no statement in the facts that the police had determined Sally to be underage, or that Sally had complained to the police and was prepared to testify against Dunn. The police may argue that when a man carries a woman into a room after they've been kissing, it's more likely than not that they will engage in intercourse. It will also claim that the charge against Dunn is supported by Buck's statement that Sally had stayed in Dunn's apartment overnight on two occasions. But neither of these arguments is sufficient to establish probable cause to arrest for the crime of statutory rape.

Was it proper to arrest Dunn without a warrant?

Assuming, again, that there was probable cause for the arrest, the fact that the police failed to obtain an arrest warrant before arresting Dunn would be immaterial. A suspect who has committed a felony may be taken into custody outside his home without prior judicial approval, provided probable cause exists.

Was the search of Dunn's car proper?

Dunn will contend that even if there was probable cause to arrest him, the police had no right to search underneath the front seat of his car. But the prosecution will make two arguments in reply. First, incident to a valid arrest, the area within a suspect's immediate control may be searched. Because Dunn had just begun to enter his car, the area under the front seat was within his reach.

Dunn will reply that the area under the front seat of his car was not within his immediate control (presumably, he would need to stoop down and extend his arm under the front seat; this would be difficult with the police standing at his side). This argument is likely to fail — the Supreme Court allows the police to search the entire passenger compartment of a car, even closed containers and places that the suspect cannot possibly reach. See, *e.g.*, *New York v. Belton*, 453 U.S. 454(1981). (*See* ELO Ch.3-III(D).)

Dunn will also contend that he had not been driving the vehicle before his arrest (he was arrested *as he was entering it*), so the right of the police to inspect the car had not arisen. But the automobile exception has been interpreted broadly to include cases in which the suspect was entering or leaving the car rather than driving it. Therefore, the search of the car would probably be upheld--assuming, again, that the arrest was proper.

Summary

Since there was not probable cause to arrest Dunn, the warrantless search of his car and the marijuana seizure were improper. Similarly, the seizure of the letter was improper because the original search was not based upon probable cause or a reasonable suspicion. The charges against Dunn should be dismissed.

Answer to Question 21

1. *The marijuana seized in the garage*

Smith's standing to object to seizure of the marijuana

In order to make a Fourth Amendment challenge to an illegal government search, the suspect must have a reasonable expectation of privacy in the area searched. The prosecution will contend that Smith has no standing to object to the search of the garage, because the house in question was occupied by his estranged wife, Wanda. The facts are unclear: were Smith and Wanda separated temporarily, or was Wanda occupying the house under a court order? In the latter case, Smith probably would *not* have standing, because Wanda would presumably have been given full control of the dwelling. But if Smith's access to the house had *not* been legally extinguished (*i.e.*, re-entry into the house by Smith was permitted), Smith probably had standing. We will assume for purpose of discussion that Smith will be able to establish his right of access and his expectation of privacy with respect to the garage. (If not, the marijuana found in the garage would be admissible against him). (*See* ELO Ch.7-II(C)(2).)

Was Wanda's consent to a search of the garage effective against Smith?

Assuming that Smith had an expectation of privacy with respect to the garage, would Wanda's consent to the search nevertheless entitle the police to enter and search it. (*See* ELO Ch.3-VIII(B)(1).) The prosecution will contend that Wanda's statement, "Search everywhere," authorized them to search the garage.

The success of this position will depend in large part on whether the garage was used solely by Smith. If it was (and if the lock was under his sole control), then Wanda probably did not have authority to consent to the search. If both used the garage or had access to it (which would be the case if Wanda also had a key to the lock), then Wanda did have authority to consent. The fact that Smith might be the sole owner would not be dispositive — even if he was the sole owner, the fact that he allowed Wanda to have access to the garage would be enough to entitle her to consent.

Was the warrant validly issued?

A search warrant may be issued only if there is probable cause to believe (*i.e.*, it is more likely than not) that contraband or evidence of criminal activity will be found at the location described in the document. Whether probable cause exists depends upon the "totality of the circumstances" (*Illinois v. Gates*, 462 U.S. 213 (1983)). (*See* ELO Ch.2-IV(B).) Smith will argue--probably successfully--that Officer's statement that a reliable informant had advised him that marijuana would be delivered to Smith's apartment or the house owned by

Smith was insufficient. (The affidavit should have stated: 1) the basis for believing that the the informant was reliable; 2) the source of the informant's knowledge; and 3) the informant's knowledge of the means by which the marijuana would be transported to Smith.) Without this information, the warrant was probably *not* valid.

The prosecution will argue that when police act in **good faith** and reasonably rely upon a search warrant that is facially valid but that later turns out to be defective, evidence obtained pursuant to the warrant is nevertheless admissible. *United States v. Leon*, 468 U.S. 897 (1984). Smith could respond that any reasonable police officer or magistrate with a modicum of experience should have recognized that the affidavit was wholly conclusory and, thus, inadequate to establish probable cause. This issue would probably be resolved in favor of Smith. (For purposes of analysis, however, we will assume that the prosecution would prevail on this issue.) (*See* ELO Ch.2-V(H).)

Even if the warrant was valid, did the search of the garage exceed its scope?

Police may search only those areas described in a search warrant. Smith will contend that because the document referred only to the "house," the police had no right to search the garage. The prosecution will reply that a garage is ordinarily considered an inseparable part of a house (*i.e.*, when a person offers to sell his "house," he doesn't mean to exclude the garage). If the garage was attached to the house or immediately adjacent to it, the prosecution will probably prevail. If the garage was not contiguous with the home or within its curtilage, then Smith should win on this issue. (*See* ELO Ch.2-V(G)(6).)

Is Smith's statement attributing the marijuana to Wanda admissible against him?

When a suspect has been taken into custody, he must ordinarily be given *Miranda* warnings before an interrogation may take place. Because (1) Smith had been arrested, (2) Officer's question ("What do you keep in your garage?") probably constituted an interrogation, and (3) Smith was not given *Miranda* warnings (Officer asked his question "immediately after the arrest"), Smith's statement acknowledging the presence of marijuana in his garage would not be admissible against him. (*See* ELO Ch.5-IV(C).)

2. The marijuana in Smith's pocket

Was the arrest of Smith valid?

If the arrest of Smith was valid, then the marijuana in his pocket would be admissible as a search incident to a lawful arrest; *Chimel v. California*, 395 U.S. 752 (1969). (*See* ELO Ch.3-III(B).)

We will assume that possession of such a large quantity of marijuana in the garage constituted a felony under the applicable local law. If not, Officer was obliged to obtain an arrest warrant.

The facts are silent as to where Smith was arrested. If he was arrested in his apartment, the arrest was invalid because a warrant must ordinarily be obtained before the suspect may be taken into custody in his home. On the other hand, if Smith was arrested outside his home, no arrest warrant was needed. (*See* ELO Ch.3-II(A).)

The arrest was valid only if the police had probable cause to believe that Smith was guilty of the crime charged (marijuana possession). Because evidence which has been illegally seized cannot be considered in determining whether probable cause for arrest exists, whether Smith's arrest was valid probably turns upon whether the seizure of the marijuana from his garage was proper. If it was not (as discussed above on the issuance of the search warrant), probable cause to arrest Smith did not exist. If, however, the search of the garage and seizure of the marijuana were valid, the police would appear to have had a sufficient basis to arrest Smith.

The admissibility of the additional marijuana and Smith's statement ("That's Wanda's marijuana") is directly dependent upon the validity of Smith's arrest. If Smith was not properly taken into custody, the police could not lawfully search his pocket (nor could they use the statement he blurted-out). On the other hand, if Smith's arrest was proper, the marijuana found in Smith's pocket would be admissible as the fruit of a search incident to a valid arrest.

Multiple-Choice Questions

1. Sub lived in a residential neighborhood, over which planes often flew. Sub liked his privacy, so he erected a tall fence which completely enclosed his backyard. One reason he liked his privacy was that he grew marijuana in his yard. Unbeknownst to Sub, the police had received a tip as to his activities. They rented a plane, flew overhead, used binoculars, and took pictures of the marijuana. The police accurately submitted this information to a judge, who then issued a search warrant. Executing the warrant, the police seized Sub's marijuana, which was used at trial against him. Sub's pretrial motion to suppress the marijuana was denied.

    Under the U.S. Constitution, the trial court's ruling was:

    (A) Incorrect, because individuals have a reasonable expectation of privacy with respect to items contained within the home.
    (B) Incorrect, because the marijuana was within the curtilage of Sub's home.
    (C) Incorrect, if the marijuana was not observable from ground level.
    (D) Correct, because Sub had no reasonable expectation of privacy in his backyard with respect to aerial surveillance.

2. Two police officers in a squad car received a radio message from headquarters to be on the lookout for a large green sedan occupied by two women who had just committed a bank robbery. An hour later they saw a car answering this description traveling down a main boulevard leading out of town. They pulled the car over to the side of the road and walked over to it. One of the officers told the occupants that they were under arrest for bank robbery. Doreen, the driver, suddenly put the car into gear and drove off. The Officers, unable to overtake the car and afraid they would lose sight of it in heavy traffic, shot at the car. A bullet struck Valerie, the passenger sitting next to Doreen.

    Doreen was caught five minutes later. Valerie died from loss of blood. Doreen was taken to the police station.

    The bank robbers had handed the teller a handwritten note, demanding the money. Doreen was required, over her protest, to write out the words of the note and have her fingerprints taken. She was then, for the first time, allowed to telephone a lawyer, who thereafter represented her.

    Doreen was charged with the bank robbery and the murder of Valerie.

    At trial, the prosecution, after introducing the robbers' note to the teller, also offered into evidence Doreen's exemplar of the words of the note written at the demand of the police. On appropriate objection, the court should rule that this evidence is:

(A) Admissible.

(B) Inadmissible, if Doreen was not advised that her handwriting sample could be admitted into evidence against her.

(C) Inadmissible, because Doreen was entitled to refuse to give a handwriting sample.

(D) Inadmissible, if Doreen had not been informed that she had a right to have counsel present.

3.   Jack and Paul planned to hold up a bank. They agreed that Paul would drive the car (owned by Jack) during the "getaway." Jack entered the bank while Paul remained as lookout in Jack's car. After a few moments, Paul panicked and drove off.

Soon after leaving the scene, Paul was stopped by the police for speeding. Noting his nervous condition, the police asked Paul if they could search the car. Paul reluctantly agreed. While Paul looked on, one of the police officers reached into the ignition and removed the keys. These keys were used to open the trunk, where heroin was found.

In the trial against Jack for bank robbery, the prosecution's BEST argument to sustain the validity of the search of Jack's car would be that:

(A) The search was reasonable in light of Paul's nervous condition.

(B) The search was incident to a valid arrest.

(C) Paul consented to the search.

(D) Exigent circumstances, including the inherent mobility of a car, justified the search.

4.   A grand jury was investigating a murder. The only information known to the prosecutor was a rumor that Suspect might have been involved. The grand jury subpoenaed Suspect. Without specifying why, Suspect refused to answer questions about the murder. Suspect was found in contempt and has appealed this determination. The finding of contempt will be:

(A) Affirmed, because a subpoenaed grand jury witness must answer all questions.

(B) Affirmed, because Suspect did not specifically invoke the Fifth Amendment privilege against self-incrimination.

(C) Reversed, because grand jury witnesses are not legally obliged to answer questions.

(D) Reversed, if Suspect's answer might have implicated him in a crime.

5.   Dillon held up a gasoline station. During the robbery he shot and killed a customer who attempted to apprehend him. Dillon was prosecuted for

deliberate, premeditated murder, but was acquitted. Thereafter, he was indicted for armed robbery of the station. Dillon's attorney moved to dismiss the indictment on the ground that further proceedings were unconstitutional because of Dillon's prior trial.

The motion to dismiss should be:

(A) Granted, because once Dillon was acquitted on any charge arising out of the robbery, the prosecution was constitutionally estopped from proceeding against Dillon on any other charge resulting from the same transaction.

(B) Granted, because the double jeopardy clause prohibits a subsequent trial on a lesser included offense.

(C) Denied, because there is no constitutional requirement that all known charges against Dillon be brought in the same prosecution.

(D) Denied, because estoppel never applies when the defendant is charged with committing two different crimes.

Questions 6-7 are based on the following fact situation.

Pursuant to a valid arrest warrant, Defendant was arrested in a public place for the murder of his wife. Before putting him in the police car, the police searched Defendant's entire person and found one ounce of heroin, which he had concealed in a flat plastic envelope under his belt.

6. At Defendant's motion to suppress the heroin, the court should rule that:

(A) The search was invalid, since the police did not have a search warrant.

(B) The search was invalid, since incident to a lawful arrest the police may only search a suspect's person for weapons or evidence of the crime.

(C) The search was valid, since Defendant's arrest was proper.

(D) The search was valid, because evidence of a crime was, in fact, discovered.

7. Assume that, in the above situation, the police arrested Defendant without a warrant, although they had (1) time to obtain one, and (2) probable cause to believe Defendant was his wife's murderer. In challenging the validity of his arrest and the heroin found on his person, Defendant will:

(A) Succeed, because an arrest without a warrant is an unreasonable seizure under the Fourth Amendment.

(B) Succeed, because the police must always obtain a warrant if there is sufficient time to do so.

(C) Fail, because the police had probable cause to make the arrest.

(D) Fail, because even without probable cause, the subsequent discovery of heroin would have been sufficient justification for the arrest.

Questions 8-12 are based on the following fact situation.

After a series of muggings within a 4-square-block vicinity, police conducted a comprehensive sweep of the area. The mugger was described as a white male, about six feet tall, with blond hair, and a goatee. While on patrol in this area, uniformed Officer O'Leary noticed Byron walking nervously down the street with his hands in his pockets. O'Leary could tell that Byron was white, about 6 feet tall, and had blond hair, but could not, from her angle of view, determine if he had a goatee. When O'Leary attempted to approach Byron for the purpose of determining if he had a goatee, Byron (having spotted O'Leary) hurriedly entered the apartment building which was closest to him. O'Leary followed him. When she saw Byron on the lighted stairway, O'Leary noticed that Byron did have a goatee and arrested him on the spot. After handcuffing and putting him in the squad car, but before reading Byron his *Miranda* rights, O'Leary asked Byron where he'd been at 9:00 p.m. on the preceding night (the date and time of the most recent mugging). Byron broke down and confessed to that mugging and several others.

O'Leary then searched Byron's pockets and found a diamond ring, which was later identified as the one taken from a recent mugging victim.

At the station, Byron initially claimed his innocence. However, when he considered his earlier confession and the ring, he agreed to plead guilty, based on a promise by the prosecutor of a reduced sentence. Soon afterward, however, Byron made a motion to permit withdrawal of the guilty plea and the entry of a not guilty plea. The court granted Byron's motion.

At his trial, Byron took the stand and was asked just one question by his attorney, "Did you commit the robberies with which you are charged?" Byron answered, "No." The prosecution then attempted to cross-examine Byron. However, the prosecution was prevented from doing so by the court when Byron's attorney asserted the Fifth Amendment privilege against self-incrimination. The court also prevented the prosecution's attempt to introduce evidence of Byron's confession to O'Leary for the purpose of impeachment.

8. Which of the following statements describes most accurately Byron's standing to object to the introduction into evidence of the diamond ring?

    (A) Byron has standing, because he was inside a residential structure when the ring was seized.

    (B) Byron has standing, because the ring was in his pocket.

(C) Byron does not have standing, because he was unlawfully on the premises of the apartment house.

(D) Byron does not have standing, because he did not own the ring.

9. If Byron contends that the search which produced the ring violated his Fourth Amendment rights, the most accurate statement is:

(A) Byron is correct, because exigent circumstances did not exist.

(B) Byron is correct, because there was no probable cause to arrest him.

(C) Byron is correct, because there was no probable cause to believe Byron had the ring on his person.

(D) Byron is incorrect, because O'Leary had probable cause to make the arrest.

10. Assume, for the purpose of this question only, that Byron's confession and the ring were inadmissible. On which of the following grounds, if factually true, could the court properly allow Byron to withdraw his plea of guilty prior to sentencing?

I.   A criminal defendant is permitted to withdraw a guilty plea at any time.

II. Byron was under the mistaken impression that the confession was admissible when he pleaded guilty.

III. The guilty plea was "involuntary" because it was induced by the promise of a lighter sentence.

(A) I only.

(B) II and III only.

(C) II only.

(D) None.

11. Did the trial court correctly prevent the prosecution from cross-examining Byron based on the Fifth Amendment's privilege against self-incrimination?

(A) Yes, because Byron did not make an incriminating statement when he took the stand.

(B) Yes, because by taking the stand merely to deny guilt Byron did not waive the privilege.

(C) No, because by taking the stand to deny guilt Byron waived the privilege.

(D) No, because Byron's right to rely on the privilege did not arise unless and until he was actually asked a question which could incriminate him.

12. Did the trial court correctly prevent the introduction into evidence of Byron's confession?

(A) Yes, because the confession was made in violation of the *Miranda* rule.

(B) Yes, because the confession was made pursuant to an invalid arrest.

(C) No, because the confession is admissible for all purposes.

(D) No, because the confession is admissible for impeachment purposes.

Questions 13-14 are based on the following fact situation.

Defendant sold some heroin to Morgan. One hour later, Morgan was stopped by police for going five miles per hour over the speed limit. The police ordered Morgan out of the car and then searched the entire vehicle. They did so solely because they thought the car might contain drugs, even though they had no concrete reason to suspect that drugs would be found. In fact, the police found the heroin concealed under the rear seat. Defendant is charged with possessing illegal drugs because his fingerprints were found on the bag of heroin.

13. Defendant's motion to suppress introduction of the heroin into evidence will probably be:

    (A) Granted, because the heroin was not in plain view.

    (B) Granted, because the search of the car's interior was unlawful.

    (C) Denied, because Defendant had no standing to object to the search.

    (D) Denied, because the search was proper as incident to a valid, full custodial arrest.

14. Assume for this question that Morgan was also charged with illegal possession of heroin. His motion to prevent introduction of the heroin into evidence will probably be:

    (A) Granted, because the heroin was not in plain view.

    (B) Granted, because the police had no justification for stopping Morgan.

    (C) Denied, because he was properly stopped.

    (D) Denied, because the search was proper as incident to a valid, full custodial arrest.

Questions 15-16 are based on the following fact situation.

Lucky was tried and convicted of arson in a State X court. She appealed her decision to the State X Supreme Court. Yesterday, the U.S. Supreme Court issued a decision indicating that peremptory challenges, when used by the prosecution to systematically exclude blacks from a jury, require automatic reversal. Lucky's jury was identical in composition to the jury which was invalidated in the Supreme Court case.

15. Lucky's appeal will be:

(A) Successful, because Supreme Court decisions pertaining to criminal procedure are ordinarily given retroactive effect in cases pending on direct appeal.

(B) Successful, because improper jury formation is always grounds for reversal.

(C) Unsuccessful, if the new decision is a "clear break" from previous precedent.

(D) Unsuccessful, if reversal would cause a serious disruption to the administration of criminal justice.

16. If Lucky's appeal was predicated on a *writ of habeas corpus*, whether the recent Supreme Court decision would be given retroactive effect would:

(A) Depend on whether the new decision was a "clear break" from the past.

(B) Depend upon the purpose of the new rule, reliance on the old rule, and the effect which retroactive application would have on the criminal justice system.

(C) Be contingent upon applicable state law.

(D) None of the above.

17. After Dexter was arrested and formally indicted for rape, Dexter's photograph (along with several photos of other persons with similar features) was shown to Sally, a rape victim. Sally identified Dexter as her assailant. The prosecutor failed to notify Dexter's attorney that he was going to conduct a photographic identification by Sally. If Sally dies before Dexter's trial, the results of the photo display will be:

(A) Admissible, because there is no right to counsel at photo displays.

(B) Inadmissible, if Dexter's counsel had specifically requested to be present at any photo displays.

(C) Inadmissible, because Dexter's Sixth Amendment right to counsel was violated.

(D) Inadmissible, because this particular photo display was overly suggestive.

18. Trish went to a public high school. One of her rivals saw her smoking marijuana in the girl's room and informed the principal, who immediately asked Trish to see him. When the principal was advised that Trish was not at her assigned class, he searched Trish's locker (without obtaining Trish's permission to do so). There was no lock on the locker, so it was easily opened. The principal found a gun and other illegal drugs in Trish's locker. In a criminal prosecution against Trish, the gun and drugs will be:

(A) Admissible, because Trish had not reached the age of majority.

(B) Admissible, because Trish was not in her assigned classroom.

(C) Admissible, because the locker was in plain view.

(D) Admissible, because the principal had a reasonable suspicion that Trish had engaged in criminal conduct.

19. Detective received information from Informant, who had given reliable information many times in the past. Specifically, Informant said that, two days before, he had visited Harry's apartment with Bill and saw Harry sell Bill some heroin. Detective knew that Informant, Harry, and Bill were friends. Thereafter, Detective put this information into affidavit form, appeared before a magistrate, and secured a search warrant for Harry's apartment. The search turned up a supply of heroin. Harry's motion to suppress introduction of the heroin into evidence probably will be:

(A) Granted, because a search warrant cannot validly be issued solely on the basis of an informant's information.

(B) Granted, because the information supplied to Detective concerned an occurrence too remote in time to justify a finding of probable cause.

(C) Denied, because there was reasonable cause to believe a crime had been committed.

(D) Denied, because there was probable cause to issue the warrant.

20. The police had reason to believe that the four Jones sisters had committed a robbery. This suspicion arose because they all claimed to have been out of town when the crime occurred. In order to check their suspicions, the police arrested all four and fingerprinted them. The sisters demanded to see an attorney before the fingerprinting occurred, but their demands were ignored. The prints of Donna Jones (one of the sisters) matched those found at the crime. The fingerprinting procedure was:

(A) Unlawful, because it was done pursuant to an unlawful seizure.

(B) Unlawful, because the police rejected the Jones sisters' request for an attorney.

(C) Lawful, because fingerprints are nontestimonial in nature.

(D) Lawful, because an individual has no reasonable expectation of privacy in her fingerprints.

Questions 21-25 are based on the following fact situation.

Willy was validly arrested on a charge of drunken driving. Over Willy's objection, the police took Willy's car to a lot which was owned by the police department and inventoried the contents of the car. Under the front passenger seat, the police found a plastic bag containing heroin. On the rear seat, there was a suitcase which was sealed by a zipper. The police unzipped the suitcase, opened it, and found two illegal machine guns. In the locked trunk of the car (which the police broke into), the police discovered a dead body.

21. The police impoundment of Willy's car was:

    (A) Lawful, because Willy was lawfully arrested.
    (B) Lawful, because Willy impliedly consented to this action.
    (C) Lawful, if done pursuant to standardized police procedures.
    (D) All of the above.

22. Is the heroin admissible against Willy in a criminal prosecution for unlawful possession of that substance?

    (A) No, because the vehicle was not searched at the time Willy was arrested.
    (B) Yes, if the impoundment was lawful.
    (C) No, because the police did not have probable cause to search the interior of the vehicle.
    (D) No, because, while probable cause existed to search the car, no warrant was ever obtained by the police.

23. In a prosecution against Willy for unlawful gun possession, the firearms discovered in his car are:

    (A) Admissible, because Willy was validly arrested.
    (B) Admissible, because the police had probable cause to believe the vehicle contained evidence of criminal activity.
    (C) Inadmissible, because the police lacked probable cause to believe the vehicle contained evidence of criminal activity.
    (D) Inadmissible, because the contents of the suitcase were not in plain view.

24. In a prosecution of Willy for murder, the body which was discovered in the truck is:

    (A) Inadmissible.
    (B) Admissible under the inventory exception.
    (C) Admissible under the homicide scene exception.
    (D) Admissible under the "search incident to arrest" exception.

25. For this question only, assume that: (1) in a single trial, Willy was tried for possession of heroin, possession of an illegal firearm, and murder; (2) the body found in the trunk of the car was admissible; (3) the prosecution proved that Willy's victim was poisoned (*i.e.*, she was killed in a deliberate, premeditated manner); and (4) as part of the guilty verdict, the jury sentenced

Willy to death. On appeal, Willy's best argument for overturning the death
sentence portion of the verdict is:

(A) The murder charge had to be tried separately from the possession charges.

(B) The death sentence is cruel and unusual punishment.

(C) A sentence of death in these circumstances would violate the principle of
proportionality.

(D) There was not a separate sentencing phase on the death sentence.

26. John and David rob a liquor store. As they leave, David turns and shoots the
shopkeeper, Bill. John is caught by the police a few hours later, but David is
never caught.

John is indicted, tried and convicted of first-degree robbery, a felony. Three
months after the conviction, Bill dies from the injuries he suffered during the
robbery. Immediately after Bill's death, John is indicted, tried and convicted
of felony murder for the death of Bill. John appeals his conviction for felony
murder, arguing that the second indictment and trial were prohibited by the
double jeopardy Clause.

The appellate court will:

(A) Uphold the second conviction, because the conviction for robbery establishes that John is responsible for any murder committed during the
course of the robbery.

(B) Overturn the second conviction, because the double jeopardy Clause prohibited John's prosecution for felony murder following his conviction for
robbery.

(C) Uphold the second conviction, because Bill died after John's trial for robbery.

(D) Overturn the second conviction, because both the robbery and the felony
murder arose from the same event.

27. The police observed what appeared to be a drug transaction between Joe
Seller and Bill Buyer on a sidewalk corner. When they approached Buyer to
arrest him, he swallowed his purchase and began to run. After three blocks,
however, the police caught and arrested Buyer. Within a two-hour period, the
police obtained a warrant (based upon the foregoing facts) which authorized
them to inject Buyer with a solution which would cause him to vomit.
Laboratory analysis of the vomitus revealed partially digested heroin.
Assuming there was probable cause to issue the warrant, the heroin would
probably:

(A) Be suppressed.

(B) Not be suppressed, because the heroin would dissipate within Buyer's system without injection of the solution (*i.e.*, exigent circumstances existed).

(C) Not be suppressed, because the police had obtained a warrant.

(D) Both (B) and (C).

Questions 28-32 are based on the following fact situation.

The police received an anonymous telephone call that Paul was engaged in illegal gambling operations consisisting of betting on professional sporting events. The informant did not say how he knew any of this information. Officers Laverne and Shirley went to Paul's place of business (Joe's Restaurant, where Paul worked as a waiter) and were given permission to speak to him. They advised Paul that they had full knowledge of his involvement in illegal gambling operations, and that he would probably be sent to jail as a consequence of these activities. When Paul responded, "I've got nothing to say to you gals," he was told that he should consider himself under arrest. Before Paul was advised of his *Miranda* rights, Officer Shirley told Paul, "Confession is good for the soul," and asked Paul if he would like to make a statement about his illegal activities. Paul hesitated, but then informed the officers that he did "take" bets on sporting events.

He then voluntarily led the officers back to the garage adjacent to his home, where he showed them notebooks in which were written the names of bettors, the amounts of money they had wagered, and the corresponding events. The police also searched Paul's person and found a pocket notebook which revealed bets that had been placed with Paul that day. The police then advised Paul that they were too busy to take him to the station house for booking then, but that they were confiscating the notebooks as evidence. Paul did not protest this action.

About two weeks later, Paul was subpoenaed to appear before a grand jury investigating illegal gambling. He appeared with an attorney whom he had retained, but was advised that he was not entitled to have counsel present. In a rage, Paul walked out. He has refused to return until his lawyer is allowed to be with him, even though he has been warned that he could be cited for contempt.

28. In the grand jury proceedings, Paul's confession as to his involvement in illegal gambling is:

   I.   Admissible, because a *Miranda* rights violation does not result in suppression.

   II. Inadmissible, because it was given after Paul was improperly arrested.

   III. Inadmissible, because it was obtained in violation of Paul's *Miranda* rights.

(A) I only.

(B) II only.

(C) III only.

(D) II and III.

29. Can Paul be compelled to appear as a witness at the grand jury proceedings?

(A) No, because the police initially lacked probable cause to arrest him.

(B) No, because he was not given *Miranda* warnings.

(C) Yes, despite the lack of *Miranda* warnings.

(D) Yes, but only if the grand jury has reason to believe that Paul was involved in gambling operations, without reference to Paul's confession.

30. Which of the following statements is correct?

(A) Paul had an absolute right to have counsel present at the grand jury proceedings.

(B) There is no right to have counsel present at grand jury proceedings.

(C) Paul had no right to have counsel present at the grand jury proceedings if the evidence obtained from him was inadmissible in a criminal case.

(D) Paul had a right to have counsel present because he was arrested in connection with the purpose of the grand jury proceedings.

31. As a consequence of Paul's refusal to answer any questions, which of the following is correct?

I.   Paul could be convicted of perjury.

II. Paul could be convicted of contempt.

III. Paul cannot be convicted of any crime, because the evidence obtained from him is inadmissible in a criminal case.

(A) I only.

(B) II only.

(C) III only.

(D) None of the above.

32. In the subsequent trial of Paul for the crime of participating in an illegal gambling operation, which of the following items of evidence obtained by the police officers would be admissible?

(A) Paul's confession, but nothing else.

(B) The regular size notebooks, but nothing else.

(C) The pocket notebook, but nothing else.

(D) None of the evidence.

33. Jay was angry with John for stealing his girlfriend, Sue. Jay wanted to get even. He called John up and told John there were no "hard feelings" and that he wanted to take over a bottle of wine. Actually, Jay had heard that John had some marijuana around and wanted to tell the police where it was located. John let Jay into his home on the assumption that Jay wanted to share a drink. After the two drank the wine, Jay asked John if he had any "stash." John obliged by going to his bookcase and taking some marijuana from a hollowed out book. Shortly after they had begun smoking some marijuana cigarettes, John had to answer a telephone call. After he left the room, Jay grabbed the book which contained the marijuana and took it to police headquarters. He then told the police exactly how he obtained it from John.

    If John is charged with possession of an illegal substance on the basis of this evidence and Jay's testimony, John would probably:

    (A) Win, because the marijuana is inadmissible (Jay gained entrance into John's home through a ruse).
    (B) Win, because this type of conduct "shocks the conscience."
    (C) Lose, because the evidence would be admissible.
    (D) Win, because the evidence, even if admissible, would be insufficient as a matter of law.

34. Officer Donald obtained a valid warrant to search Vic's apartment for a stolen television. When he arrived at Vic's apartment, Vic was home. After Officer Donald announced his authority and purpose, Vic permitted him to enter. Vic stated, however, that he had an important business meeting to attend, and therefore wanted to leave. Officer Donald advised Vic that he was obliged to remain until the search was completed. When Officer Donald discovered the television set in question, Vic blurted out, "OK, I took it. How else was I going to see the World Series?"

    Vic's confession is:

    (A) Inadmissible, because he had specifically requested to leave.
    (B) Inadmissible, because no arrest warrant for Vic had been obtained.
    (C) Inadmissible, because Officer Donald had no reasonable suspicion that Vic had engaged in criminal activity when he forbade Vic to leave the premises.
    (D) Admissible.

35. Sharon's phone was bugged by federal agents for 90 consecutive days on the strength of a court order which authorized a "tap" for four months. The tap

revealed that Sharon was engaged in unlawful vice activities. Sharon wishes to exclude the electronically obtained evidence. Assuming the warrant authorizing the tap was based upon probable cause, Sharon's best argument is:

(A) Electronic surveillance violates the Fourth Amendment.
(B) A federal wiretap can only be for a maximum period of 30 days, unless there is a renewal.
(C) The wiretap did not exceed the period authorized by the order.
(D) A federal wiretap can only be for a maximum period of 60 days, unless there is a renewal.

36. Huffer was involved in illegal gambling activities, but the government had never been able to assemble enough evidence to prosecute him. Insider, who had been indicted for a similar offense, offered to help the government prosecute Huffer in return for a lighter sentence in his case. The FBI agreed. Insider purposefully engaged Huffer in several conversations, during which Huffer made incriminating statements. If the government seeks to have Insider testify about these conversations, his testimony will be:

(A) Admissible, because Huffer spoke to Insider voluntarily.
(B) Admissible, because Insider was a private party.
(C) Inadmissible, because there was no court order authorizing the governmental action.
(D) Inadmissible, because the conversations violated Huffer's Sixth Amendment rights.

Questions 37-38 are based on the following fact situation.

Dr. Carla (a private physician) saw Jones loitering on the public street in front of her house. Assuming that Jones was "casing" her home for a future robbery, Dr. Carla went outside and ordered Jones to remain there while she summoned the police. When Jones started to walk quickly away, Dr. Carla tackled Jones and told a passerby to call the police. While Jones was struggling to extricate himself from Dr. Carla's hold, a vial of heroin dropped from Jones' jacket. Dr. Carla grabbed the vial and held it until the police arrived. Assume that under applicable state law, (1) Dr. Carla had no legal right to restrain Jones under these circumstances, and (2) as a consequence of her actions, Dr. Carla could be liable to Jones for assault, battery, and false imprisonment.

37. The police subsequently arrived. They arrested Jones and confiscated the heroin. Jones was charged with possession of heroin. If Jones moved to suppress this evidence at trial, he would probably be:

(A) Successful, since it was derived from an invalid arrest.

(B) Successful, since Dr. Carla had no legal right to restrain Jones.

(C) Unsuccessful, if it could be proven by a preponderance of the evidence that Jones actually intended to burglarize Dr. Carla's home.

(D) Unsuccessful, because the heroin was discovered as a consequence of Dr. Carla's actions.

38. Assume, for this question only, that the vial of heroin had not fallen out of Jones' jacket prior to the time the police arrived. Assume also that, based upon Dr. Carla's assertion that Jones had "attempted to rob" her, Officer Brown arrested Jones. The vial was discovered when the items in Jones' possession were inventoried at the police station. Jones was then charged with possession of heroin. If Jones moved to suppress this evidence at trial, he would probably be:

(A) Successful, because it was derived from an invalid arrest.

(B) Successful, because the search of Jones at the police station was conducted without a warrant.

(C) Unsuccessful, because there was probable cause to arrest Jones.

(D) None of the above.

Questions 39-40 are based on the following fact situation.

While his mobile home was parked in the parking lot of a state operated recreational park, Reggie solicited illegal drug sales. Buyers would make the actual purchase inside the motor home. Bill, an off-duty police officer vacationing at the campsite, heard about Reggie's activities from other campers. One individual, who had just left Reggie's motor home, showed Bill amphetamines which he had bought from Reggie. When Reggie left to pick up some supplies in town, Bill (taking his badge and gun) searched Reggie's motor home. Bill found illegal amphetamines in a closed suitcase. When Reggie returned from town, he was placed under arrest by Bill. Reggie was then taken to the police station and strip searched. He was then put in a jail cell and formally charged.

39. The search of Reggie's motor home was:

(A) Lawful, because Bill was off-duty when the search was made.

(B) Lawful, because Bill had probable cause to believe it contained contraband.

(C) Unlawful, because Reggie had a reasonable expectation of privacy in his motor home.

(D) Unlawful, because the amphetamines were in a sealed container.

40. The strip search of Reggie at the station house was:

    (A) Lawful, as a "booking" search.
    (B) Lawful, because "exigent circumstances" existed.
    (C) Unlawful, if it revealed nothing.
    (D) Unlawful, because Reggie's arrest was invalid.

41. Officer Jane, having obtained a valid arrest warrant for Defendant, went to Defendant's home. There, Defendant's wife told Officer Jane (1) that Defendant was visiting Friend, and (2) Friend's address. Officer Jane then went to Friend's home. Friend answered the doorbell and (after Officer Jane announced her authority and purpose) said to Officer Jane, "Beat it, I've got no love for cops." Officer Jane then advised Friend that unless he opened the door, it would be broken down. Friend let Officer Jane enter. Inside, Jane arrested Defendant and seized heroin belonging to Friend (the heroin was on the table at which Defendant was sitting). Friend is now being prosecuted for heroin possession. If Friend moves to suppress the heroin, his motion should be:

    (A) Granted, because Officer Jane unlawfully entered Friend's house.
    (B) Granted, because the heroin was inadvertently discovered by Officer Jane.
    (C) Denied, because Friend consented to Officer Jane's entry.
    (D) Denied, because the heroin was discovered incident to a valid arrest.

42. Officer Joe was walking his beat one day when Kathy (the local candy store owner) advised him that Billy (a 26-year-old who, unfortunately, had the intelligence of a 15-year-old) had just taken $50 from Kathy's cash register. Billy had done this by locking Kathy in the supply room (where she had gone to obtain a candy bar requested by Billy). As Officer Joe and Kathy were talking, Billy appeared on the other side of the street. When Billy saw Kathy talking with Officer Joe, he turned and ran. Officer Joe gave chase and shouted at Billy to stop. Officer Joe, who was losing ground to Billy, fired a shot over Billy's head, but Billy kept running. Finally, Officer Joe fired at Billy's leg. But the shot accidentally hit Billy in the back, causing him to become permanently paralyzed. Assume that Billy's actions in Kathy's store constituted burglary (a felony) under applicable state law. The shooting of Billy was:

    (A) Lawful, because Officer Joe had probable cause to arrest Billy.
    (B) Lawful, because Billy's prior conduct constituted a felony.
    (C) Unlawful, because Officer Joe's conduct was unreasonable.
    (D) Unlawful, because shooting Billy under these circumstances constituted cruel and unusual punishment.

Questions 43-44 are based on the following fact situation.

Defendant, a 17-year-old, was arrested (as she walked to school) for setting fire to a building on Main Street. She was given *Miranda* warnings and then asked if she would like to make a statement about the Main Street arson. Defendant answered, "I'll talk to you, provided you don't start hasslin' me." In the course of the interrogation, Officer Bill asked Defendant about a fire at a store on First Street. Defendant admitted committing that arson. The police then told Defendant that someone had died as a result of the fire. Defendant was subsequently charged with felony-murder.

43. Defendant's admission is:

   (A) Admissible, if the police had probable cause to arrest Defendant for the Main Street fire.
   (B) Inadmissible, because prior to her confession she was not told that anyone died at the First Street Fire.
   (C) Inadmissible, because she had not fully waived her *Miranda* rights.
   (D) Inadmissible, because she was arrested only for the Main Street fire.

44. Assume, for purposes of this question only, that Defendant was validly arrested, but that she suffered from an unreasonable delusion that Officer Bill would kill her if she didn't answer his questions. Under these circumstances, Defendant's admission is:

   (A) Admissible.
   (B) Inadmissible, because she was a minor.
   (C) Inadmissible, because her delusion would invalidate her *Miranda* waiver.
   (D) Inadmissible, because she was arrested only for the Main Street fire.

45. A gun and bullets were stolen from a gun shop. The owner immediately called the police. They combed the area, searching for the person who met the description furnished by the owner. About two hours after the theft, Jack emerged from a movie house. Because he closely fit the description of the person who had robbed the gun shop, Officer John accosted Jack with his revolver drawn. Jack froze when he saw Officer John approach and placed his hands behind the back of his head. Officer John then asked Jack, "Where's the gun?" Jack said, "I'm not answering any questions, I know my rights." Officer John responded, "Come on, there are kids inside that movie." Jack then led Officer John to the gun (which he had taped to the underside of a seat in the theatre). At Jack's trial, the gun should be:

   (A) Admissible, if Jack had committed a felony.

(B) Admissible, because Officer John was concerned about a threat to the public safety.

(C) Admissible, because Jack, who had not been arrested, was not in "custody" for *Miranda* purposes.

(D) Inadmissible, because the police had no right to question Jack without prior *Miranda* warnings.

46. Although no arrest warrant had been obtained, Pat was arrested by the police as she walked home from work. She was told, "You have the right to remain silent. You have the right to have an attorney present during questioning. Anything said to us may be used against you." Pat then asked for a drink of water, which she received. Officer Jones then asked, "Would you like to make a statement? It might make you feel better." Pat responded, "I know I got a right to a lawyer, but I want to tell you the truth anyway." She then confessed to shooting Arthur. The confession is probably:

(A) Inadmissible, because the waiver of *Miranda* warnings was not voluntary.

(B) Inadmissible, because *Miranda* warnings were not given effectively.

(C) Inadmissible, if there was no probable cause to arrest Pat.

(D) Admissible, whether or not probable cause existed to arrest Pat.

47. Locust was convicted of murder in a State X court. The evidence used to convict him at trial was illegally obtained. However, Locust's attorney neglected to make the proper motions to suppress the improper evidence. After Locust had exhausted his direct appellate rights, he filed a writ of *habeas corpus* with the proper federal court. Locust asserted that his Fourth Amendment rights had been violated by admission of the illegally obtained evidence. The writ will probably be:

(A) Granted, because Locust's counsel had negligently failed to raise a Fourth Amendment violation.

(B) Granted, if there was a fair showing that Locust's conviction would have been overturned but for the admission of the illegal evidence.

(C) Denied, because Fourth Amendment issues will not be considered in a federal *habeas corpus* proceeding if the defendant had a full and fair opportunity to raise them in the state proceeding.

(D) Granted, because Locust's Sixth Amendment right to effective counsel may have been violated.

48. Defendant was arrested and charged with distributing controlled substances. As part of its case, the prosecution wanted to show that a huge quantity of illegal drugs had been seized at a summer cabin owned by Defendant. However, at a suppression hearing which preceded the trial, the evidence

discovered at the cabin was excluded because no search warrant had been obtained. At trial, Defendant took the stand and testified that, while his brother was heavily involved in the drug trade, he was completely innocent of the charges against him. When Defendant was asked on cross-examination if he ever had drugs in his possession, on advice of counsel, he claimed that he was privileged to refuse to answer since it might "tend to incriminate him." Although the judge ordered Defendant to answer the prosecution's question, Defendant still refused. The prosecution was then permitted to introduce into evidence the drugs which had been illegally seized at Defendant's summer home.

The prosecution's use of the illegally seized evidence was:

(A) Proper, because it was used to impeach Defendant.
(B) Proper, because Defendant improperly refused to answer the prosecution's question.
(C) Improper, because the evidence had been suppressed at a pre-trial hearing.
(D) Improper, because Defendant's refusal to answer the prosecution's question was on the instructions of his attorney.

49. A pen register was installed, at the request of the police, at a privately owned telephone company. The register listed all of the telephone numbers dialed from Darlene's residence. The police suspected that Darlene was selling drugs. No warrant was obtained by the police to install this pen register. The telephone numbers subsequently disclosed by the pen register suggested that Darlene was associating with several known drug addicts. As a result of this information, the police questioned the drug addicts and obtained incriminating evidence against Darlene. Darlene was charged with distribution of illegal drugs.

If Darlene moves to suppress the evidence attributable to the pen register, her motion should be:

(A) Granted, because the telephone company acted as a governmental agent.
(B) Granted, because no search warrant was obtained.
(C) Denied, because Darlene had no reasonable expectation of privacy in the resulting evidence.
(D) Denied, if the police acted in good faith.

Questions 50-51 are based upon the following fact situation.

Bob was convicted in the state of Midwest. The main evidence used against Bob was the result of a warrantless entry upon his land and search of a fenced-in area located about 50 feet away from his house. Bob had grown marijuana within the enclosure, and was successfully prosecuted under a Midwest law for possession of an illegal substance. However, the Midwest Supreme Court reversed the conviction, concluding that "pursuant to the Midwest Constitution, Bob had an expectation of privacy in the area searched."

50. The state has appealed the decision to the appropriate federal court. The appeal will be:

(A) Successful, if there was a "No Trespassing" sign on the fence which surrounded the marijuana.

(B) Successful, because there is no expectation of privacy in "open fields."

(C) Unsuccessful, because Bob was afforded greater constitutional protection from the state than that given by the U.S. Constitution.

(D) Successful, because the area invaded was completely fenced.

51. Assume, for this question only, that the decision of the Midwest Supreme Court was upheld by the federal court. The federal government then indicted Bob for an identical offense under U.S. law. The federal prosecution:

(A) Violates due process.

(B) Violates the double jeopardy clause.

(C) Is precluded by the principle of collateral estoppel.

(D) Is permissible.

52. Officer Judy validly arrested Defendant and gave Defendant correct *Miranda* warnings. Defendant stated, "I want to see my lawyer." The police then allowed Defendant to call his attorney, who was out of his office. Defendant then said to Officer Judy, "You know, I've heard confession is good for the soul. I think I'd like to make a statement after all." Officer Judy stated the *Miranda* warnings again. Defendant then confessed. The confession is:

(A) Admissible, because Defendant waived his *Miranda* rights.

(B) Admissible, if Defendant had been arrested for a misdemeanor only.

(C) Inadmissible, because Defendant had requested to talk to his attorney.

(D) Inadmissible, because the police were obligated to provide Defendant with another attorney until the first lawyer arrived.

Questions 53-56 are based on the following fact situation.

Informant was known to be reliable. He had given information to Officer Joe on several occasions. Informant told Officer Joe that (1) he had talked to Suspect a few minutes before, and (2) there was a bulge in the pocket of her suit, which probably indicated that Suspect was carrying an illegally concealed weapon. Officer approached Suspect (who was seated in her car) and asked, "Can I see some ID, please?" Suspect shrugged and began to reach toward her pocket, saying, "I'll show you my license." Officer grabbed Suspect's hand and held it. Officer then patted the outside of the pocket, felt what he reasonably concluded was a gun, reached into Suspect's pocket, and pulled out what was indeed a gun. Officer Joe then arrested Suspect. Suspect was prosecuted for concealing an illegal weapon (a misdemeanor).

53. If Suspect moves to suppress the gun, her motion will be:

   (A) Granted, because the weapon was the product of an unlawful detention.
   (B) Granted, because Officer Joe had failed to obtain a warrant.
   (C) Denied, because there was a valid detention and frisk.
   (D) Denied, because Officer Joe had probable cause to believe Suspect was engaged in criminal activity.

54. Suspect was convicted of the misdemeanor, which is punishable by a maximum term of three months imprisonment. Prior to her trial, Suspect asked to be tried by a jury, but her request was denied. If Suspect appeals the conviction on this basis, the trial verdict will be:

   (A) Affirmed, since there is no constitutional right to a jury trial in criminal cases.
   (B) Affirmed, since the right to a jury trial exists only when the offense is punishable by a prison term of at least six months.
   (C) Reversed, since there is a right to a jury trial in all criminal cases.
   (D) Reversed, since there is a right to a jury trial whenever a criminal defendant affirmatively requests it.

55. Assume Suspect had requested that an attorney be appointed for her, but one was not. Suspect appeals upon the ground that she was denied the right to counsel. Her appeal is based upon an assumption which is:

   (A) Correct, because there is a right to counsel in all criminal cases.
   (B) Correct, because Suspect's crime was punishable by imprisonment.
   (C) Correct, if Suspect was actually imprisoned.
   (D) Incorrect, because there is no right to counsel for crimes punishable by imprisonment of six months or less.

56. For purposes of this question only, assume that: (1) Suspect was sentenced to three months imprisonment, but was immediately paroled; and (2) she filed a *writ of habeas corpus* with the appropriate U.S. District Court, contending that the failure to appoint counsel for her constituted a Sixth Amendment violation. Suspect's appeal should be:

(A) Denied, if she has not exhausted all of her state court remedies.

(B) Denied, because one must be in custody to assert *habeas corpus*.

(C) Denied, because there is no right to petition for *habeas corpus* from a
state court to a federal court.

(D) Granted, because there is a constitutional right of *habeas corpus* review
by a federal court with respect to all state court criminal cases.

Questions 57-59 are based on the following fact situation.

Two federal agents arrested Jake for bank robbery. The arrest took place on the
sidewalk in front of Jake's house. He was watering his front lawn at the time. Jake
requested that he be allowed to go into the kitchen where the telephone was
located in order to call his wife (who was at work). The agents agreed, but first
handcuffed Jake's arms behind his back. One of them dialed the number and held
the receiver up to Jake's face. As Jake talked to his wife, the second agent noticed
the corner of a $10 bill protruding from a closed breadbox located on the same
counter as the phone, approximately five feet from where Jake was standing.
Remembering that a number of $10 bills had been taken during the bank robbery,
the second agent opened the breadbox and seized the bill. It was later determined
from the bill's serial number that it had, in fact, been taken from the bank.

57. The prosecution's best theory in opposing a motion to suppress the $10 bill
from evidence is:

(A) The bill was in "plain view."

(B) The second agent acted in good faith in searching the breadbox.

(C) The bill was seized incident to Jake's arrest.

(D) Exigent circumstances existed.

58. Jake's arrest was:

(A) Valid, if in addition to these facts, an Assistant United States Attorney had
approved the arrest in advance.

(B) Valid, if the agents had probable cause to believe Jake had committed the
robbery.

(C) Invalid, if the agents had sufficient time to obtain an arrest warrant.

(D) Invalid, because a neutral judicial officer did not independently determine
if there was probable cause for the arrest.

59. As the federal agents were taking Jake to their car, Jake's friend, Fred, was
coming up Jake's walkway. One of the agents, speculating (without any
specific grounds) that Fred might have been Jake's accomplice in the bank
robbery, ordered Fred to stop and frisked him. Feeling a small packet of

something, he told Fred to hand the item to him. Fred did. The packet contained a substance which was subsequently determined to be heroin.

If Fred moved to suppress the heroin from evidence at his trial for violation of U.S. law, its seizure would probably be deemed:

(A) Invalid, under the Fifth Amendment.

(B) Invalid, under the Fourth Amendment.

(C) Invalid, under the Sixth Amendment.

(D) Valid.

Questions 60-61 are based on the following fact situation.

Denise was charged with the crime of aggravated battery (a serious felony) in State X. She asked Lawyer Lon to defend her. Lon agreed. Lon was a highly qualified lawyer who was licensed to practice law in two states, but not in State X. Lon applied to the State X Supreme Court, requesting to defend Denise on a *pro hac vice* basis. This application was denied. Denise then chose Ron, an in-state attorney. Denise had some reservations about Ron's approach to her case, but the strategy was competent. A 9-1 verdict of guilty was returned against Denise by the 10-member jury.

60. The State X Supreme Court's denial of Lon's petition to defend Denise:

(A) Violated Denise's right to effective counsel.

(B) Violated Denise's right to a fair trial.

(C) Violated Denise's due process rights.

(D) Did not violate any of Denise's rights.

61. Denise has argued on appeal that her Sixth and Fourteenth Amendment jury trial rights were violated. Her appeal should:

(A) Succeed, because she did not have a 12-person jury.

(B) Succeed, because the jury's verdict was not unanimous.

(C) Succeed, because she was not represented by counsel of her choice.

(D) Fail.

62. Linda was charged with committing arson. She was indigent, so a public defender, Mary, was appointed for her. Linda was convicted. Mary appealed Linda's case to the state intermediate appellate court (as was Linda's right under existing law), but the appeal failed. Linda requested Mary to appeal her case gratuitously to the State X Supreme Court. Mary, due to her own time constraints, refused Linda's request. Linda filed her own petition for review

with the State X Supreme Court. Under State X law, there is no right of appeal in criminal cases to the State X Supreme Court. Linda's petition was denied.

Linda was:

(A) Denied the right to effective counsel, because Mary refused to pursue the case to the State X Supreme Court.

(B) Denied the right to effective counsel, because no attorney appealed her case to the State X Supreme Court.

(C) Denied the right to counsel, if she can show that her appeal would probably have been successful if conducted by an attorney.

(D) Not denied the right to effective counsel, since this was a discretionary appeal.

Questions 63-65 are based on the following fact situation.

Wanda was prosecuted for petty theft (a misdemeanor). She was indigent and requested that counsel be appointed for her. This request was denied. Wanda was convicted and immediately put on probation.

Two months later, Wanda was arrested for shoplifting a diamond ring and indicted for grand theft. She was offered a public defender, but refused. Against her wishes, a standby attorney was appointed who occasionally coached Wanda at trial. Wanda was again convicted.

Under the state's sentencing statute, repeat theft offenders are obliged to serve an additional three years in prison. Wanda was sentenced to a term of five years imprisonment for the second offense.

63. When the state denied the right to counsel to Wanda in her petty theft trial:

(A) There was a reversible constitutional error.

(B) There was error, but it will be deemed harmless unless Wanda can prove she would have prevailed.

(C) There was no error, because Wanda was charged only with a misdemeanor.

(D) There was no error, because no imprisonment resulted.

64. When the state appointed "standby" counsel for Wanda in her grand theft trial:

(A) She was denied the right to defend herself.

(B) She was denied her due process rights.

(C) She was denied the right to effective counsel.

(D) There was no constitutional error.

65. Wanda's five-year sentence is:

    (A) A violation of the principle of proportionality.

    (B) A violation of the double jeopardy clause.

    (C) A violation of her right to effective counsel.

    (D) Constitutionally permissible.

Questions 66-67 are based on the following fact situation.

Bill killed Tom. He was originally tried in a State X court on a charge of voluntary manslaughter. Although the prosecution introduced sufficient evidence to support a determination of guilty, the jury was unable to reach a verdict. Bill was then re-tried for the same offense. This time, the jury returned a verdict of guilty. However, their determination was overturned by the trial judge, based upon the weight of the evidence.

66. Bill's re-trial was:

    (A) Barred by the double jeopardy clause, because jeopardy had previously attached.

    (B) Barred by the double jeopardy clause, because the jury had been impaneled and sworn.

    (C) Not barred by the double jeopardy clause, because there was a hung jury in the first trial.

    (D) Barred by the double jeopardy clause, because a verdict had been returned in the first trial.

67. Can Bill be re-tried a third time?

    (A) No, because the initial trial ended in a hung jury.

    (B) No, because re-trial is barred after a reversal resulting from insufficient evidence.

    (C) Yes, because a re-trial is not barred after a reversal based on the weight of the evidence.

    (D) No, because only a single re-trial is permissible.

68. Six workers had just cashed their weekly paychecks in a liquor store when they were robbed at gunpoint in the liquor store's parking lot. The State X prosecutor charged and prosecuted Jim with the robbery of Joe (one of the workers). Jim's sole defense was an alibi defense. Jim was acquitted.

    The State X prosecutor has now charged Jim with the robbery of Allan (another of the workers). Jim:

(A) Can have the charge dismissed, because the prosecution is obliged to bring all criminal charges arising from a single incident, transaction, or occurrence in one case.

(B) Can have the charge dismissed, because he was successful in the initial case based upon an alibi defense, equally applicable to the second case.

(C) Cannot have the charge dismissed, because the charge against Jim for robbery of Allan constitutes a different case for purposes of the double jeopardy clause.

(D) Cannot have the charge dismissed, because there are different issues in this instance.

Questions 69-71 are based on the following fact situation.

The police in the city of Smud were conducting a lineup as part of a murder investigation. Wanting to conform to constitutional safeguards, Officer Green decided that they would need five persons in the lineup in addition to the suspect, Jones. Jones had been arrested without a warrant one hour earlier while walking home from work. Jones had not yet been charged with the murder in question. Because Jones was white and there were only three other persons at police headquarters who were white, Officer Green walked outside to find a citizen who would "volunteer" to be in the lineup.

Green spotted Mr. Bad Lad sitting on a bench. He approached Bad Lad and asked him to volunteer. Bad Lad refused. However, when Green taunted him about not fulfilling his civic duties, Bad Lad agreed to be placed in the lineup.

Jones, the suspect, was 6'5", Bad Lad was 6'2", and the rest of the participants were 5'9" to 6'0".

Green placed Bad Lad next to Jones and then brought Witness into the room. As soon as Witness saw Bad Lad he pointed at Bad Lad and shouted, "Hey, that guy robbed my store this morning." Green immediately asked, "What about the guy standing to his right [referring to Jones]?" Witness replied, "He looks like the guy who shot my brother, yeah, that's him."

Bad Lad tried to run from the elevated stage, but Green grabbed him by the wrist. Green told other officers to take Jones away. Green searched Bad Lad and found a small handgun on him. Bad Lad then exclaimed, "Man, this ain't my day, I might as well confess." Green then read Bad Lad his *Miranda* warnings, after which Bad Lad refused to speak.

Bad Lad and Jones were indicted shortly thereafter. Witness died of natural causes prior to trial.

69. At Jones' trial, the prosecution submitted into evidence Witness' statement at the line-up identifying Jones. (You may assume that a hearsay objection to this evidence would *not* be successful.) An objection to this evidence by Jones should be:

    (A) Sustained, on the grounds that Jones did not have assistance of counsel at the lineup.
    (B) Sustained, on the grounds that Jones' right to due process of law was violated because the lineup procedure was impermissibly suggestive.
    (C) Overruled, because no constitutional violation occurred in obtaining this evidence.
    (D) Overruled, whether or not the police lacked probable cause to arrest Jones.

70. If Bad Lad was tried for the robbery of Witness' store, the gun would be:

    (A) Admissible, because Bad Lad's arrest was valid.
    (B) Inadmissible, because no warrant had been obtained for Bad Lad's arrest.
    (C) Inadmissible, because Bad Lad had not been given the *Miranda* warnings.
    (D) Inadmissible, because Bad Lad had been illegally detained.

71. If Bad Lad was tried for the robbery of Witness' store, Bad Lad's statement ("I might as well confess") would be:

    (A) Inadmissible, because he had not been given the *Miranda* warnings.
    (B) Admissible, because *Miranda* warnings were not necessary.
    (C) Inadmissible, because it was the product of an illegal detention.
    (D) Inadmissible, because counsel was not appointed for Bad Lad immediately after Witness's identification.

Questions 72-79 are based on the following fact situation.

Mel, an FBI agent, was advised by a reliable informant that she had personally seen Ann printing counterfeit money in her house. Mel went to the office of the Assistant United States Attorney on the same day and asked her whether she felt there was enough evidence to arrest Ann. The Assistant United States Attorney answered affirmatively.

Mel then went to Ann's house. As he arrived at Ann's door, Mel realized that he had once heard from a source he could not remember that Ann had a violence-prone boyfriend. As a consequence, Mel decided to be careful. He knocked on the door. A young female voice asked, "Who's there?" Mel replied, "A friend of Ann's." The door was opened by Ann's 15-year-old daughter, Suzy. Mel started into the house but, less fearful now, told Suzy before he crossed the threshold that he was an FBI agent who wanted to arrest Ann. Suzy then tried to close the door, but Mel was able to slip into the house before Suzy was able to slam the door shut.

Mel found Ann taking a nap in her bedroom and placed her under arrest. Mel saw a small, but sophisticated stenography machine (which could be used to print counterfeit money) next to the bed where Ann was napping. He thought about seizing it, but decided against it.

After taking Ann to the jail to await arraignment, Mel obtained a search warrant. It authorized him to search Ann's bedroom for, and seize, the machine. As Mel left to execute the search warrant, the Assistant United States Attorney said, "Mel, seize anything else that looks good while you're out at Ann's." (Although probably not the case, you may assume that the search warrant was validly issued.)

When Mel arrived back at Ann's house, he knocked on the door. Suzy answered. Mel properly identified himself and told her he had a warrant to search the house. Suzy then let Mel in. On the way to the bedroom, Mel saw a closed door in the living room (which he thought led to a closet, as indeed it did). Thinking that Ann's boyfriend might be hiding there, he opened the closet door. No one was inside, but Mel saw a sawed-off shotgun on a shelf. Because possession of such a firearm violated federal law, he seized it. He then went to the bedroom and saw that the machine was no longer on the floor. Mel then opened a jewelry box on Ann's desk and found chemicals and dyes used in counterfeiting. He seized them, too. Mel then opened the bedroom closet door, saw the stenography machine sitting on the floor along with a number of bills (which later proved to be counterfeit). Mel seized the machine and the bills.

72. Mel's arrest of Ann was:

  (A) Invalid, because he had failed to obtain an arrest warrant.
  (B) Valid, because the Assistant United States Attorney had approved the arrest.
  (C) Valid, if Mel had probable cause to arrest her.
  (D) Valid, if Ann's conduct constituted a felony.

73. Mel's first entry into Ann's home was:

  (A) Valid, if there was probable cause to arrest Ann.
  (B) Invalid, since Suzy's consent to Mel's entry was vitiated because she was a minor.
  (C) Valid, since sufficient exigent circumstances existed.
  (D) Invalid.

74. When Mel saw the stenography machine at the time he arrested Ann:

    (A) He could legally have seized it, since it was in plain view.
    (B) He could not seize it, because he did not have a warrant for Ann's arrest.
    (C) He could not seize it, because it was located beyond Ann's immediate control.
    (D) He could not seize it whether or not the arrest was proper, because he did not have a search warrant for the machine.

75. Mel's seizure of the sawed-off shotgun was:

    (A) Invalid, because his second entry into Ann's house was invalid.
    (B) Invalid, because the sawed-off shotgun was not connected to the counterfeiting scheme.
    (C) Valid, because the sawed-off shotgun was contraband.
    (D) Invalid, because the search was outside the scope of the warrant.

76. Mel's seizure of the chemicals and dyes in Ann's jewelry box was:

    (A) Invalid, because police officers executing a proper warrant may not seize items not described in the document.
    (B) Valid, because the jewelry box was in plain view.
    (C) Invalid, because the stenographic machine could not reasonably have been contained in the jewelry box.
    (D) Valid, because Mel was entitled to seize any evidence pertaining to the counterfeiting scheme found in Ann's bedroom.

77. Mel's seizure of the stenography machine in the bedroom closet was:

    (A) Invalid, because it was not in plain view.
    (B) Invalid, because it was not where Mel had previously seen it.
    (C) Valid, because Suzy's consent to Mel's entry into the house entitled him to search the entire premises.
    (D) Valid, because the stenography machine was found while Mel was in the process of properly executing the warrant.

78. Mel's seizure of the counterfeit bills on the floor of Ann's bedroom closet was:

    (A) Invalid, because he had no reason to believe that the bills were evidence of a crime.
    (B) Valid, because they were in plain view.

(C) Invalid, because an Assistant United States Attorney has no authority to expand the scope of a search warrant.

(D) Valid, because Mel had a warrant covering the evidence.

79. Assuming Ann moved to suppress the chemicals and dyes found in her jewelry box, their seizure could best be attacked on the grounds that:

(A) They are privileged under the Fifth Amendment.

(B) The seizure was in violation of the Sixth Amendment (since Ann was arrested prior to the search).

(C) The seizure was in violation of the Fourteenth Amendment.

(D) The seizure was in violation of the Fourth Amendment.

Questions 80-85 are based on the following fact situation.

Badluck called FBI Agent Hoover and told him that he had (1) participated in a bank robbery the previous day with Eddie Fingers, and (2) since seen in Eddie's living room closet both the gun that Eddie used in the bank robbery and the stolen money. The bills were marked. Badluck described Eddie's home as a one-story frame house located at 823 *Howard* Street. Badluck also told Hoover that he had heard a rumor that Fingers had given his brother-in-law, Donald Doyle, some of the proceeds of the robbery to repay a debt, and that Doyle had joked about the money feeling "kinda hot to the touch."

Later the same day, Hoover saw Doyle standing outside a massage parlor downtown. Hoover approached Doyle, identified himself, and told Doyle that he was a suspect and to raise his hands. Doyle complied. Hoover then "frisked" Doyle, feeling what Hoover thought to be a wallet in his back pocket. Hoover told Doyle that he wanted to see the contents of the wallet, and Doyle handed it over. After Hoover found in the wallet a map of the bank which had been robbed, he arrested Doyle. As he was leading Doyle to his (Hoover's) car, Hoover passed Doyle's car and noticed that it matched the description and bore the license plate of the robbery getaway car. Peering through a rear window, Hoover saw pants and a shirt on the floor. These items matched the description of those worn by one of the robbers. Hoover opened the closed (but unlocked) back door and seized the clothes.

After depositing Doyle at the federal jail, Hoover obtained a search warrant for the living room of Fingers' home. The "probable cause" affidavit detailed the information given to him earlier in the day by Badluck. A warrant was issued, but it mistakenly described Fingers' address as 823 *Harold* Street.

Hoover went to Fingers' home at 823 *Howard* Street without noticing the mistake in the warrant regarding the street name. He knocked on the door. When Fingers asked who it was, Hoover replied, "Fuller Brush." Fingers opened the door.

Hoover then stated that he was really an FBI agent with a search warrant. Fingers told him to come in and was promptly arrested by Hoover. Following Fingers' arrest, Hoover searched the hall closet and found money on the floor which had been taken from the bank. He seized the money and then opened the living room closet, where he found the gun described in the warrant. On the floor on his way out of the house, Hoover saw an unopened envelope addressed to Fingers from Doyle. Hoover opened the envelope and found a letter to Fingers from Doyle, thanking Fingers for the bank robbery opportunity.

Fingers asked to be allowed to go to his bedroom and put on shoes and socks. Hoover agreed, and accompanied Fingers to the bedroom. While Fingers was seated on the side of the bed lacing his shoes, Hoover noticed and seized a wig which protruded from underneath the pillow. The wig matched the description of one worn by one of the robbers.

80. Hoover's seizure of the map from Doyle's wallet was:

    (A) Proper, as incident to a valid arrest.
    (B) Proper, because Doyle consented.
    (C) Proper, as incident to a valid detention.
    (D) Improper, because Doyle's detention was unreasonable.

81. Hoover's search of Doyle's car, and seizure of the pants and shirt, was:

    (A) Valid, as incident to Doyle's arrest.
    (B) Valid, because there was a suspect at large who might have access to the car.
    (C) Invalid, because no warrant had been obtained.
    (D) Valid, because probable cause to search the car existed.

82. Hoover's arrest of Fingers was:

    (A) Proper, as incident to the execution of the search warrant.
    (B) Improper, because Hoover had sufficient time to obtain an arrest warrant and failed to do so.
    (C) Proper, because Hoover had probable cause to arrest Fingers.
    (D) Proper, because Hoover did not need an arrest warrant.

83. The entry of Hoover into Fingers' home was:

    (A) Invalid, because he obtained entry by ruse.
    (B) Valid, because the error in the address would not make the warrant invalid.

(C) Valid, because the presence of the gun in the house constituted exigent circumstances.

(D) Invalid, because the street address was incorrect.

84. Assuming Fingers moved to suppress the contents of the envelope, Hoover's seizure and search of the envelope was:

(A) Invalid, because only items described in a search warrant may be seized by police.

(B) Valid, because it was in "plain view."

(C) Valid, as incident to Fingers' arrest.

(D) Invalid, because Hoover had no probable cause to believe that the envelope contained evidence of a crime.

85. The seizure of the wig was:

(A) Invalid, because it resulted from a search incident to an invalid arrest.

(B) Invalid, because it was outside the scope of the warrant.

(C) Invalid, because the warrant was defective.

(D) Valid, if the wig was within Fingers' control.

86. Brawler was suspected by the FBI of illegal gambling. The FBI convinced Brawler's brother, Smitch, to place a bet through Brawler and to wear a recording device during the attempt. Smitch arrived at Brawler's home on July 4th and told Brawler that he would like to make a wager. Brawler said, "OK, even though, as a patriot, I don't normally do this type of thing on holidays." Brawler accepted the bet and was later prosecuted. The federal prosecutor introduced the taped recording of the conversation into evidence at Brawler's trial.

Smitch's recording of his conversation with Brawler was:

(A) Constitutionally valid.

(B) Done in violation of Brawler's Fourth Amendment rights.

(C) Done in violation of Brawler's Fifth Amendment rights.

(D) Done in violation of Brawler's Sixth Amendment rights.

Questions 87-90 are based on the following fact situation.

Chiseler borrowed Employer's car to pick up his brother at the train station. However, he actually used the car to rob a bank. After returning the car and returning to work, Chiseler remembered that he had left his wallet underneath the driver's seat of the vehicle. As he was returning to the car, Chiseler was arrested by the FBI (although they did not have an arrest warrant). They took Chiseler directly to the bank to determine whether any of the tellers could identify him. Chiseler requested a lawyer, but his request was refused. Tillie Teller was the only witness able to positively identify Chiseler at the bank. On the following day, the FBI seized Employer's car and found Chiseler's wallet. Chiseler was then indicted for federal bank robbery.

87. Does Chiseler have standing to object to the FBI's seizure of Employer's car on Fourth Amendment grounds?

(A) Yes, if the FBI seized Employer's car without a warrant.

(B) Yes, if the FBI lacked probable cause to believe that Employer's car was involved in the robbery.

(C) No, because Chiseler was not the owner of the car.

(D) No, because the FBI's seizure of Employer's car was justified by exigent circumstances.

88. Can Chiseler successfully object to the introduction of his wallet into evidence?

(A) Yes, because the police failed to obtain a warrant.

(B) Yes, because the wallet was still his property.

(C) Yes, if the police lacked reasonable cause to believe that Chiseler's wallet was in the car when Employer's vehicle was seized.

(D) No.

89. Assume for the purposes of this question only that Chiseler had not yet been given his *Miranda* warnings. In response to a taunting inquiry by one of the arresting officers ("A bank? Why rob a bank? You'd have had better luck robbing a pushcart"), Chiseler blurted out that he had driven Employer's car on the day of the bank robbery, but that he did not rob the bank. At trial, Chiseler testified in his own defense that he was in Mexico on the day of the robbery. The prosecutor then attempted to offer Chiseler's statement into evidence. The statement is:

(A) Admissible, if it was voluntary and the jury is instructed by the court that it can only be considered on the issue of Chiseler's credibility.

(B) Admissible, because the statement was not a specific admission of any element of the crime for which Chiseler was being tried.

(C) Inadmissible, unless Chiseler's statement was involuntary.

(D) Inadmissible, because Chiseler was not given *Miranda* warnings prior to a custodial interrogation.

90. Assume for the purposes of this question only that Chiseler objected to an alleged error at trial. Which of the following is the MOST accurate statement of the law on "reversible error"?

    (A) An error of constitutional dimension made during trial requires reversal.

    (B) Only trial errors relating to involuntary confessions or a prejudiced judge require reversal.

    (C) An error of constitutional dimension at trial requires reversal, if the prosecution cannot show beyond a reasonable doubt that the error did not contribute to the verdict.

    (D) An error of constitutional dimension requires reversal, unless all other evidence introduced at the trial overwhelmingly proves a defendant's guilt.

91. Over the years, Mark and his neighbor Phil have come to despise each other. Most recently, Phil has neglected to return a power saw borrowed from Mark. Mark has asked Phil to return the item many times. But each time, Phil merely replies, "No problem," and then fails to return the saw. Mark has became so angry, he decides to kill Phil. He makes a list called "Six ways to do away with Phil." One entry on the list is "Buy new hammer to bash Phil's skull in." Mark finally decides he's had enough and buys the hammer.

    The next day, Mark sees Phil lounging in his backyard hot tub. Mark shoves the "6-Ways List" into his pocket, grabs his new hammer, and creeps up behind Phil as the latter sits in the hot tub. Yelling "You lazy bum!", Mark strikes Phil in the skull with the hammer several times, killing him. Betty, Phil's wife hears Mark's yell and rushes out to find Phil dead. She calls the police and tells them (1) that Phil and Mark hated each other, and (2) that she heard Mark's yell and saw him near the body. The police then arrest Mark for murder. When Mark is booked at the police station, his clothes are searched and the "6-Ways List" is found in his pocket.

    If the "6-Ways List" is introduced into evidence by the prosecution at trial, it is most likely that:

    (A) It is admissible, if Mark was validly arrested.

    (B) It is admissible, if Mark had waived his *Miranda* rights.

    (C) It is inadmissible, because a valid search warrant had not been obtained.

    (D) It is inadmissible, if Mark's prior consent to the search had not been obtained.

92. Jason is a "Slurpee-aholic." He felt the need for a "Slurpee fix," but he had no money. He grabbed his brother's toy handgun and walked into the local 7-Eleven store. Jason brandished his "gun" and demanded ten Slurpees. After

guzzling the Slurpees, Jason pointed the gun at the cashier and demanded several Pogs. He put the Pogs in his pocket and ran out of the store. The cashier immediately called the police and gave them a physical description of Jason. She also told them what direction Jason had taken when he ran off.

Officer Johnson started driving in Jason's direction. He saw Jason and immediately arrested him. He began to search Jason and found the Pogs in his pocket.

If the prosecution attempts to introduce the Pogs at trial, it is most likely that:

(A) The Pogs are admissible if Officer Johnson had a reasonable suspicion that Jason was the perpetrator.
(B) The Pogs are admissible if Officer Johnson had, based upon the cashier's description, probable cause to arrest Jason.
(C) The Pogs are inadmissible because no search warrant was obtained.
(D) The Pogs are inadmissible if Jason was not apprised of his *Miranda* rights prior to the search.

93. Jack and Maria were married for more than ten years. Their relationship was very vitriolic, and Jack hit Maria on several occasions. One time, Maria called the police and pressed charges. Maria and Jack finally divorced. Determined not to let any other man have her, one night when Maria came home late from a date, Jack shot and killed her. There were no witnesses.

When the police searched Jack's room under a valid warrant, no weapon was found. But pants that appeared to have a speck of Maria's blood on them were found stuffed in a laundry hamper. At his trial, Jack did not take the stand.

The prosecution wishes to comment upon Jack's failure to testify at his trial. Which of the following is true:

(A) The prosecution may comment on Jack's failure to take the stand because this is a murder case.
(B) The prosecution may comment on Jack's failure to take the stand; but the defense can then request that the jury be advised that no adverse inference may be drawn from Jack's failure to testify.
(C) The prosecution is not allowed to comment; and if requested to do so by the defense, the judge must advise the jury that no adverse inference may be drawn from Jack's failure to testify.
(D) The prosecution is not allowed to comment; but the jury need not be advised that no adverse inference may be drawn from Jack's failure to testify.

94. Cynthia and Phyllis are attorneys who work at Morgan, Taller and Jacobs, a large law firm in downtown Mindenville. Cynthia and Phyllis have been rivals for 12 years, ever since they attended the same law school. Cynthia knew that Phyllis was up for partnership consideration, and deliberately sabotaged her chances by surreptitiously hiding files and destroying telephone messages. As a result, Phyllis was passed over for partnership. Sensing that Cynthia was responsible for her disappointment, Phyllis deliberately struck Cynthia with her car while Cynthia was crossing a street, and then sped off.

There were several witnesses to the hit-and-run, and Phyllis was arrested. Minutes after the arrest and prior to receiving her *Miranda* warnings, Phyllis was confronted by a police officer, who said , "I'll bet that Cynthia was a real SOB, wasn't she." Phyllis angrily replied, "You betcha! I'm only sorry that she dented my car."

If the prosecution tries to have the police officer testify as to Phyllis' incriminating statement at trial, it is most likely that:

(A) The statement is not admissible because police officers may not talk with a suspect prior to giving her *Miranda* warnings.

(B) The statement is not admissible if the officer's comment was reasonably calculated to elicit an incriminating response by Phyllis.

(C) The statement is admissible because Phyllis waived her *Miranda* rights by responding to the officer.

(D) The statement is admissible because Phyllis' blurt-out occurred before the police officer had an opportunity to recite her *Miranda* warnings.

95. Gina is a favorite gown designer for many Hollywood stars. In fact, she has been called the "designer to the stars." Lately, however, a young upstart designer, McClaren, has been gaining popularity. In fact, several actresses who are up for the Best Actress award have ordered dresses from McClaren. One of these actresses was previously a long-standing client of Gina's.

The night before the Oscars, Gina took several old dresses and drove to McClaren's shop. She put the dresses in a bundle near the door, and set them afire. Because the outside of the building was comprised of glass and metal, the fire did little damage. The fire department arrived several minutes later and extinguished the burning dresses. A witness identified Gina (who had remained at the scene), and she was immediately arrested.

Unaware that an arrest had been made, a fireman on the scene held up one of the burnt dresses, shook his head, and said to Fireman Cole, "Who would be so stupid as to start a fire with some old trashy dresses." Gina happened to overhear this remark as she was being led away, and spontaneously responded, "What do you know about dresses. They make a great fire; go back to the Firemen's Academy, Bozo."

If the prosecution attempts to introduce Gina's statement at trial, it is most likely that:

(A) The statement is inadmissible because Gina was arrested without a warrant.

(B) The statement is inadmissible because it was made in response to a calculated effort to elicit incriminating information from Gina.

(C) The statement is admissible if we assume that Gina was given her *Miranda* warnings before her statement.

(D) The statement is admissible because it was not made in response to an interrogation.

96. Madolyn yearned for a suit in the window of The Chanel Shop. Unable to restrain her desire, she drove her Rolls-Royce to the Shop, ran into the place brandishing a small pistol, took the suit from the window display, and then drove off.

The store manager called the police, and described Madolyn and her Rolls-Royce. The police immediately began to search for her. Meantime, a few blocks away, Madolyn double-parked outside her manicurist and went inside for a quick touch-up. She had the gun in her purse and quickly hid the gun between the cushions of her chair. When the police entered the salon after spotting her Rolls-Royce, Madolyn ran toward the back door exit. She was tackled and arrested.

Before Madolyn could be given her *Miranda* rights, a police officer sternly asked her, "Where's the gun? Give it to me before someone gets hurt." Madolyn walked to her chair, removed the gun, and handed it to the officer.

If the prosecution attempts to introduce the gun into evidence at Madolyn's trial, it is likely that:

(A) The gun is admissible because it represented a threat to the public safety.

(B) The gun is admissible because Madolyn impliedly waived her *Miranda* rights.

(C) The gun is inadmissible because the police lacked probable cause to arrest Madolyn.

(D) The gun is inadmissible because it was obtained in a coercive manner.

97. Marcus is fired by the manager of Marcy's Department Store after serving the store for over thirty years. Furious, Marcus hires "Mr. X" to kill the manager.

Marcus' "hired gun" succeeds only in shooting the manager in the foot. Mr. X is arrested and implicates Marcus, who is then arrested and charged with conspiracy to commit murder. Tony, a police informant, is put in the cell with Marcus, and pretends to befriend Marcus. After Marcus "makes bail," Tony and Marcus are released together. Tony leads Marcus into a conversation about Mr. X and the wounding of Marcy's manager. During the conversation, Marcus says, "What a bungler I picked. Someone else will finish the job."

If the prosecution attempts to introduce this statement at trial, it is most likely that:

(A) The statement is inadmissible because Tony tricked Marcus into making it.

(B) The statement is inadmissible because Tony's questioning is attributable to the police.

(C) The statement is admissible because Tony was not a police officer.

(D) The statement is admissible because Marcus was no longer in custody when he made it.

98. Baldonado, a local gangster, enters Joe's Butcher Shop. He tells Joe that, unless he (Joe) pays Baldonado "protection money" of $1,000 per month, his shop "might accidentally get burned to the ground." Unbeknownst to Baldonado, Joe is an undercover FBI special agent put in the store to investigate a local drug gang. Baldonado's threats are captured on both audio and videotape. Baldonado is tried in state court for attempted extortion, but his "friends" manage to "talk" to several of the jurors, and he is acquitted.

If the U.S. Attorney's Office then proceeds to prosecute Baldonado under RICO and/or other applicable federal statutes, it is most likely that the:

(A) Prosecution is not barred if the federal crimes have at least one additional legal element not existing in the state crime of extortion.

(B) Prosecution is not barred because double jeopardy principles are inapplicable.

(C) Prosecution is barred under double jeopardy principles.

(D) Prosecution is barred if there is at least one common legal element in both the state and federal crimes.

99. Madison is a dangerous serial killer. One night, three coeds from a sorority at Gregor University are brutally murdered. Witnesses at the scene observe a yellow "Bug" (identified as Madison's vehicle) driving quickly away. Using DMV records, the police arrest Madison. The coroner establishes the time of the deaths at about 1:00 a.m. on January 5th. At Madison's trial in state court for the murder of one of the coeds, a defense witness, Sheila, testifies that

Madison was with her from 9:00 p.m. on January 4th until 8:00 a.m. on January 5th. Sheila also testifies that she lived two hours from the scene of the murders. Sheila is the only witness presented by the defense. The jury believes Sheila's alibi testimony, and Madison is acquitted.

The prosecution subsequently indicts Madison for the murders of the two other individuals.

Based upon the foregoing::

(A) Madison can be tried for murdering the other women because double jeopardy is inapplicable to a case involving different victims.
(B) Madison can be tried for murdering the other women because the *res judicata* principles inherent in double jeopardy are inapplicable to different victims.
(C) Madison cannot be tried for murdering the other women because the jury determined in the initial action that he was not at the scene.
(D) Madison can be tried for murdering the other women if the prosecution can show that Sheila committed perjury.

100. Margot was arrested for shoplifting a red sweater from Marcy's Department Store. Shoplifting is a misdemeanor in this jurisdiction. At her arraignment, Margot told the judge that she couldn't afford an attorney, and requested that one be appointed for her. The judge, who saw that Margot was dressed in expensive clothes and was carrying a designer purse, denied her request. Margot refused to hire a lawyer, and represented herself at trial. She was subsequently convicted. Because it was her first offense, Margot was merely placed on one month's probation. Concerned about having a criminal conviction on her record, Margot appealed her conviction, claiming that her right to appointed counsel had been violated.

The appellate court will most likely rule that:

(A) Margot's right to counsel was not violated because she was not actually imprisoned.
(B) Margot's right to counsel was not violated because the charge against her was only a misdemeanor.
(C) Margot's right to counsel was violated when her request was wrongfully denied.
(D) Margot's right to counsel was violated because she was convicted.

101. Mandy and Douglas had dated for over two years. Although Mandy attempted to break off the relationship, Douglas called Mandy several times a day, had flowers delivered to her house, and ultimately began stalking her. But Douglas never threatened Mandy with physical violence or death.

Several months after the breakup, Mandy was found shot to death in her bedroom. There were no signs of illegal entry into her home. On Mandy's bedside table was a card from Douglas which read: "I know it's over, and I know I'll never see you again until we meet again in heaven."

Policewoman Carla, Mandy's sister, knowing that Douglas had stalked her sister, immediately suspected him. She began to follow him during her off hours. One evening, after Douglas left a bar, she saw him commit several driving misdemeanors (*e.g.*, exceeding the speed limit by 5 to 10 miles per hour, crossing the yellow line, etc.). Carla put on her flashing lights just as Douglas arrived home. When he saw the flashing lights, Douglas ran into his home and locked the door. Carla ran after him and forced the door open. She walked into the kitchen where Douglas, distraught, was sitting. She advised Douglas that he was under arrest, and recited his *Miranda* rights. She then asked him if he had anything to say. When Douglas looked up and saw that it was Carla, he whispered, "I'm sorry that I killed Mandy."

Douglas' confession is:

(A) Inadmissible because Carla broke into Douglas's house.

(B) Inadmissible because Carla saw that Douglas was distraught.

(C) Admissible because Douglas voluntarily waived his *Miranda* warnings.

(D) Admissible because Carla had personally seen Douglas commit several misdemeanors.

102. Marcus, a high school Honors student, is very nearsighted. One day, Marcus was on his way to attend the monthly chess club meeting at the home of a friend he'd never visited before. He was carrying a small duffle bag which he'd borrowed from his friend, Stan. Marcus had filled the bag with expensive chess pieces. Unfamiliar with the area, Marcus walked slowly down the street peering at addresses. Two policemen in an unmarked car observed Marcus. They accosted Marcus and asked him, "Do you have any stash?" Marcus thought the police had asked him, "Do you have any cash?" Marcus, who had $5 in his wallet, replied, "Yes." He was promptly arrested.

Unbeknownst to Marcus, Stan had placed several packets of cocaine within an inner lining of the duffle bag. The police found the cocaine, investigated all the circumstances and arrested Marcus' friend.

If Stan is indicted but his attorney objects to admission of the cocaine, it is most likely that:

(A) It is inadmissible because Marcus misunderstood the police officer's question.

(B) It is inadmissible because Marcus was never given his *Miranda* rights.

(C) It is admissible because the police officers had a reasonable suspicion that Marcus was involved in criminal activity.

(D) It is admissible because Stan had given the bag to Marcus.

103. Anita is a compulsive shoplifter. One day, Anita was observed by Jack, a manager at Marvin's Department Store, stealing some scarves. Jack, who knew Anita's parents and wanted to avoid causing her any humiliation, did not report the theft immediately. However, the following day, Jack informed the police that he had observed Anita leaving the store with stolen scarves in her bag. This information was communicated to Officer Johnson, who patrolled the neighborhood in which Anita lives. He drove by her house and saw her watering the front lawn. Officer Johnson stopped his car, and arrested Anita for shoplifting, a misdemeanor. After receiving *Miranda* warnings, Anita stood silently for a moment. Officer Johnson then said, "Come on, you'll feel better if you tell the truth." Anita then confessed.

If the prosecution attempts to introduce Anita's confession at her trial, it is most likely that the confession is:

(A) Admissible because it was made voluntarily.

(B) Admissible because Officer Johnson had probable cause to arrest Anita.

(C) Inadmissible because Officer Johnson should have ceased asking Anita any questions when she remained silent.

(D) Inadmissible if Officer Johnson had failed to obtain an arrest warrant.

Multiple-Choice Answers

1. **D** There is no reasonable expectation of privacy from aerial surveillance of an area over which there is an established aerial route; *California v. Ciraolo*, 476 U.S. 227 (1986). The fact that the police used a relatively unsophisticated mechanical device like binoculars probably doesn't change this result (though use of a very unusual or sophisticated spying device to see something that couldn't be seen by the naked eye from public airspace might make a difference). Since Sub had no reasonable expectation of privacy with respect to items in his backyard which were visible from the sky, use of the photos to obtain a warrant was proper. (*See* ELO Ch.2-II(D)(5).) Choice **A** is legally true (there is a reasonable expectation of privacy with respect to items contained *within* one's home), but it's incorrect here because Sub had no reasonable expectation of privacy with respect to surveillance made from a plane within the established aerial route over his home. (Remember, just because an answer is legally true does not make it the best answer.) Choice **B** is incorrect because, despite the fact that the evidence was within the curtilage of Sub's home, it was viewable to anyone within the established air route. Finally, Choice **C** is incorrect because the marijuana could be seen from the air. In the *Ciraolo* case, the defendant built a fence around the marijuana to prevent it from being seen from the ground, but the aerial evidence was nonetheless found admissible.

2. **A** Compelled production of a handwriting exemplar triggers neither Fifth nor Sixth Amendment protections; *U.S. v. Mara*, 410 U.S. 19 (1973). (*See* ELO Ch.6-II(B)(2).) Because the evidence obtained from Doreen was of a *nontestimonial* nature, the Fifth Amendment privilege against self-incrimination was *not* applicable. Also, because Doreen had apparently not been formally charged, her Sixth Amendment right to counsel had not yet attached. In any event, the handwriting exemplars were required at a non-critical stage of the proceedings; *Gilbert v. California*, 388 U.S. 263 (1967). (*See* ELO Ch.6-IV(C)(1).) The Fourth Amendment was not violated. Asking someone suspected of a crime to furnish relevant physical evidence may be a "seizure," but it is not an "unreasonable" seizure (the Fourth Amendment protects only against "unreasonable searches and seizures"). Finally, Doreen's due process (Fourteenth Amendment) rights do not appear to have been violated because the police did nothing which unfairly prejudiced her ability to defend against the outstanding charges. Choice **B** is incorrect because there is no legal requirement that a suspect be advised that a handwriting exemplar may be used against her. Choice **C** is legally incorrect (Doreen did not have a constitutional right to refuse to give a handwriting exemplar — our explanation shows that no Fourth, Fifth, Sixth or Fourteenth Amendment rights were violated, and there are no other relevant consti-

tutional provisions). Choice **D** is incorrect because, as discussed above, Doreen had no right to have counsel present when the handwriting exemplar was demanded.

3.   **C**   A search warrant is unnecessary where consent to a governmental search is voluntarily given by someone with authority to do so; *Schneckloth v. Bustamonte*, 412 U.S. 218 (1973). (*See* ELO Ch.3-VII(B).) Paul was driving Jack's car with Jack's consent and in furtherance of a criminal conspiracy. However reluctantly, Paul did agree to the search and he did allow the officer to remove the ignition keys and search the trunk. Paul will be deemed to have consented to the search. Even though Paul didn't own the car, his consent as co-conspirator would probably be enough to extinguish any complaint Jack might assert that his Fourth Amendment rights were violated. Choice **A** is incorrect because Paul's nervousness alone would not constitute sufficient "probable cause" to search the entire car. Choice **B** is incorrect because Paul had not been arrested at the time the search occurred. Finally, Choice **D** is incorrect because Paul was stopped for a minor traffic violation and exigent circumstances did not exist.

4.   **B**   The Fifth Amendment privilege against self-incrimination may be invoked at a grand jury hearing. However, that privilege must be specifically claimed in order to become effective. Because Suspect failed to invoke the privilege specifically, the contempt finding will probably be sustained. (*See* ELO Ch.9-I(D).) Choice **A** is incorrect because the privilege against self-incrimination under the Fifth Amendment may be asserted at grand jury hearings. Choice **C** is incorrect because witnesses at grand jury hearings must ordinarily answer all relevant questions, unless they assert a privilege entitling them to refuse to answer. Finally, Choice **D** is incorrect because, while his answer may have implicated him in a crime, Suspect was nevertheless obliged to assert a legal basis for refusing to respond.

5.   **C**   The double jeopardy clause does not (unless collateral estoppel is applicable) preclude a subsequent prosecution of the same defendant for a different crime, even though the latter crime may have arisen from the same transaction presented in the earlier trial. Because the crime of armed robbery contains at least one element which is different from the elements of premeditated murder, the prosecution would *not* be estopped from prosecuting Dillon for armed robbery. (*See* ELO Ch.9-VIII(H).) Choice **A** is legally incorrect. The prosecution may charge a defendant with different crimes resulting from the same transaction, if (1) the later prosecution involves a crime which contains at least one

element which is different from the earlier offense, **and** (2) no issue essential to conviction for the subsequent crime was actually litigated and necessarily resolved in the defendant's favor in the earlier case. Choice **B** is both legally and factually incorrect. The clause does not prohibit trial on a lesser offense if a new element is present at the second trial; and armed robbery is not a lesser offense included within the crime of premeditated murder; the two crimes are defined by different elements. Finally, Choice **D** is legally incorrect (estoppel may apply when the defendant is charged with committing two different crimes if the double jeopardy doctrine is invoked). Prosecution for an second offense would not be possible if there was a finding in favor of the defendant in the first trial on a factual element essential to conviction on the second offense.

6. **C** Pursuant to a valid arrest, police may make a full search of the area within the suspect's immediate control; *Chimel v. California*, 395 U.S. 752 (1965). Because Defendant was arrested pursuant to a valid warrant, a search of his outer clothing was appropriate. Thus, the heroin found in his outer clothing was admissible. (*See* ELO Ch.3-III(B).) Choice **A** is incorrect because a "search incident to a valid arrest" constitutes a recognized exception to the requirement of obtaining a prior search warrant. Choice **B** is incorrect because a search incident to a valid arrest is *not* limited to weapons or indicia of the crime which the person arrested is suspected of having committed. Finally, Choice **D** is incorrect because the law does not validate an otherwise illegal search simply because indicia of a crime is, in fact, discovered in the search. See *Smith v. Ohio*, 494 U.S. 541 (1990).

7. **C** Provided probable cause exists, an arrest by a police officer is valid without a warrant, unless made (1) within the suspect's home, or (2) for a misdemeanor perpetrated out of the arresting officer's presence; *Payton v. New York*, 445 U.S. 573 (1980). Because the police had probable cause to believe Defendant had killed his wife, and the arrest was made in a public area, no warrant was necessary. The search was therefore valid because it was incident to a valid arrest. (*See* ELO Ch.3-II(A)(B).) Choice **A** is incorrect because an arrest warrant is not required when there is probable cause and the arrest is made in a public area. Choice **B** is legally incorrect (an arrest warrant need *not* be obtained where probable cause exists and the arrest is made in a public area). Finally, Choice **D** is incorrect because an illegal arrest is not validated by the discovery of criminal evidence during the search.

8. **B** A suspect has standing to object to the search of an area in which he has a legitimate expectation of privacy; *Rakas v. Illinois*, 439 U.S. 128 (1978). Because the ring was in Byron's physical possession at the time of his arrest, he had a legitimate expectation of privacy in the item. (*See* ELO Ch.7-II(C).) Choice **A** is incorrect because Byron had no expectation of privacy in the apartment building which was not his home. It's not his presence on the stairway that gives him standing, but the possession of the ring. Choice **C** is incorrect; the fact that Byron may have been trespassing when arrested does not lessen his expectation of privacy with respect to items in his physical possession. Finally, Choice **D** is incorrect because ownership is not a *per se* requirement of standing; here, the key factor was possession.

9. **D** Probable cause to arrest exists when, considering all the circumstances, the police officer reasonably believes it is more probable than not that the suspect has committed a crime.(*See* ELO Ch.2-III(B)(1).) Because Byron fit the mugger's description, was in the vicinity where the muggings had occurred, and sought to avoid O'Leary as she attempted to approach him, it is likely that probable cause was present. Therefore, the search of Bryon's outer clothing was proper as a search incident to a valid arrest. (*See* ELO Ch.3-III(B).) Choice **A** is incorrect because, while exigent circumstances may not have existed, O'Leary nevertheless had probable cause to arrest Bryon. Choice **B** is factually incorrect (there was probable cause to arrest Byron). Finally, Choice **C** is incorrect because it is not necessary to believe that a suspect has a particular item in his possession in order to be able to use all the evidence discovered in a valid search. Because the arrest was valid, any evidence found within Byron's immediate control could be used against him.

10. **C** A court may permit a defendant to withdraw a guilty plea prior to sentencing whenever there is a "fair and just reason" for doing so; FED.R.CRIM.P. 32(e). If Byron was under the mistaken impression that the confession and ring would be admissible against him at a trial when he agreed to plead guilty, the mistaken impression would probably constitute a "fair and just" reason for permitting him to withdraw his plea. (It is not clear that the court *would* so decide, but the court "could" decide this way without abusing its discretion, and the question asks you on what grounds the court could allow withdrawal.) (*See* ELO Ch.9-III(E)(1).) Choice **A** is legally incorrect (a criminal defendant cannot withdraw a guilty plea that is fairly and voluntarily made). Choice **B** is incorrect because a guilty plea is not "involuntary" simply because it was induced by the prosecution's offer of a sentence which was lighter than might otherwise have been exacted under the circumstances.

Finally, Choice **D** is incorrect because, as described above, Byron probably would be permitted to withdraw his guilty plea under these circumstances.

11. **C**   When an accused takes the stand to testify in his own defense, the Fifth Amendment privilege against self-incrimination is waived. When Byron chose to testify in his own behalf, he waived his Fifth Amendment right to refuse to answer questions about the crime charged. (*See* ELO Ch.9-VII(D)(1)(a).) Choice **A** is incorrect. Byron did *not* preserve his Fifth Amendment privilege merely because he hadn't incriminated himself during his direct testimony. Choice **B** is factually incorrect (*i.e.*, Byron did waive his Fifth Amendment privilege against self-incrimination by taking the stand to deny his guilt). Finally, Choice **D** is incorrect because, having voluntarily chosen to testify in his own behalf, Byron could not subsequently refuse to answer questions which might tend to incriminate him. The right to assert the privilege arises when the defendant makes the decision to testify or not to testify.

12. **D**   A voluntary statement obtained in violation of the *Miranda* rule may be utilized to impeach the accused; *Harris v. New York*, 401 U.S. 222 (1971). Byron's statement could not be used by the prosecution for its case-in-chief because it was not preceded by *Miranda* warnings. However, since it appears to have been made voluntarily, it may be used to impeach Byron's testimony. (*See* ELO Ch.5-XII(B).) Choice **A** is incorrect because the confession is being utilized in cross-examination of Byron's testimony (rather than as part of the prosecution's case-in-chief). Choice **B** is incorrect because, as discussed above in the answer to Question 9, Byron's arrest was probably valid. Finally, Choice **C** is incorrect because statements obtained in violation of the *Miranda* rule are not admissible as direct evidence against the accused. (*See* ELO Ch.5-IV(H).)

13. **C**   An individual ordinarily has standing to object to a governmental search of areas in which he has a reasonable expectation of privacy. (*See* ELO Ch.7-II(C).) Because the heroin was found in *Morgan's* car (an area in which Defendant would have no expectation of privacy), Defendant lacked standing to object to the search which resulted in discovery of the heroin. Nor did Defendant have standing to object to search of the bag because it was no longer his and he had lost his expectation of privacy with respect to it. Choice **A** is incorrect because, while factually true (the heroin was not in plain view), Defendant lacked standing to object to the search. Choice **B** is incorrect because, while probably true (the search of the car's interior was probably unlawful), Defendant lacked

standing to object to it. Pursuant to a routine stop for the purpose of issuing a citation for a minor traffic violation, the police may peer into the vehicle (even with a flashlight, if the stop occurs during the evening). They may not, however, search the car's interior (unless they have probable cause to believe, or reasonable suspicion, that indicia of criminal activity or concealed weapons will be found). (*See* ELO Ch.3-VI(L).) Choice **D** is incorrect because (1) a routine stop for a minor traffic violation does not constitute a full custodial arrest, and (2) Defendant had no standing with respect to items found in Morgan's car.

14. **A**   In a stop for a traffic violation for the purpose of issuing a ticket, even when the ticket is issued, the police may *not* search the vehicle's interior. (*See* ELO Ch.3-VI(L).) (They may, however, conduct a protective sweep for weapons if they have a concrete reason to fear that the driver will get control of a weapon, but the facts here indicate no such fear.) (*See* ELO Ch.3-IX(H).) Since the heroin was not in plain view (it was underneath the rear seat), the search of the area underneath the rear seat was unlawful. Thus, the heroin would *not* be admissible into evidence against Morgan. Choice **B** is factually incorrect (the police were justified in stopping Morgan, because he was driving five miles per hour over the speed limit). Choice **C** is incorrect because, though factually true (Morgan was properly stopped), the stop alone would not validate the search of his car's interior. Finally, Choice **D** is incorrect because stopping a driver for a minor traffic violation does *not* constitute a full custodial arrest. Thus, a search of the vehicle in places which were not in plain view was unlawful.

15. **A**   Supreme Court decisions pertaining to constitutional aspects of criminal procedure must be given retroactive effect to cases pending on *direct* appeal; *Griffith v. Kentucky*, 479 U.S. 314 (1987). Choice **B** is incorrect because not *all* errors in the formation of a jury constitute grounds for automatic reversal [*e.g.*, some errors (not including the exclusion of jurors of a particular race or ethnic group) are tested by the "harmless error" standard]. Choice **C** is incorrect because use of the "clear break" test for determining when a Supreme Court decision should be given retroactive effect to a case on direct appeal was overruled in the *Griffith* case. Finally, Choice **D** is incorrect because, under *Griffith*, an adverse impact upon the administration of criminal justice is *not* a factor to be considered in determining whether a Supreme Court decision should be given retroactive effect.

16. **D**   New constitutional decisions of the Court will generally not be applied on collateral appeals, unless: (1) the new decision decriminalizes previously criminal conduct; *or* (2) the new decision expands the truth-finding functions at trial and enhances the fundamental fairness of the trial. See *Teague v. Lane*, 489 U.S. 288 (1989); *Sawyer v. Smith*, 497 U.S. 227 (1990). Choices A and B are incorrect because the "clear break" test was overruled by *Griffith*. To have retroactive effect, it is no longer necessary that the Supreme Court decision represent a clear break with the past. Choice **C** is incorrect because the retroactivity of constitutional decisions is a matter of federal, not state, law.

17. **A**   There is ordinarily no right to counsel with respect to photo identifications made outside the defendant's presence; *United States v. Ash*, 413 U.S. 300 (1973). (*See* ELO Ch.6-IV(B).) Choice **B** is incorrect because Dexter's counsel had no legal right to be present at the photo displays. Choice **C** is incorrect because, although Dexter's Sixth Amendment right to counsel was effectuated by his arrest, it was not violated in this instance (because photo displays are not a "critical" stage of a criminal proceeding). Finally, Choice **D** is incorrect because the facts indicate that several photographs of other persons with similar features were shown to the victim.

18. **D**   A student's personal effects may be searched by school personnel when they have a reasonable basis for suspecting criminal conduct or a violation of school rules; *New Jersey v. T.L.O.*, 469 U.S. 325 (1985). (Note that the Court in *T.L.O.* did not specifically address the issue of whether students have a "legitimate expectation of privacy in lockers, desks, or other school property provided for the storage of school supplies." *Id.*) (*See* ELO Ch.3-X(I)(4)(a).) Therefore, Choice **D** is the *best* answer here. Because the principal had been informed by an eyewitness that Trish was engaging in illegal conduct on school grounds, the principal had a reasonable suspicion that Trish was engaged in criminal activity. An argument can also be made that since Trish had no lock on the locker, she did not have an expectation of privacy as to the locker. Choice **A** is incorrect because minors do have constitutional rights. While probable cause is *not* required, school officials cannot act unless they have a reasonable suspicion that criminal conduct or a violation of school rules has occurred. Choice **B** is incorrect because no right to search Trish's locker arose simply because she was not in the appropriate classroom when summoned by the principal. The search was not reasonably related to any school rule which may have been violated by her being in another

room. Finally, Choice **C** is incorrect because the contents of Trish's locker were not in "plain view" (*i.e.*, seen from the vantage point which the principal had a right to be in).

19. **D**   Probable cause is determined from the totality of the circumstances; *Illinois v. Gates*, 462 U.S. 213 (1983). A specific statement by a reliable informant who was an eyewitness to the event described in the affidavit would probably constitute the "probable cause" necessary to issue a search warrant. Additionally, there is corroborating evidence in that Detective knew that Harry, Bill and Informant were friends. (*See* ELO Ch.2-IV(B)(1).) Choice **A** is legally incorrect (a search warrant may be validly issued on the basis of information received from an informant). Choice **B** is incorrect because the information probably was *not* too remote in time (Informant saw Harry sell narcotics to Bill just two days earlier). Finally, Choice **C** is incorrect because (1) search warrants must be based upon probable (rather than "reasonable") cause, and (2) the mere fact that a crime was committed at the location would not necessarily be sufficient to support a search warrant (rather, there must be probable cause that incriminating evidence will be found when the search is made).

20. **A**   Provided probable cause exists, arrests by the police without a warrant are valid unless made (1) within the suspect's home, or (2) for a misdemeanor perpetrated outside the arresting officer's presence. (*See* ELO Ch.3-II(A),(B).) Because the police merely "believed" (*i.e.*, did not have probable cause) that the Jones sisters were involved in a robbery, the arrest of the group was unlawful. As a consequence, evidence derived from the illegal arrest would be inadmissible as "fruits of the poisonous tree." (*See* ELO Ch.7-III(B)(2).) Choice **B** is incorrect because there is no right to counsel prior to the time a suspect has been formally charged. (*See* ELO Ch.8-IV(B).) Choice **C** is incorrect because, while fingerprint evidence is nontestimonial in nature, it is inadmissible in this instance because the seizure of Donna (from whom the fingerprints were taken) was illegal. Finally, Choice **D** is legally incorrect (an individual does have a reasonable expectation of privacy in his or her fingerprints).

21. **C**   Pursuant to standardized police procedures, the police may impound a vehicle whose driver has been lawfully arrested. That is, the individual police officer must not be given--and must not exercise--any discretion about whether and when to impound. Because Willy was validly arrested under a charge of drunk driving, the police (if acting pursuant to standardized procedures) would be permitted to impound his car, so as to prevent theft or vandalism. The impoundment would fall under the

"inventory" exception to the search-warrant requirement. See *Florida v. Wells*, 495 U.S. 1 (1990). (*See* ELO Ch.3-VI(J).) Choice **A** is incorrect because the fact that Willy was arrested on a public highway would not, in itself, constitute a constitutional basis for the police to ***impound*** his car. Choice **B** is incorrect because there is no indication in these facts that Willy either explicitly or impliedly consented to impoundment of his vehicle. Finally, Choice **D** is incorrect because Choice **C** is the only right answer.

22. **B**   The police may "inventory," *i.e.*, inspect, items that come lawfully into their possession; because Willy's arrest and impoundment of the car were, by hypothesis, lawful, the inventory was, too. (As an alternative rationale, pursuant to a valid, full custodial arrest of the occupants of a vehicle, the police may search its interior, including any closed containers. *New York v. Belton*, 453 U.S. 454 (1981). (*See* ELO Ch.3-III(D).) This right is not forfeited simply because the search is made at a point in time subsequent to the arrest; *Chambers v. Maroney*, 399 U.S. 42 (1970). (*See* ELO Ch.3-VI(B).) Choice **A** is incorrect because a warrantless search of the vehicle, proper at the time of arrest, was still proper at a reasonably later point in time. Choice **C** is incorrect because probable cause is not required to search the interior of a vehicle after its occupants have been lawfully arrested (and because the search here was a valid "inventory search" as explained above). Finally, Choice **D** is incorrect because these circumstances constitute an exception to the normal rule requiring a search warrant.

23. **A**   Pursuant to a valid, full custodial arrest of the occupants of a vehicle, the police may search its interior (including closed containers); *New York v. Belton*, 453 U.S. 454 (1981). This right is not forfeited merely because the search is made at a later time. Since Willy (the operator of the car) had been validly arrested, the police had the right to search the interior of the vehicle (including containers such as the suitcase). (*See* ELO Ch.3-VI(B).) Choice **B** is factually incorrect (there is nothing to indicate that the police had probable cause to believe the vehicle contained indicia of criminal activity when they stopped Willy). Choice **C** is incorrect because probable cause was not required to search the passenger compartments of Willy's car. Finally, Choice **D** is incorrect because, while the contents of the suitcase were not in plain view, the police were entitled to search closed containers in Willy's car.

24. **B**   The police are permitted to inventory effects lawfully within their possession if they act pursuant to standard operating procedures; *Florida v. Wells*, 495 U.S. 1 (1990). This rule is known as the "inventory" excep-

tion. (*See* ELO Ch.3-VI(J).) Choice **A** is incorrect because the body is admissible, provided this police department routinely allowed for inventory searches at impoundment lots. Choice **C** is incorrect because there is no "homicide scene" exception to the warrant requirement; *Mincey v. Arizona*, 437 U.S. 385 (1978). (*See* ELO Ch.3-IV(B)(3).) Finally, Choice **D** is incorrect because the victim's body was in the trunk. Incident to the arrest of the occupant of an automobile, police may search the car's passenger compartment and the contents of any container found in the compartment, but not the trunk. *New York v. Belton*, 453 U.S. 454 (1981); ELO Ch.3-III(D).

25. **D**   Sentencing in a capital punishment case must be made in a separate proceeding from the verdict phase of the accused's trial; *Gregg v. Georgia*, 428 U.S. 153 (1976). Thus, Willy would be entitled to a new trial on the issue of the death sentence. Choice **A** is legally incorrect (the murder charge did not have to be tried separately from the other offenses for which Willy was indicted). Choice **B** is also legally incorrect (capital punishment is not, *per se*, cruel and unusual punishment). Finally, Choice **C** is incorrect because the principle of proportionality (*i.e.*, a sentence should be reversed when it is too severe under the circumstances) is inapplicable. The jury's verdict establishes that it had found the elements supporting the death penalty--the intentional taking of another's life; and most statutes have decided that the death penalty under these circumstances is not excessively severe.

26. **C**   Under the double jeopardy clause, a person cannot be prosecuted for a crime which arises from the same event or set of facts as another crime for which that person has already been acquitted or convicted. (*See* ELO Ch.9-VIII(H)(1).) The rule is a narrow one which requires that the facts relating to both crimes be the same. The clause does not apply if the facts relating to the second crime are essentially different or if the prosecution is unable to try both crimes together for reasons that are not the prosecution's fault. (*See* ELO Ch.9-VIII(H)(3).) Here, Bill was still alive at the time of John's trial and conviction for robbery. The prosecution could not indict John for felony murder until *after* Bill had died. *Diaz v. U.S.*, 223 U.S. 442 (1912). Therefore, the double jeopardy clause does not prohibit John's later conviction for felony murder. Note: It's important to this answer that the second crime is a greater crime than the first. If the first crime tried had been the greater one, the second would have been barred on double jeopardy grounds despite the subsequent development of new facts. The correct answer is C. (*See* ELO Ch.9-VIII(H)(3).) Choice **A** is not correct because the elements of the crime of murder were not considered or tried during the trial for robbery.

There was no felony murder issue until Bill's death. Choice **B** is incorrect because the Double Jeopardy clause did not bar the later trial for murder for the reasons cited above. The prosecution could not bring the charges until Bill's death. Finally, Choice **D** is incorrect because robbery and felony murder are two distinct crimes even though they may grow out of the same event or the same set of facts. An indictment or conviction for one does not preclude an indictment or conviction for the other. If this were not the case, the entire concept of felony murder would collapse. By definition, felony murder is a crime which arises from the commission of another crime. Strict application of the double jeopardy rule in a trial for felony murder would preclude the trial itself.

27. **A** Police may not conduct a search or seizure in a manner which shocks the conscience; *Rochin v. California*, 342 U.S. 165 (1952). In *Rochin*, the Supreme Court held that "stomach pumping" a suspect to obtain evidence of a crime violated the due process clause. Moreover, certain highly invasive body intrusions, even if supported by probable cause, are "unreasonable" under the Fourth Amendment; *Winston v. Lee*, 470 U.S. 753 (1985). (*See* ELO Ch.2-V(G)(8).) Choice **B** is incorrect because, even if the heroin would dissipate within Buyer's system (and thereby be lost), the loss of evidence is outweighed by the severe trauma caused to Buyer by injection of the solution into him. Choice **C** is incorrect because, while the police had a warrant, it would be deemed invalid under these facts. Finally, Choice **D** is incorrect because Choices B and C are both wrong.

28. **A** A grand jury may consider evidence that would be inadmissible at trial; *Costello v. United States*, 350 U.S. 359 (1956). Even though Paul's confession would be inadmissible at a criminal trial (*i.e.*, besides the lack of *Miranda* warnings, the detention and arrest of Paul were not based upon probable cause), it can still be introduced at the grand jury proceeding. Most procedural protections are relaxed in grand jury proceedings because the purpose of the grand jury is simply to determine whether a crime has been committed (rather than to convict). (*See* ELO Ch.9-I(C)(2).) Choices B and C are incorrect because, while supported by the facts (*i.e.*, Paul's confession would be inadmissible in a criminal case), the evidence in question is admissible in grand jury proceedings. Finally, Choice **D** is incorrect because Choices B and C are wrong.

29. **C** Individuals (even one who may be a suspect) who are subpoenaed to appear before a grand jury must comply with the subpoena. Despite the fact that Paul was improperly arrested and not given *Miranda* warnings, he would be obliged to honor the grand jury's subpoena. (*See* ELO

Ch.9-I(C)(1).) Choices A and B are incorrect. Though both would be applicable to prevent Paul's confession from being admitted in a criminal trial, neither argument is available in a grand jury proceeding. Finally, Choice **D** is incorrect because a grand jury's subpoena must be honored, even if the grand jury has no reason to believe that the witness was involved in criminal activities.

30. **B**   There is no right to have counsel present at grand jury proceedings. (*See* ELO Ch.9-I(E).) Choice **A** is legally incorrect (there is no right to counsel at grand jury proceedings). Choice **C** is incorrect because, even if the evidence obtained from Paul was not admissible in a criminal case, he would still have no right to have counsel present. Finally, Choice **D** is incorrect (the mere fact that Paul was arrested prior to the grand jury proceedings would not entitle him to have legal counsel present).

31. **B**   A contempt citation may be issued for refusal to comply with a grand jury subpoena. Paul's refusal to remain at the grand jury proceedings despite the warning that he could be cited for contempt, can result in a conviction for contempt. (*See* ELO Ch.9-I(C)(1).) Choice **A** is incorrect because Paul had not answered any questions (and, therefore, could not be accused of lying under oath). Choice **C** is incorrect. Paul may be convicted of contempt even though the evidence in question might be inadmissible in a criminal case. Finally, Choice **D** is incorrect because Statement II is true. (It should be mentioned, however, that a witness at a grand jury proceeding may assert the Fifth Amendment privilege against self-incrimination.) (*See* ELO Ch.9-I(D).)

32. **D**   Evidence derived from an unlawful detention or arrest is inadmissible in the prosecution's case-in-chief. Because the informant was not known to be reliable and did not state the basis of his knowledge about Paul's gambling, the "totality of the circumstances" test of *Illinois v. Gates* is not met, and the police did not have probable cause to arrest Paul. Because Paul's confession, as well as the notebooks, was derived from that illegal arrest, *none* of the evidence would be admissible. (*See* ELO Ch.2-IV(B)(1).) Choices A, B and C are, therefore, incorrect.

33. **C**   The Fourth Amendment (applicable to the states via the Fourteenth Amendment) applies only to governmental conduct. Because the evidence was obtained by Jay, who was independent of any governmental influence or supervision, it would be admissible against John. From Jay's testimony and the marijuana itself , a jury could conclude beyond a reasonable doubt that John knowingly had an illegal substance in his possession. (*See* ELO Ch.1-II(D).) Choice **A** is incorrect because, while

Jay did gain entrance into John's home through a ruse, the evidence which he obtained is nevertheless admissible (because Jay was not a governmental officer). Choice **B** is incorrect because Jay was not a governmental officer. Therefore, the due process clause (which is violated by governmental conduct which "shocks the conscience") would *not* be applicable. Finally, Choice **D** is incorrect because there is sufficient evidence on these facts to enable a jury to determine that John knowingly possessed marijuana.

34. **D** Pursuant to a valid search warrant, police have the right to detain the person who has lawful possession of the premises while the search is being conducted (even though neither probable cause nor articulable basis to detain exists); *Michigan v. Summers*, 452 U.S. 692 (1981). Because the detention of Vic was legal, his "blurt out" is admissible. There is no *Miranda* problem in this instance because Vic's statement was not made pursuant to an interrogation (*i.e.*, Donald had not questioned Vic about his criminal activities). Rather, Vic simply "blurted out" his confession when he saw that Officer Donald had discovered the television set. (*See* ELO Ch.3-IX(J).) Choice **A** is incorrect because the fact that Vic asked to leave the area does not detract from Officer Donald's right to detain Vic while the search was being conducted. Choice **B** is incorrect because an arrest warrant is not necessary to detain the person in lawful possession of the premises covered by a valid search warrant. Finally, Choice **C** is incorrect because Officer Donald was permitted to detain Vic whether or not he suspected Vic of any wrongdoing.

35. **B** Federal wiretaps are valid for only 30 days. The wiretap must be renewed to be valid. (Title III of the Omnibus Crime Control and Safe Streets Act of 1968). (*See* ELO Ch.4-III(E)(3)). Since the facts indicate that the court order authorizing the wiretap extended for a period of four months, any information gained after the initial 30 days would probably be inadmissible. Choice **A** is incorrect because electronic surveillance which is based upon a proper warrant does not violate the Fourth Amendment. Choice **C** is incorrect because, although the wiretap did not exceed the period authorized by the order, the period authorized was excessive and the length of the tap was excessive. D is incorrect because the basis for a federal wiretap must be reviewed after 30 days.

36. **A** Incriminating statements made in response to police questioning (or to someone acting under police supervision or influence) are admissible, unless (1) the defendant has already been indicted (in which event, his Sixth Amendment right to counsel will apply), or (2) the statements

result from a custodial interrogation which is not preceded by adequate *Miranda* warnings. In the typical "misplaced trust" case in which an unindicted suspect makes incriminating statements to an undercover operative, the statements are admissible. Because Huffer voluntarily made his statements to Insider and had not previously been formally charged, Insider (even though acting under government supervision) could testify about Huffer's comments. (*See* ELO Ch.4-IV(D).) Choice **B** is incorrect because, while Insider was a private party, in this instance he would be viewed as a governmental agent (*i.e.*, he acted pursuant to the FBI's guidance). Choice **C** is incorrect because no court order was required in this instance. Finally, Choice **D** is incorrect because Huffer's Sixth Amendment rights did not mature in this instance (because he had not been formally charged with a crime prior to the incriminating conversations).

37. **D**   The Fourth Amendment (applicable to the states via the Fourteenth Amendment) applies only to governmental searches and seizures. Since Dr. Carla was a private party, Jones could not effectively raise a Fourth Amendment objection to her recovery of the vial of heroin and its delivery to the police. (*See* ELO Ch.1-II(D).) Choice **A** is incorrect because, despite Dr. Carla's unlawful conduct, the police had probable cause to arrest Jones. Choice **B** is incorrect because, while it is literally true (*i.e.*, Dr. Carla had no right to restrain Jones under these circumstances), the Fourteenth Amendment does not extend to evidence obtained by or derived from private parties. Thus, the fact that Dr. Carla acted unlawfully does not preclude the police from utilizing the fruits of her conduct. Finally, Choice **C** is incorrect because Jones' intention to burglarize Dr. Carla's home is irrelevant to the question of whether the heroin would be admissible in a trial against Jones for possession of heroin.

38. **C**   When an individual who has been validly arrested is booked, or within a reasonable time thereafter (provided there is a legitimate reason for the delay), the police may make a full inventory search of his person and clothes (including the contents of any unlocked containers); *Illinois v. Lafayette*, 462 U.S. 640 (1983). Because Dr. Carla told the police that Jones had attempted to rob her, the police had probable cause to arrest Jones (even though the statement made to the police by Dr. Carla was not supported by the facts). (In ascertaining whether probable cause existed, the issue is whether a reasonable officer in Officer Brown's position would conclude that it was more likely than not that Jones had committed robbery. The fact that, unbeknownst to Brown, Dr. Carla was mistaken in her statement, is irrelevant.) Thus, the vial of heroin was

obtained pursuant to a valid inventory search. (*See* ELO Ch.3-III(G)(2)(b).) Choice **A** is incorrect because the police had probable cause to arrest Jones, given Dr. Carla's statement that Jones had attempted to rob her. Choice **B** is incorrect because the police are entitled to conduct an inventory search of the belongings of an individual who has been validly arrested. Choice **D** is incorrect because Choice **C** is correct.

39. **B** The "automobile exception" to the search warrant requirement has been extended to mobile homes, at least when the home is being used as a "mobile" device (*e.g.*, in a parking lot rather than permanently anchored in a residential development); *California v. Carney*, 471 U.S. 386 (1985). Because Bill had (1) heard from several persons at the campsite that Reggie was selling illegal drugs from his mobile home, and (2) actually seen the results of one purchase, he had probable cause to believe that Reggie's mobile home contained contraband. Therefore, under the "automobile exception" to the search warrant requirement, Bill's search of Reggie's mobile home was valid. (*See* ELO Ch.3-VI(D).) Choice **A** is incorrect because Bill was acting in his capacity as a law enforcement officer (as evidenced by the fact that he took his badge and gun prior to invading Reggie's vehicle). Choice **C** is incorrect because, while Reggie had an expectation of privacy in his mobile home, this situation constitutes an exception to the normal rule requiring a search warrant to be obtained before a search or seizure of personal property occurs. Finally, Choice **D** is incorrect because the police could have obtained a warrant authorizing a search of the entire vehicle, including the contents of the sealed container.

40. **A** Pursuant to a valid, full custodial arrest, the police may make an inventory search of the suspect's person and clothes; *Illinois v. Lafayette*, 462 U.S. 640 (1983). Because Reggie was validly arrested (*i.e.*, Bill had probable cause to believe that Reggie had been engaged in criminal activity), a strip search prior to (or soon after) his incarceration was valid. A search under these conditions diminishes the risk to guards and other inmates that the suspect may have hidden weapons or contraband in his body cavities. (*See* ELO Ch.3-III(G)(2)(b).) Choice **B** is factually incorrect (there is no indication the police perceived an immediate danger to themselves or that evidence might be lost if the strip search did not occur immediately). Choice **C** is incorrect because the fact that a search was unsuccessful would not make it invalid when started. Finally, Choice **D** is incorrect because, as discussed in the answer to the preceding question, Reggie's arrest was probably valid.

41. **A**   In the absence of consent or exigent circumstances, a search warrant is required before police may enter someone's home to execute an arrest warrant for another individual; *Steagald v. United States*, 451 U.S. 204 (1981). Because Officer Jane's arrest warrant applied only to Defendant, she had no right to make a non-consensual entry into Friend's home. Because Officer Jane improperly threatened to use force to secure entry (*i.e.*, break down his door), her entrance into Friend's home was not consensual. Thus, the heroin (which would not have been discovered except for Officer Jane's unlawful entry) is inadmissible in a criminal trial against Friend. Choice **B** is incorrect because it's irrelevant how the heroin was discovered. Officer Jane had no right to be in the house at all. Choice **C** is factually incorrect (Friend cannot be said to have consented to Officer Jane's entry). Finally, Choice **D** is also factually incorrect (the heroin was not found incident to a valid arrest). Since exigent circumstances did not exist, Officer Jane had no right to enter Friend's home to arrest Defendant. (*See* ELO Ch.3-IV(E).)

42. **C**   A police officer may not use deadly force to effectuate an arrest, unless the police officer has probable cause to believe that the suspect poses a significant threat of death or serious physical injury to the arresting officer or others; *Tennessee v. Garner*, 471 U.S. 1 (1985). Because Officer Joe had no reason to believe that Billy was armed or constituted a present public danger, the use of deadly force was unreasonable. (*See* ELO Ch.3-II(D).) Choice **A**, while factually true (Officer Joe did have probable cause to arrest Billy), is incorrect because it was improper for Joe to use deadly force in effectuating Billy's arrest under these circumstances. Choice **B** is incorrect because use of deadly force in effectuating an arrest is proper only where the person seized posed a significant danger to the arresting officer or the public. Whether or not Billy's conduct constituted a felony under applicable local law is irrelevant. Finally, Choice **D** is incorrect because the Eighth Amendment (applicable to the states via the Fourteenth Amendment) prohibition against cruel and unusual punishment applies to legislative or judicial conduct (not the actions of police officers).

43. **A**   Interrogation with respect to a crime unrelated to the arrest does not invalidate an adequate *Miranda* waiver; *Colorado v. Spring*, 479 U.S. 564 (1987). Assuming the police had probable cause to arrest Defendant for the Main Street fire (the facts are silent on this point), Defendant's confession would be admissible (even though unrelated to the crime for which she was arrested). (*See* ELO Ch.5-X(C)(7).) If the police lacked probable cause to arrest Defendant, her confession would be inadmissible (even though she voluntarily waived her *Miranda* rights), because it

would have been derived from an unlawful arrest. Choice **B** is incorrect because the police are under no obligation to inform a suspect of the implications of her confession. Choice **C** is factually incorrect (Defendant had waived her *Miranda* rights by her statement that she would answer questions, unless the police officers began "hassling her"). Finally, Choice **D** is incorrect because the fact that Defendant was arrested for one crime does not preclude questioning her with respect to a different crime.

44. **A** A waiver of *Miranda* rights is not invalidated by the disability of the accused; *Colorado v. Connelly*, 479 U.S. 157 (1986). Because Defendant voluntarily waived her *Miranda* rights (*i.e.*, there was no overreaching by the police), her confession is admissible. (*See* ELO Ch.5-X(C)(8)(d).) Choice **B** is incorrect because the fact that Defendant was a minor does not, *per se*, invalidate her *Miranda* waiver. However, the court will review the waiver more closely and more critically to determine whether the suspect really understood what she was doing. ELO Ch.-5(D). Choice **C** is incorrect because Defendant's confession was not coerced by police conduct. Defendant's erroneous perception of the situation would **not** make her statement legally involuntary for *Miranda* purposes. Finally, Choice **D** is incorrect because the fact that Defendant was validly arrested for one crime would not preclude the police from questioning her with respect to another offense (after, of course, proper *Miranda* warnings were given and waived). (*See* ELO Ch.5-X(C)(7).)

45. **B** Evidence derived from a custodial interrogation is admissible, even in the absence of prior *Miranda* warnings, if the statements were voluntary, and the questions were reasonably prompted by a concern for the public safety; *New York v. Quarles*, 467 U.S. 649 (1984). Jack had just emerged from the movie house. It was reasonable for Officer John to suspect that the gun might have been hidden in the move house by Jack and that it would be found by a child. Officer John could reasonably conclude that a threat to public safety existed. Thus, the questioning (as well as its fruits) was proper. Jack may argue that his statement was not voluntary because Officer John had pointed a gun at him, but Jack was not compelled to answer. (*See* ELO Ch.5-VIII(B).) Choice **A** is incorrect because, in the absence of exigent circumstances, the lack of proper *Miranda* warnings would prevent the evidence from being admitted (whether or not Jack's crime was a felony). Choice **C** is factually incorrect (because Officer John approached Jack with his gun drawn, Jack would probably be deemed to be in "custody" for *Miranda* purposes).

Finally, Choice **D** is incorrect. When a threat to public safety is present, the fruits of the interrogation are admissible, even in the absence of *Miranda* warnings.

46. **C**   Evidence derived from an illegal arrest is ordinarily inadmissible. If the police lacked probable cause to arrest Pat, any information derived from her arrest would ordinarily be inadmissible as the fruits of an illegal arrest (regardless of whether *Miranda* rights had been effectively waived). (*See* ELO Ch.7-III(J).) Choice **A** is factually incorrect (Pat's waiver of her *Miranda* rights appears to have been made voluntarily). The fact that her request for a drink of water was honored, and that she was spoken to in soft tones, does not make her *Miranda* waiver involuntary. Choice **B** is incorrect because, while the *Miranda* warnings were not absolutely complete (*i.e.*, Pat was not told that she had a right to appointed counsel if she was indigent), the court will probably conclude that there was substantial compliance with the necessary requisites. Any confusion or inadequacy was probably resolved when Pat acknowledged her entitlement to an attorney. (*See* ELO Ch.5-IX(A).) Finally, Choice **D** is incorrect because, if there was no probable cause to arrest Pat, her subsequent confession would be inadmissible (regardless of any *Miranda* waiver).

47. **C**   A defendant in a state criminal case may not obtain release through a federal *habeas corpus* proceeding on the ground that evidence used to convict him was obtained in violation of his Fourth Amendment rights, unless he/she was not given a full and fair opportunity to raise those issues in state court; *Stone v. Powell*, 428 U.S. 465 (1976). Here, it was Locust's counsel's incompetence, not the state's procedures, that prevented Locust from getting a state court hearing on his Fourth Amendment claim. (This incompetence may raise a Sixth Amendment claim, but that does not preserve Locust's Fourth Amendment claim.) (*See* ELO Ch.1-II(E)(1)(b).) Choices A and B are incorrect for the reasons just stated. Choice **D** is incorrect because the facts stipulate that Locust was relying only on a violation of his **Fourth** Amendment rights. If Locust had raised a **Sixth** Amendment violation (*i.e.*, he was deprived of effective counsel by reason of the latter's failure to object to particular evidence), a federal *habeas corpus* proceeding might have been appropriate. *Withrow v. Williams*, 507 U.S. 680 (1993).

48. **A**   Illegally seized evidence can be used *to impeach* a defendant who voluntarily takes the witness stand; *United States v. Havens*, 446 U.S. 620 (1980). Because Defendant took the stand to deny the allegations against him, the evidence seized illegally at his summer home could be

used for the purposes of impeachment. (*See* ELO Ch.7-IV(B)(1)(a).) Choice **B** is incorrect because the prosecution can use illegally seized evidence to impeach a defendant's testimony under any circumstances, not just when the defendant improperly refuses to answer cross-examination questions. Choice **C** is incorrect because, while factually true (the evidence had been suppressed and, therefore, could not be used in the prosecution's case-in-chief), illegally seized evidence may be used to impeach the credibility of an accused. Finally, Choice **D** is incorrect because the fact that an accused asserts the Fifth Amendment upon advice of counsel does not preclude the prosecution from impeaching him with illegally seized evidence.

49. **C**   An individual has no reasonable expectation of privacy with respect to objects, items or information held out to the public; *Smith v. Maryland*, 442 U.S. 735 (1979). The numbers one dials on his telephone are deemed to be "held out to the public," so police use of a pen register does not violate the caller's Fourth Amendment rights. (*See* ELO Ch.2-II(E)(2).) Choice **A** is incorrect. Although privately owned, the telephone company was acting at the request of the police. It was, indeed, acting as a governmental entity for Fourth Amendment purposes. But this fact did not make its actions illegal. On the contrary, it was acting with the same authority as the police would have under the same circumstances. Choice **B** is incorrect because, having no legitimate expectation of privacy with respect to the search (*i.e.*, the installation of the pen register), Darlene could **not** successfully complain about the absence of a valid warrant. Finally, Choice **D** is incorrect because the actions of the police are not measured by their "good faith." The police are required to comply with all the constitutional safeguards which the courts have confirmed over many years. In the absence of compliance, any evidence obtained will not be admitted.

50. **C**   A state may give its citizens greater protection than that afforded to them by the U.S. Constitution; U.S. CONST. amend. X. (*See* ELO Ch.1-II(F).) Under the U.S. Constitution, Bob had no expectation of privacy with respect to items within a detached fenced-in area (even if there was a "No Trespassing" sign on the enclosure and even if the fenced in area was only 50 feet from his house); *Oliver v. U.S.*, 466 U.S. 170 (1984). (*See* ELO Ch.2-II(C)(6)(b).) However, the State of Midwest (via its Constitution) affords its citizens greater protection than that provided by the U.S. Constitution, and the federal courts must respect that greater protection. Thus, the state's appeal will be unsuccessful. Choice **A** is incorrect because the fact that there was a "No Trespassing" sign on the enclosure would argue for a greater expectation of privacy in the area

searched. Therefore, it would ***not*** constitute a reason why the state should succeed on its appeal. Choice **B** is incorrect because, while Bob had no expectation of privacy with respect to the area searched under the U.S. Constitution, the State of Midwest affords protection to its citizens under these circumstances. Finally, Choice **D** is incorrect because the fact that the area involved was fenced and locked would arguably create a greater expectation of privacy with respect to the enclosed marijuana. Therefore, it would ***not*** constitute a reason for granting the state's appeal.

51. **D**   The double jeopardy clause does not preclude prosecution for the same offense by a different sovereign. (*See* ELO Ch.9-VIII(G).) Although Bob was initially tried by State of Midwest authorities, the federal government could prosecute him for exactly the same offense. Choice **A** is incorrect because there is no case law supporting the proposition that the Due Process Clause precludes multiple prosecutions for the same offense by different sovereigns. Choice **B** is incorrect because the double jeopardy doctrine applies only to prosecutions by the the *same sovereign* for a second offense based on the same elements as the first. Finally, Choice **C** is incorrect because the defense of collateral estoppel in a criminal case (an element of the Fifth Amendment's guarantee against double jeopardy) applies only to *issues of fact* that were necessarily decided in the accused's favor in the first proceeding; the issue here is a legal issue not affected by collateral estoppel.

52. **A**   Once a defendant asserts the right to consult a lawyer, he may then waive his *Miranda* rights only when (1) he initiates subsequent discussion with the police, (2) proper *Miranda* warnings are reiterated before any statement, ***and*** (3) there has been no intervening interrogation by the police; *Oregon v. Bradshaw*, 462 U.S. 1039 (1983). Here, Defendant asserted his *Miranda* rights, but the three-part test necessary to invoke a *Miranda* waiver was also satisfied when Officer Judy restated the warning. (*See* ELO Ch.5-X(C)(9)(e).) Choice **B** is incorrect because *Miranda* rights must be given even when a minor offense is involved; *Berkemer v. McCarty*, 468 U.S. 420 (1984). (*See* ELO Ch.5-VI(A).) Choice **C** is factually true (Defendant had requested to speak with his attorney), but the request for an attorney does not preclude a subsequent waiver by the accused. Finally, Choice **D** is legally incorrect (the police are not legally obliged to provide an accused with a substitute lawyer when the lawyer of his choice is delayed.)

53. **C** If an officer reasonably suspects that a person who has been detained for questioning may be armed, he may conduct a limited "pat down" of the suspect's outer clothing; *Terry v. Ohio*, 392 U.S. 1 (1968). Although Informant was known to be reliable, he did not actually see a gun in Suspect's pocket. Officer Jones can be said to have had only a reasonable suspicion (rather than probable cause) to believe that criminal activity was afoot. On the basis of his suspicion, however, Officer Joe was entitled to question Suspect. When Suspect made a move toward her pocket, Officer Joe was entitled to protect himself by restraining her until he could evaluate the danger to him. He would not, however, have been justified in reaching directly into Suspect's pocket. That action would have gone beyond a simple "pat-down" or frisk, which must be limited to the detainee's *outer* clothing. See *Minnesota v. Dickerson*, 508 U.S. 366 (1993). But Officer Joe was justified in conducting the pat down of Suspect's outer clothing; and once he felt what he reasonably believed to be a weapon, he was justified in taking the further step of reaching into the pocket to retrieve the weapon in order to prevent possible harm to himself. Thus, the weapon was seized in a constitutional manner. (*See* ELO Ch.3-IX(G).) Choice **A** is incorrect because the weapon was *not* the product of an unlawful detention. Officer Joe did have a reasonable suspicion that Suspect might be engaged in criminal activity. Choice **B** is incorrect because evidence can be obtained without a warrant under circumstances like those described here. Finally, Choice **D** is incorrect because Officer Joe did *not* have probable cause to believe Suspect was engaged in criminal activity — when Officer Joe approached Suspect, he merely had a reasonable suspicion that she might be involved in criminal conduct.

54. **B** The right to a jury trial exists only with respect to those crimes punishable by imprisonment for over six months; *Baldwin v. New York*, 399 U.S. 66 (1970). Because the offense involved carried a maximum prison term of three months, Suspect had no right to a jury trial. (*See* ELO Ch.1-II(C)(2).) Choice **A** is legally incorrect (there is a constitutional right to a jury trial in all criminal cases in which a defendant may be imprisoned for a term longer than six months). Choice **C** is legally incorrect (there is no absolute right to a jury trial in *all* criminal cases). Finally, Choice **D** is legally incorrect: there is no right to a jury trial simply because an accused affirmatively requests it (*e.g.*, the request will be rejected when the charge carries a maximum prison term of under six months). There is a grain of truth in this choice's use of the phrase "affirmatively requests;" a defendant may generally waive her right to a jury trial (in a case in which the right does exist) by neglecting to assert it.

55. **C**   Under the Sixth Amendment, an absolute right to counsel exists in situations in which imprisonment, however short, is ***actually imposed*** upon the defendant; *Scott v. Illinois*, 440 U.S. 367 (1979). If Suspect was actually imprisoned (even for one day), her Sixth Amendment right to counsel was violated by the refusal to provide her with an attorney. (*See* ELO Ch.8-III(A)(2).) Choice **A** is legally incorrect (there is no right to counsel in *all* criminal cases). Choice **B** is incorrect because the fact that a crime is potentially punishable by imprisonment does not, *per se*, result in a right to counsel. Imprisonment must be imposed before the right to counsel can be used as the basis for appeal. Finally, Choice **D** is legally incorrect (the right to counsel is violated in the case of a prisoner who is incarcerated even if the crime charged is punishable by imprisonment for less than six months).

56. **A**   A prisoner in a state court proceeding must generally exhaust all available state court remedies before seeking *habeas corpus* in a federal court; *Delo v. Stokes*, 495 U.S. 320 (1990). If Suspect has not exhausted her state court remedies, a writ of *habeas corpus* made to a federal court will usually be denied. Choice **B** states a correct legal conclusion but is incorrect on the facts; the term "custody" for purposes of federal *habeas corpus* includes parole; *Fay v. Noia*, 372 U.S. 391 (1963). Choice **C** is legally incorrect (there is a right of *habeas corpus* from state court to federal court in many instances). Finally, Choice **D** is incorrect because there is no constitutional right of review by a federal court through a writ of *habeas corpus* in *all* instances. For instance, where a state defendant contends that evidence was used to convict her in violation of the Fourth Amendment, *habeas corpus* will ordinarily be denied (unless the defendant can show that she was not given a full and fair opportunity to raise the Fourth Amendment issues in state court); *Stone v. Powell*, 428 U.S. 465 (1976). (*See* ELO Ch.1-II(E).)

57. **A**   Under the "plain view" doctrine, when a police officer who is lawfully positioned sees (or hears or smells) any item which, in reliance on his knowledge or experience, he has probable cause to believe is (1) contraband, or (2) the proceeds or instrumentalities of a crime, he may seize the item; *Horton v. California*, 496 U.S. 128 (1990). Because Jake implicitly consented to the police officer's being in the kitchen (he asked to make a call, knew that the phone was in the kitchen, and knew that the police would not allow him to walk to the kitchen alone), the second agent lawfully saw the $10 bill from a vantage point where he had a right to be. Because (1) the second agent knew that a number of $10 bills had been taken during the bank robbery, and (2) people do not ordinarily put $10 bills in breadboxes, the second agent arguably had proba-

ble cause to believe that the $10 bill in question had been taken during the bank robbery. Therefore, the item was seized constutionally. (*See* ELO Ch.3-V(B).) Choice **B** is incorrect because "good faith" alone is not a proper basis for making a warrantless search. Choice **C** is incorrect because Jake's arms were handcuffed behind his waist; under this restraint, the $10 bill was not within his immediate control, and the search-incident-to-arrest exception to the warrant requirement applies only to areas within the suspect's control; *Chimel v. California*, 395 U.S. 752 (1969). (*See* ELO Ch.3-III(C)(1).) Finally, Choice **D** is incorrect because exigent circumstances did not exist (*i.e.*, there is no indication that the evidence would be destroyed or otherwise lost during the time a warrant was being obtained). We have to assume, of course, that the wife did not know or notice the money was in the breadbox and that she would not have destroyed or removed it.

58. **B**   If probable cause exists, an arrest by a police officer is valid without an arrest warrant unless the arrest is made (1) within the suspect's home, or (2) for a misdemeanor perpetrated out of the arresting officer's presence; *Payton v. New York*, 445 U.S. 573 (1980). A felony arrest outside the suspect's home is valid if the arresting officers had probable cause to believe Jake had committed the robbery in question. (*See* ELO Ch.3-II(B)). Choice **A** is legally incorrect (there is no requirement for U.S. Attorney approval and no significance to the fact that an Assistant United States Attorney did or did not give advance approval to the arrest). Choice **C** is incorrect because the agents did not have to procure an arrest warrant. So long as the officers have probable cause and the other conditions exist (see above), an arrest is valid without a warrant. Finally, Choice **D** is incorrect because Jake was arrested on the sidewalk *in front of his house and not in the house*; therefore, the police officers were not required to obtain an arrest warrant or to submit an affidavit to a neutral magistrate.

59. **B**   The Fourth Amendment protects persons from unreasonable searches and seizures by the federal government. Since the conduct in question was undertaken by federal agents, the Fourth Amendment would be applicable. Detention of an individual can ordinarily be made only when an officer has a reasonable suspicion that criminal activity may be afoot. The facts 1) that Jake had an accomplice and 2) that Fred was walking into Jake's home, probably would *not* constitute "reasonable suspicion" that Fred had engaged, or was about to engage, in illegal conduct. (*See* ELO Ch.3-IX(D).) Choice **A** is incorrect because the Fifth Amendment protects individuals only from compelled disclosures of a testimonial nature. Choice **C** is incorrect because the Sixth Amendment right to

counsel does not apply until an accused has been formally charged. Finally, Choice **D** is incorrect because the conduct violated the Fourth Amendment.

60. **D**   An accused has no constitutional right to be represented by out-of-state counsel. While an accused who is being prosecuted for a serious felony is entitled to counsel, she has no right to insist upon being represented by an attorney who is not licensed to practice law in the jurisdiction in which she's being tried. Choice **A** is incorrect because a defendant's Sixth Amendment right to effective counsel is not violated unless the attorney's performance (1) falls below an objective standard (*i.e.* he performs below the level of competence reasonably expected of lawyers handling the same or similar matters); and (2) "but for" the lawyer's incompetence, there is a reasonable probability that the result of the case would have been different (*i.e.*, the attorney's errors were of such magnitude as to undermine confidence in the outcome of the case); *Strickland v. Washington*, 466 U.S. 668 (1984). (*See* ELO Ch.8-VI(A)(1).) Finally, Choices B and C are incorrect because there is no case law supporting the proposition that a criminal defendant's rights to due process and a fair trial are violated by her inability to obtain representation by an attorney who is not licensed to practice law in the jurisdiction.

61. **D**   Although *federal* criminal trials require a 12-person jury and a unanimous verdict, the U.S. Supreme Court has declined to impose either of these requirements for state court trials. (But there must be a "substantive" majority; a bare majority – *e.g.*, 5-4 – would not suffice.) The Court has upheld a 9-3 verdict; *Johnson v. Louisiana*, 406 U.S. 356 (1972). On that reasoning, a 9-1 verdict presumably would be valid. (*See* ELO Ch.1-II(C)(2).) Choice **A** is incorrect because a 12-person jury is not required in *state* court criminal proceedings. Choice **B** is incorrect because unanimity is not always required in *state* court criminal proceedings. Finally, Choice **C** is incorrect because there is no established case law supporting the proposition that an accused may insist on being represented by a lawyer who is not licensed to practice law in that state.

62. **D**   The Sixth Amendment right to counsel for indigent criminal defendants does not extend to discretionary appeals; *Ross v. Moffitt*, 417 U.S. 600 (1974). Linda was *not* denied her right to effective counsel because her appeal to the State X Supreme Court was discretionary with the court. (*See* ELO Ch.8-II(D)(3), IV(J).) Choice **A** is incorrect because an indigent criminal defendant has no right to appointed counsel with respect to a discretionary appeal. Choice **B** is incorrect because, as discussed

above, Linda had no right to appointed counsel in this instance. Finally, Choice **C** is incorrect because, even if Linda could show that her chances of being successful on appeal would be greatly enhanced by the assistance of counsel, she has no right to appointed counsel in this instance (her appeal being discretionary in nature).

63. **D**   The right to counsel is deemed to exist in criminal prosecutions if imprisonment, however short, is actually imposed; *Scott v. Illinois*, 440 U.S. 367 (1979). Because Wanda was not imprisoned, the denial of her request for counsel did not violate her Sixth Amendment rights (applicable to the states via the Fourteenth Amendment). (*See* ELO Ch.8-III(A)(2).) Choice **A** is legally incorrect (there was no constitutional error). Choice **B** is incorrect because there was no error and the "harmless error" standard does not arise (Wanda had no right to be represented by counsel at the initial trial). Finally, Choice **C** is incorrect because the conclusory phrase does not explain why there was no error: there was no error because Wanda was not imprisoned, not because she was charged with a misdemeanor.

64. **D**   A defendant has an absolute right to waive counsel, as long as this is done knowingly and intelligently; *Faretta v. California*, 422 U.S. 806 (1975). (*See* ELO Ch.8-V(C).) Notwithstanding the waiver, the court may appoint a back-up attorney who will intervene on her client's behalf as long as the defendant's basic right of self-representation is not undermined. That is, the defendant must both appear to be in control and be in actual control. *McKaskle v. Wiggins*, 465 U.S. 168 (1984). Choice **A** is incorrect since Wanda is still primarily responsible for her own defense. Choice **B** is incorrect because there is no case law supporting the proposition that a criminal defendant's due process rights are violated by the appointment of standby counsel. Finally, Choice **C** is incorrect because (1) Wanda chose to represent herself, and (2) standby counsel would promote (rather than impair) Wanda's right to effective representation.

65. **D**   An earlier conviction of an indigent defendant, even though she was constitutionally denied counsel because no imprisonment was imposed, can be used under an enhancement statute to increase the sentence for a subsequent conviction; *Nichols v. United States*, 511 U.S. 738 (1994). (*See* ELO Ch.8-III(A)(3).) Choice **A** is incorrect because a five-year sentence for a conviction for grand theft would probably ***not*** be deemed disproportionate . Choice **B** is legally incorrect (a recidivist sentencing statute does not, *per se*, violate the double jeopardy clause). Finally, Choice **C** is legally incorrect (the enhanced sentence imposed upon

Wanda because of her previous conviction does not violate her Sixth Amendment rights) because she was not imprisoned after the first conviction.

66. **C**   When a first trial of a suspect ends in a hung jury after the prosecution has introduced all its proof of guilt, the double jeopardy clause of the Fifth Amendment (applicable to the states via the Fourteenth Amendment) does not prevent re-trial of the suspect on the same charge. *Richardson v. U.S.*, 468 U.S. 317 (1984). (*See* ELO Ch.9-VIII(D)(2)(a)(i).) Choice **A**, while legally true (*i.e.*, jeopardy had attached because the jury had been impaneled and sworn), is incorrect because the double jeopardy clause does not prevent re-trial when (1) the initial proceeding resulted in a hung jury, and (2) the prosecution introduced sufficient evidence to support a guilty verdict. Choice **B**, while factually true (the jury had been impaneled and sworn), is incorrect because the double jeopardy clause does not prevent re-trial when the original proceeding ends in a hung jury after the prosecution has introduced the evidence necessary to support a finding of guilt. Finally, Choice **D** is factually incorrect (no verdict was returned in the first trial).

67. **C**   A criminal defendant may be re-tried when reversal on appeal is based on the *weight*, rather than sufficiency, of the evidence; *Tibbs v. Florida*, 457 U.S. 31 (1982). Because the court decided that the verdict was against the weight of the evidence (rather than that the prosecution had failed to introduce sufficient evidence to support the verdict), Bill may be re-tried a third time. (*See* ELO Ch.9-VIII(E)(2).) Choice **A** is incorrect because re-trial after a hung jury is not precluded by the double jeopardy clause, unless the prosecution has failed to introduce sufficient evidence to meet its burden of proof; *Burks v. U.S.*, 437 U.S. 1 (1978). While Choice **B** states the law correctly (double jeopardy would bar re-trial if the earlier proceeding had been reversed due to the prosecution's failure to produce sufficient evidence), the facts establish that reversal in the second case was based upon the *weight* (rather than sufficiency) of the evidence. Finally, Choice **D** is legally incorrect (there is no rule permitting only a single re-trial).

68. **B**   Under the double jeopardy clause, a defendant may not be tried for a crime when the jury in a previous trial has found for the defendant on a fact essential to the prosecution of the crime; *Ashe v. Swenson*, 397 U.S. 436 (1970). Because Jim in the first trial persuaded the jury that he had a valid alibi, an issue essential to the prosection has been resolved in the defendant's favor and may not be relitigated. (This was the only issue Jim raised in his defense). State X may not retry Jim for robbery of any

of the other workers. Choice **A** is legally incorrect (the prosecution is ordinarily ***not*** obliged to bring all criminal charges arising from a single incident or occurrence in one case). Unless double jeopardy has attached, a sovereign may bring several different prosecutions against an individual as a consequence of a single occurrence or incident (provided each subsequent charge requires proof of at least one element which was not resolved in the earlier trial). Choice **C** is incorrect because, while factually accurate (the charge against Jim for the robbery of Allan does constitute a different case), Jim cannot be prosecuted because the "alibi" issue has been litigated and resolved in Jim's favor. Finally, Choice **D** is incorrect because, while there may be different issues in the case against Jim for the robbery of Allan, resolution of the "alibi" issue in Jim's favor precludes his prosecution for the offense in question.

69. **B** An identification procedure which is so suggestive as to create a substantial likelihood of misidentification at trial is violative of due process. Under this principle, an in-court identification which is predicated upon an unlawful out-of-court identification is not admissible; *Stovall v. Denno*, 388 U.S. 293 (1967). Although Jones was taller than each of the other participants in the lineup (they were between 5'9" and 6'2"), this disparity would probably not by itself be deemed so unnecessarily suggestive as to create a substantial likelihood of misidentification. However, Green's question to Witness, "What about the guy standing to his right?" is very suggestive, and undermines the purpose of a lineup. The height disparity and Green's question, taken together, would probably lead a court to conclude that the whole procedure was unduly suggestive, in which case the identification of Jones by Witness would be excluded at trial. (*See* ELO Ch.6-V.) Choice **A** is incorrect because Jones did not have a right to counsel at that time because he had not been formally charged with a crime. Choice **C** is incorrect because the undue suggestiveness was a constitutional violation. Finally, Choice **D** is incorrect. If the police lacked probable cause to arrest Jones, his objection to this evidence would be sustained (*i.e.*, the identification at the lineup would have been derived from an illegal arrest).

70. **A** Pursuant to a valid arrest, police may search the area within the suspect's immediate control; *Chimel v. California*, 395 U.S. 752 (1969). (*See* ELO Ch.3-III(B).) Because (1) Witness identified Bad Lad as the person who had robbed him that morning, and (2) Bad Lad immediately attempted to flee, Officer Green had probable cause to arrest Bad Lad. As a result, items found in Bad Lad's outer garments would be admissible against him. Choice **B** is incorrect because an arrest which is based upon probable cause ordinarily requires no warrant (unless effectuated

in the suspect's home or for a misdemeanor committed outside the arresting officer's presence). Choice **C** is incorrect because *Miranda* warnings need not be given prior to the search of an individual pursuant to a valid arrest. Finally, Choice **D** is incorrect. The fact that Green had taunted Bad Lad into discharging his civic duties and cooperating in a legitimate police activity could not reasonably be construed as inducing an unlawful detention.

71. **B**   Evidence derived from a custodial interrogation is inadmissible in the prosecution's case-in-chief, unless voluntarily obtained and preceded by adequate *Miranda* warnings. But no interrogation had taken place here (Bad Lad simply blurted out the statement, "I might as well confess"). The fact that *Miranda* warnings had not yet been given does not preclude Bad Lad's statement from being admitted into evidence. (*See* ELO Ch.5-VII(A)(2).) Choice **A** is incorrect because no interrogation had occurred and *Miranda* warnings were not necessary. Choice **C** is incorrect because, as we've discussed, no illegal detention had occurred. Finally, Choice **D** is incorrect because Bad Lad (even if indigent) was not entitled to the appointment of counsel until he was formally charged, an event which had not yet occurred.

72. **A**   Police may ***not*** make a warrantless arrest of an individual in her home, unless exigent circumstances exist; *Welsh v. Wisconsin*, 466 U.S. 740 (1984). Since exigent circumstances were not present, Mel was obliged to obtain an arrest warrant before arresting Ann in her home. (*See* ELO Ch.3-II(A)). Choice **B** is incorrect because approval by a law officer, even a U.S. Attorney, does not negate the necessity for following the procedures necessary for a valid arrest warrant. Choice **C** is incorrect. Probable cause alone is not sufficient to justify arrest of a suspect in her own home; exigent circumstances must exist. Finally, Choice **D** is incorrect because, even if Ann's conduct constituted a felony, a warrant was necessary to effectuate the arrest in her home.

73. **D**   When consent to enter premises is obtained on the basis of a lie or false statement, the consent is ordinarily invalid. Because Mel obtained entrance to Ann's house by means of a ruse (*i.e.*, representing that he was one of her friends), his entrance into the house was invalid. (*See* ELO Ch.3-VII(F).) Choice **A** is incorrect because, in the absence of consent, Mel needed a warrant to enter Ann's home to arrest her (even if probable cause existed). Choice **B** is factually incorrect; Suzy did ***not*** consent to Mel's entry into the apartment (she tried to slam the door on him). Finally, Choice **C** is factually incorrect (the facts do not indicate that exigent circumstances existed).

74. **B**   Evidence derived from an unlawful search or seizure is ordinarily inadmissible. (*See* ELO Ch.7-I(A).) Because Mel was not lawfully in Ann's house and could not lawfully arrest her, the prosecution can not utilize or assert the "plain view" doctrine. (*See* ELO Ch.3-V(B).) Choice **A** is incorrect because the machine was not in "plain view." Mel had no right to be in the place which enabled him to see it. Choice **C** is incorrect because Mel could not lawfully seize any evidence, whether or not it was within her immediate control. Finally, Choice **D** is incorrect. Had the arrest been proper Mel would have been able to seize the evidence (*i.e.*, the machine) which was within Ann's control without a search warrant.

75. **C**   Under a valid search warrant, police are permitted to scan the entire premises if they have reasonable suspicion that an armed accomplice is present; *Maryland v. Buie*, 494 U.S. 325 (1990). (*See* ELO Ch.3-III(E).) Because Mel had a reasonable suspicion that Ann's "violence-prone boyfriend" might be present, he had a right to conduct a "sweep" of the premises to locate the boyfriend, including the closed closet (a good hiding place) where the gun was found. Choice **A** is incorrect because, having obtained a valid search warrant, Mel was entitled to enter the apartment. Choice **B** is incorrect because the fact that the shotgun was not directly connected to the counterfeiting scheme, alone, would not invalidate its seizure (*e.g.*, if it were in plain view, it could be seized as contraband). Finally, Choice **D** is incorrect for the same reasons that Choice **C** is correct.

76. **C**   When a search warrant specifies the items to be found, police officers may not search into areas in which the items cannot possibly be located. Because the stenography machine could not possibly have been enclosed within the jewelry box, Mel had no authority to open the box (even though it was in Ann's bedroom). Choice **A** is incorrect because it is overly broad. Officers executing a search warrant may seize items not described in the warrant if they are related to criminal activity and in plain view. Choice **B** is incorrect. Although the jewelry box was in plain view, Mel had no right to open it because the warrant was limited to the machine and the box could not reasonably be related to the crime of counterfeiting. Choice **D** is incorrect because, in addition to the machine, Mel was entitled to seize any contraband or potential evidence which was in "plain view," but not to open closed containers that could not have contained any item listed on the warrant or been related to criminal activity. ELO Ch. 2-V(G)(6)-(7)).

77. **D**   Evidence seized pursuant to a valid search warrant is admissible.
Because the warrant permitted Mel to search Ann's bedroom, Mel could
lawfully search the entire room until (1) the item was located, or (2) the
entire area had been investigated. Choice **A** is incorrect because the warrant entitled Mel to search Ann's entire bedroom, including closets, if
necessary, to locate the machine. Choice **B** is incorrect because the fact
that the item wasn't where Mel had previously seen it did not affect his
authority to search the entire bedroom. Finally, Choice **C** is incorrect
because Ann's consent was not material or necessary to the search. Mel
was proceeding under the authority of a valid search warrant.

78. **B**   Under the "plain view" doctrine, when a lawfully positioned police
officer sees (hears or smells) an item which (relying on his knowledge
or experience) he has probable cause to believe is (1) contraband, or (2)
the proceeds or instrumentalities of a crime, he may seize the item;
Texas v. Brown, 460 U.S. 730 (1983). Because Mel had the right to
search Ann's entire bedroom (including the closet), he was able to
observe the counterfeit bills from a vantage point which he had a right to
be in. (*See* ELO Ch.3-V(B)(1).) Mel had probable cause to believe that
the bills were counterfeit (*i.e.*, they were near the machine and people do
not normally throw real currency onto a closet floor). (*See* ELO Ch.3-
V(B)(2).) Choice **A** is factually incorrect. As discussed above, Mel had
probable cause to believe that the bills were counterfeit and, thus, contraband. After all, Mel's concern was to obtain proof of the crime of
counterfeiting. Choice **C** is incorrect because, while factually true (an
Assistant United States Attorney can not expand the scope of a search
warrant), the counterfeit bills were in plain view. Finally, Choice **D** is
factually incorrect (Mel's warrant covered the machine, not the counterfeit bills).

79. **D**   The Fourth Amendment prohibits unreasonable searches and seizures by
federal officers. Because Mel is a federal governmental official, Ann's
objection would be asserted under the Fourth Amendment. (*See* ELO
Ch.2-I(A).) Choice **A** is incorrect because the Fifth Amendment protects
individuals only from compelled disclosures of a testimonial nature.
Choice **B** is incorrect because the police may obtain a warrant to search
for additional evidence even after a person is arrested. (In any event, it's
not clear from the facts whether Ann had actually been arrested.)
Finally, Choice **C** is incorrect because the Fourteenth Amendment
applies to actions by the state.

80. **C** Police may not ordinarily detain someone without a warrant for the purpose of questioning him unless they have an articulable, objective basis for believing that criminal activity may be underway; *Terry v. Ohio*, 392 U.S. 1 (1968). This exception to the requirement of probable cause has been extended to investigations of ***completed crimes*** when the police have a "***reasonable suspicion***, grounded in specific and articulable facts," that a person was involved in the previous crime; *U.S. v. Hensley*, 469 U.S. 221 (1985). (*See* ELO Ch.3-IX(K).) Because Hoover had heard a rumor that Doyle had knowingly received stolen money, he had a reasonable suspicion of Doyle, and, therefore, was permitted to detain him in a "stop and frisk," even though Hoover lacked probable cause (a rumor would not constitute substantial reason to believe that Doyle had received stolen money). Choice **A** is incorrect because Hoover had not arrested Doyle at the time of the search, but had merely detained him as part of a "stop and frisk." Therefore, the search was not incident to arrest. Choice **B** is incorrect because Hoover told Doyle that he was a suspect and instructed him to raise his hands; Doyle was not asked whether he consented to the search. Choice **D** is incorrect because, as stated above, the detention was valid and reasonable, based on Hoover's reasonable suspicion.

81. **D** When a vehicle is at rest on a public street and the police have probable cause to believe that it contains contraband or evidence of a crime, a warrantless search of the vehicle and its contents may be made, limited in scope, however, to the search that would be authorized by a judicial officer. Hoover saw the contents of Doyle's car as he was leading him away after Doyle's arrest. He was also able to see that the car matched the description of the getaway car and had the same license plate. Hoover had probable cause to believe the car would yield evidence of the robbery and was justified in searching it. *U.S. v. Ross,* 456 U.S. 798 (1982). Choice **B** is factually incorrect (Doyle had been arrested, and, therefore, was not "at large"). If the suspect referred to was not Doyle but Fingers, the fact that Fingers might have a key to the ignition would not justify a warrantless search of Doyle's car. Choice **C** is incorrect because the circumstances constitute an exception to the rule requiring a warrant to search and seize personal property. Choice **A** is incorrect because it's not as good an answer as D. Although the search of the car followed almost immediately on the heels of Doyle's arrest, Doyle was not in control of the car at the moment of the arrest. For this reason, it cannot be said that the search was incident to the arrest.

82. **B**   Provided probable cause exists, an arrest by a police officer is valid
without a warrant, unless made (1) within the suspect's home, or (2) for
a misdemeanor perpetrated outside the arresting officer's presence; *Payton v. New York*, 445 U.S. 573 (1980). Because Fingers was at his home
and no exigent circumstances existed, Hoover was obliged to obtain an
arrest warrant. (*See* ELO Ch.3-II(A)). Choice **A** is incorrect because
there is no right to arrest a person in his home simply because there is an
outstanding warrant to search the home, unless there is also an outstanding arrest warrant. (The police are, however, entitled to detain the persons in lawful possession of an area being searched pursuant to a lawful
search warrant; *Michigan v. Summers*, 452 U.S. 692 (1981)). (*See* ELO
Ch.3-IX(J).) Choice **C** is incorrect. Although Hoover may have had
probable cause to arrest Fingers, he was obliged to obtain an arrest warrant in this instance (Fingers was in his own home). Finally, Choice **D** is
incorrect because an arrest warrant is required for an arrest made at the
suspect's home without exigent circumstances.

83. **B**   Searches of areas which were intended to be covered by a search warrant (but which, because of an error in transcription, are not accurately
described in the warrant) are ordinarily valid. Hoover's entry into Finger's home was valid because the home was the target of the search and
the location which the warrant was meant to describe. (*See* ELO Ch.2-V(D)(1).) Choice **A** is factually incorrect. Hoover did *not* gain entry by a
ruse. Although Hoover misrepresented his identity when he announced
his presence at Fingers' home, he described his authority and purpose
accurately before entering the premises. Choice **C** is incorrect because
the fact that there may be a firearm on the premises does not, in itself,
constitute "exigent circumstances" entitling a police officer to enter a
dwelling without a warrant. Hoover was not in hot pursuit of Fingers,
there was no indication that Fingers had the gun in his possession, (on
the contrary, Badluck had told Hoover the gun was in a closet), and
Hoover was not in danger of death or injury. Finally, Choice **D** is incorrect because the error in transcription probably would not make the
search invalid. A warrant which is issued in good faith can support the
search and seizure of evidence, even though probable cause was lacking;
U.S. v. Leon, 468 U.S. 897 (1984). *A fortiori*, an error in the warrant
which did not prevent the police from identifying and searching the correct premises would not appear to affect the validity of the warrant and
of the resulting search. (*See* ELO Ch.2-V(H).)

84. **D**   Under the "plain view" doctrine, when a lawfully positioned police
officer sees (hears or smells) an object which he has probable cause to
believe is (1) contraband, or (2) the proceeds or instrumentalities of a

crime, he may seize the item. Because Hoover had no reason to believe that the envelope contained evidence of a crime, his seizure of that item was invalid. (*See* ELO Ch.3-V(B)(2).) Choice **A** is incorrect because, under a valid search warrant, police may seize, in addition to the items described in the warrant, all contraband or instrumentalities of crime which are in plain view. Choice **B** is incorrect because, although the envelope was in plain view from a position which Hoover had a right to occupy, Hoover had no reason to suspect that it was related to the bank robbery. Finally, Choice **C** is incorrect because (1) the arrest of Fingers was probably invalid, and (2) the facts fail to indicate that the envelope was within Fingers' control.

85. **A**   Evidence derived from an illegal arrest is ordinarily inadmissible. While the information supplied by Badluck may have been sufficient for a search warrant, it did not meet the requirements for probable cause to arrest. If Hoover had found incriminating evidence under the search warrant, then probable cause would have existed to arrest Fingers. Because Fingers was arrested *before* any incriminating evidence was discovered, his arrest was invalid. (*See* ELO Ch.2-III(B)(2).) "But for" the illegal arrest of Fingers and the resulting "privilege" by Hoover to accompany Fingers through the house (a police officer has a right to "accompany" the prisoner after a valid arrest), Hoover would have no right to enter Fingers' bedroom, since the search warrant was limited to the living room. Choice **B** is incorrect as overbroad. Instrumentalities of a crime (such as the wig) may be seized (even though they are not specifically described in the warrant), if they are in plain view in the area described in the warrant. Choice **C** is incorrect because a typographical error does not render a search warrant constitutionally defective; only a deliberate falsehood or reckless disregard of the truth by the affiant will render a search warrant constitutionally invalid. Finally, Choice **D** is incorrect. The rule is that items within the suspect's control may be seized under a valid arrest warrant, but Fingers' arrest was probably *not* valid. He was arrested in his home without an arrest warrant, and before probable cause to arrest was established. (*See* ELO Ch.3-II(A).)

86. **A**   Any individual who makes statements to another individual is deemed to assume the risk that his trust may be "misplaced," *i.e.,* that the individual will disclose his statements and even testify against him as to their content. Because Brawler's statements to Smitch were made voluntarily, they can be used against him, even though they were recorded without his consent or knowledge; *United States v. White*, 401 U.S. 745 (1971). (*See* ELO Ch.4-IV(C)-(D).) Choices B, C, and D are incorrect because no violation of Brawler's constitutional rights occurred. Choice

B is incorrect because, even though Smitch would be deemed to be a governmental agent (he was acting under the police's supervision), no Fourth Amendment right ordinarily exists with respect to statements made voluntarily by one individual to another. Choice **C** is incorrect because Brawler's statements were not obtained by the FBI in a compulsory or involuntary manner. Therefore, no Fifth Amendment due process rights were implicated. Also, no *Miranda* violation occurred. Although statements made in response to police questioning are inadmissible at trial if the statements resulted from a custodial interrogation which was not preceded by adequate *Miranda* warnings, here, *Miranda* warnings were not required. Brawler was not in custody. Finally, Choice **D** is incorrect. Brawler's Sixth Amendment rights had not matured because Brawler had not yet been formally charged with a crime.

87. **C**   To have standing to object to an allegedly unreasonable search or seizure, an accused must have a reasonable expectation of privacy in the area searched or the items seized; *Rakas v. Illinois*, 439 U.S. 128 (1978). Because Chiseler did not own the automobile in question, he had no expectation of privacy with respect to it and could not object to its search. (*See* ELO Ch.7-II(C).) Choice **A** is incorrect. Even though the FBI proceeded without a warrant, Employer is the only party who can object to the warrantless seizure of his car. Choice **B** is incorrect. Chiseler has no standing to raise the issue of probable cause or any other issue arising from the seizure of Employer's car. Finally, Choice **D** is incorrect. Chiseler has no standing to raise this issue either, and, in any event, the facts fail to indicate that evidence would have been lost or destroyed if the police had failed to seize the vehicle immediately.

88. **D**   To have standing to object to an unreasonable seizure, an accused must have a reasonable expectation of privacy in the items seized. Chiseler lost control of his wallet when he left it in Employer's car. Even though the wallet belonged to Chiseler, his expectation of privacy in the item ceased when he lost control of it. Therefore, Chiseler lacks standing to object to the seizure of his wallet and cannot suppress it. (*See* ELO Ch.2-II(C)(2)(b).) Choice **A** is incorrect because only Employer can object to an invalid search and seizure of his vehicle. Choice **B** is incorrect. Although the wallet was Chiseler's property, Chiseler had no expectation of privacy with respect to the contents of Employer's car. Finally, Choice **C** is incorrect because only Employer can object to a warrantless search and seizure of his car.

89. **A**   A ***voluntary*** statement obtained in violation of an accused's Fifth
Amendment right to *Miranda* warnings may be used to impeach the
accused if he testifies in his defense at trial; *Harris v. New York*, 401
U.S. 222 (1971). Since Chiseler chose to take the stand in his own
defense, his statement to the police in response to their inquiry could be
used to impeach him, despite the lack of *Miranda* warnings. (*See* ELO
Ch.5-XII(B).) Choice **B** is incorrect. While factually true (Chiseler's
statement did not specifically bear upon any of the elements of the crime
of bank robbery), it would tend only to contradict his testimony (unless
Chiseler lived on the Mexican border, he could not drive Employer's car
on the day of the robbery and be in Mexico on the same day). The statement is therefore inadmissible as substantive evidence but admissible
for impeachment purposes. Choice **C** is incorrect because, if Chiseler's
statement was made involuntarily, it would be inadmissible for all purposes. Thus, Choice **C** provides a justification for excluding (rather than
admitting) Chiseler's statement. Finally, Choice **D** is incorrect because a
voluntary statement made in response to a custodial interrogation is
admissible for impeachment purposes, even though the suspect was not
given *Miranda* warnings.

90. **C**   The admission of illegally seized evidence at trial ordinarily necessitates
reversal of an adverse judgment against the accused, unless the prosecution can show, beyond a reasonable doubt, that the evidence did not contribute to the conviction (*i.e.*, that the error was harmless); *Chapman v.
California*, 386 U.S. 18 (1967). Choice **A** is incorrect because "harmless" errors, even those of constitutional dimensions, do not necessarily
require reversal. Choice **B** is legally incorrect (prejudicial errors other
than admission into evidence of involuntary confessions or a prejudiced
judge, may necessitate reversal of an adverse judgment against the
defendant). Finally, Choice **D** is not as good an answer as Choice **C**.
Choice **C** is a more accurate statement of the law, and, thus, the correct
answer.

91. **A**   After a person has been validly arrested and booked, the police may
make an "inventory" search of his person and his clothes, and of any
items he may be carrying. The purpose of an inventory search is to avoid
a claim that the accused's property is later mislaid or appropriated by the
police and to confiscate dangerous weapons. The search does not
require a warrant; the need to obtain an inventory of a prisoner's personal effects provides its own rationale for seizing and searching those
effects; *Illinois v. Lafayette*, 462 U.S. 640 (1983). Since Mark's arrest
was valid, his personal effects were properly inventoried and are admissible at trial. (*See* ELO Ch.3-III(G)(2)(b).) Choice **B** is incorrect because

an inventory search may be made whether or not *Miranda* rights have been waived. Choice **C** is incorrect because no search warrant is necessary for an inventory search. Finally, Choice **D** is incorrect. The suspect's consent to an inventory search is not necessary.

92. **B**   Incident to a valid arrest, the police may make a full search of the area within the suspect's immediate control in order to prevent him from destroying evidence. It's not necessary to a valid search that the police officer fear for his own safety; *Chimel v. California,* 395 U.S. 752 (1969). Because Jason "matched" the perpetrator's description, and was running in the direction pointed out by the cashier, Officer Johnson had probable cause to arrest him. The search was incident to a valid arrest and the area within Jason's immediate control, including Jason's person himself, could be searched. (*See* ELO Ch.3-III(B)(2)(a).) Choice **A** is incorrect because "reasonable suspicion" only entitles a police officer to question a possible suspect; it does not justify an arrest. Choice **C** is incorrect because no warrant was needed for a search on these facts. Finally, Choice **D** is incorrect because a recitation of *Miranda* rights is not necessary for a valid search in these circumstances.

93. **C**   Neither the prosecution (nor the judge) may make any adverse comment to the jury about the refusal of a criminal defendant to testify. Upon a defense request, the jury must be advised that no adverse inference may be drawn from an accused's failure to testify. Therefore, the prosecution may not comment upon Jack's failure to testify. (*See* ELO Ch.9-VII(D)(2).) Choice **A** is incorrect because no comment may be made about an accused's failure to testify. Choice **B** is incorrect for the same reason. Finally, Choice **D** is incorrect. The jury must be advised, if the defense requests the instruction, that no adverse inference may be drawn from a criminal defendant's failure to testify.

94. **B**   Police comments which are reasonably calculated to elicit an incriminating response by a suspect constitute interrogation for purposes of interpreting and applying the *Miranda* rule; *Rhode Island v. Innis,* 446 U.S. 291 (1980). If the police officer's comment about Cynthia was designed to provoke an incriminating response from Phyllis and a *Miranda* statement was not made, Phyllis' statement will be inadmissible. (*See* ELO Ch.5-VII(A)(3).) Choice **A** is incorrect because police officers are permitted to talk with a suspect prior to giving her *Miranda* warnings. The prosecution is, however, precluded from utilizing any response to the questions by the defendant (except for impeachment purposes). Choice **C** is incorrect because Phyllis did not waive her Miranda rights. She was never given *Miranda* warnings. Finally, Choice **D** is

incorrect because Phyllis' response to the comment is not a "blurt-out." A blurt-out occurs where a suspect makes a comment without being subjected to a police interrogation.

95. **D**   To constitute an interrogation within the *Miranda* rule, the defendant must not only be under arrest but must also be the object of questioning by a police officer. Interrogation by private citizens does not invoke the rule. (*See* ELO Ch.5-VII(D).) Some courts have included probation officers and IRS agents in the category of police officers, but no court has extended the designation to firemen. The remark by the fireman did not constitute an interrogation, and the facts show that Gina was not asked a question by any police officer. The correct answer is Choice **D**. Choice **A** is wrong because it's immaterial to *Miranda* issues whether the arrest was under a warrant. So long as the defendant is in custody, *Miranda* applies. Choice **B** is wrong because it's inconsistent with the facts. There is nothing to indicate that the fireman's remark was part of a calculated police plan to draw a confession from Gina. The fireman was acting on his own. Choice **C** is incorrect. Even if Gina had been given her *Miranda* rights, this would not have constituted an interrogation. Further, if we assume Gina had received her *Miranda* warning before her outburst, as the question suggests, she probably waived them by responding to the fireman's remark.

96. **A**   Evidence derived from a custodial interrogation is admissible, even in the absence of prior *Miranda* warnings, if there is a risk to the public safety at the time of questioning (and especially if the questioning helps to eliminate the risk); *New York v. Quarles,* 467 U.S. 649 (1984). Because the police knew that Madolyn had used a gun and had reason to believe that the gun was hidden either on her person or somewhere in the premises, the police officer's questioning was proper and the gun is probably admissible. (*See* ELO Ch.5-VIII(B).) Choice **B** is incorrect because *Miranda* warnings are not necessary under these circumstances. Choice **C** is incorrect because the police had probable cause to arrest Madolyn because she and her Rolls fit the description given by the store manager and because she attempted to flee. Finally, Choice **D** is incorrect because questioning someone "sternly" about a public safety hazard does not constitute obtaining information in a coercive manner.

97. **B**   The question assumes that Marcus was not given his *Miranda* rights at any stage prior to the conversation with Tony. Tony was acting as a police agent and his questions must be construed as interrogation by a police officer. Once a person has been formally charged with a crime, he is entitled to have an attorney present at every critical stage of the case

thereafter; *Moore v. Illinois,* 434 U.S. 220 (1977). Because Marcus had been charged and was out on bail, he was entitled to have an attorney present at every stage of police questioning. (*See* ELO Ch.6-III(B).) Choice **A** is incorrect because evidence is not necessarily inadmissible because it's been obtained by tricking the defendant. (If Marcus had not previously been charged, his statement to Tony would be admissible.) Choice **C** is incorrect because Tony was acting as agent for the police. Finally, Choice **D** is incorrect because although no longer in custody, Marcus had been charged with a crime and was entitled to legal representation prior to police questioning.

98. **B**   The double jeopardy clause of the Fifth Amendment, applicable to the states via the Fourteenth Amendment, precludes prosecution by any sovereign for a crime previously charged and tried by that sovereign. For purposes of this definition, each state is a separate sovereign from every other state and the federal government is a separate sovereign from each state. In this case, because the former prosecution was conducted in a state court, double jeopardy does not bar retrial of Baldonado for similar federal crimes in a federal court, even though the facts giving rise to each set of crimes may be similar. (*See* ELO Ch.9-VIII(G).) (Note, however, that federal prosecutors will not always prosecute when there has already been a state prosecution for substantially the same act or acts. In this case, a RICO prosecution is really different in nature from the specific crime of extortion and, under the circumstances, the prosecutor would not be reluctant to prosecute.) Choice **A** is incorrect because there is no necessity under double jeopardy rules that the federal crimes contain an additional legal element to the state court offense. Choice **C** is incorrect because, as explained above, double jeopardy does not bar Baldonado's federal prosecution. Finally, Choice **D** is incorrect because prosecution is not barred even if there is a common element in the crimes charged in the state and federal courts.

99. **C**   The double jeopardy doctrine draws from the principles of collateral estoppel. When an issue of ultimate fact--in this case, that Madison was not at the scene of the crime--has been determined by the jury in one criminal trial, that issue cannot again be litigated in any future trial by the same sovereign; *Ashe v. Swenson,* 397 U.S. 436 (1970). The issue whether Madison had an alibi or not was resolved in his favor by the jury at the initial trial. It was established that Madison was two hours away at the time of the crime. He may not be prosecuted for the murder of the other two coeds, even if the prosecution is later able to prove that Sheila committed perjury. (*See* ELO Ch.9- VIII(E)(1). Choice **D** is incorrect because the prosecution is not permitted to challenge a jury's

verdict after acquittal, even if the essential testimony was perjured. Choice **A** is incorrect because double jeopardy does preclude a second prosecution after a jury verdict of acquittal on the same facts. Finally, Choice **B** is incorrect because the double jeopardy principle (which encompasses *res judicata* and collateral estoppel) are applicable even as to different victims if the jury has already accepted as fact an element which results in acquittal.

100. **A**   Under the Sixth Amendment, the right to counsel for a criminally accused indigent exists for both felonies and misdemeanors, but only when imprisonment, however short, is actually imposed; *Scott v. Illinois,* 440 U.S. 367 (1979). If the sentence is a fine or probation, the defendant is not entitled to counsel even if the offense is one which can be punished by imprisonment. Because Margot was not actually imprisoned, she had no constitutional right to appointed counsel. (*See* ELO Ch.8-III(A)(2).) Choice **B** is incorrect because an indigent accused is entitled to appointed counsel even when a misdemeanor is involved, if the charge results in imprisonment. The right to appointed counsel exists as long as imprisonment occurs. Choice **C** is incorrect because Margot was not imprisoned. Finally, Choice **D** is incorrect. The fact of conviction is immaterial. What matters is whether the defendant is imprisoned or not.

101. **A**   In the absence of exigent circumstances, such as the imminent destruction of evidence, the threat of harm to persons, or a search in "hot pursuit" of a suspect, an arrest warrant is constitutionally required before the police may enter private premises to arrest a suspect. Although Carla had observed Douglas committing several misdemeanors, there were no exigent circumstances allowing Carla to enter Douglas' house without a warrant. Once Douglas had entered his home, Carla was obliged to obtain an arrest warrant. (*See* ELO Ch.3-II(A)). Because Carla had not obtained a warrant, the arrest was invalid and Douglas' subsequent confession was inadmissible. Choice **B** is incorrect because the fact that a suspect appears distraught does not prevent the police from questioning him. Choice **C** is incorrect because Douglas could not waive his *Miranda* rights under the circumstances of an illegal arrest. Finally, Choice **D** is incorrect, since (even though she had seen him commit several misdemeanors) Carla was constitutionally obliged to obtain an arrest warrant prior to entering Douglas' home. An arrest warrant is constitutionally required when police wish to enter private premises to arrest a suspect.

102. **D** A defendant may assert the exclusionary rule only to bar evidence
obtained through a violation of his own constitutional rights. And, in
search and seizure cases, a defendant may seek to exclude evidence
derived from an illegal search or seizure only if his "legitimate expectation of privacy" was violated; *Rakas v. Illinois,* 439 U.S. 128 (1978).
Because Stan gave the duffle bag to Marcus, he had no right to prevent
Marcus or anyone else from looking through the bag, and he may not
claim that his legitimate expectation of privacy was violated when the
police searched the bag. (*See* ELO Ch.2-II(E); Ch.7-II(C)(1).) Therefore, even if the police had no right to question Marcus, Stan lacks
standing to object to that questioning because his constitutional rights
were not violated. The cocaine is admissible. Choice **C** is incorrect,
because the police probably lacked suspicion reasonably necessary to
stop and question Marcus. The mere fact that he was carrying a duffle
bag and peering at addresses does not suggest that he was involved in
any illegal activity. (*See* ELO Ch.3-IX(D).) Choice **A** is incorrect
because, if there was no basis for stopping and questioning Marcus, his
reply to the police questioning would ordinarily be inadmissible.
Finally, Choice **B** is incorrect because Marcus was not entitled to
Miranda rights (*i.e.*, he was not in custody at the time of the officer's
question) and Stan lacked standing to object.

103. **D** A police officer must obtain a warrant before he can arrest someone who
has committed a misdemeanor out of his presence. If Officer Johnson
did not have an arrest warrant, his arrest (and subsequent questioning) of
Anita was impermissible. (*See* ELO Ch.3-II(B)(2)). Choice **C** is incorrect because Officer Johnson had no right to ask Anita any questions at
all. The results of his questioning constituted "fruits of the poisonous
tree." Had Anita's arrest been valid, Officer Johnson would not have
been obliged to cease asking her questions unless she asserted her Fifth
Amendment rights. Choice **B** is incorrect because Officer Johnson was
required to obtain a warrant to arrest Anita whether or not he had probable cause. Choice **A** is incorrect because Anita's confession is inadmissible even though it may have been made voluntarily.

Table of Cases

U.S. v. — see name of party

Index

References are to the number of the question raising the issue.
"E" indicates an Essay Question; "M" indicates a Multiple-Choice Question

Confessions
See also Miranda warnings; Self-incrimination
Cat out of the bag argument, E5, E18
Voluntariness, E5

Confrontation, right of
Death, statements made in contemplation of, E16
Self-incrimination, E1, E9

Consent and approval
Arrest, entry onto premises, M73
Search and seizure, E8, E13-E15, E17, E18, E20, E21, M3

Contempt, refusal to comply with subpoena of grand jury, M31

Counsel, right to
Generally, E7, E9, M20, M55, M59, M63
Blood samples, E6
Critical stages, E6, E9
Effectiveness of representation, E6, E11, M47, M60
Grand juries, M30
Habeas corpus, M47
Handwriting exemplars, M2
Identification procedures, E16, M17
Indigent persons, M62, M100
Informants, use of, E10, E16, M36, M97
Out-of-state counsel, representation by, M60
Preliminary hearings, E6
Self-representation, right to, E18, M64
Standby counsel, appointment of, M64

Critical stages of trial, right to counsel, E6, E9

Cruel and unusual punishment
Arrest, use of deadly force to effect, M42
Capital punishment, M25
Contempt, punishment for refusal to answer question, E15
Status, imposition of criminal penalties for, E6

Curtilage of home, search and seizure, M1

Custodial nature of interrogation, *Miranda* warnings, E2, E5, E7, E8, E11, E14, E17, E18, E21, M86

Deadly force, use to effect arrest, M42

Death, statements made in contemplation of, E16

Deception
Arrest or detention, use to effect, M73
Search and seizure, use to effect, E14, M33

Detention
See Arrest or Detention

Discovery of exculpatory evidence, E11

Dog, sniff-test by, E17

Double jeopardy
Generally, E11, E12, M26
Attachment of jeopardy, E12
Collateral estoppel, E11, E12, M5, M51, M68, M99
Dual sovereignty doctrine, E12, M51, M98
Hung jury, effect of, M66, M67
Mistrial, effect of, E12
Recidivism, M65
Same or separate offense, E11, E12, M5, M26
Weight of evidence, reversal based on, M67

Dual sovereignty doctrine, E12, M51, M98

Due process
Bail and recognizance, E3
Discovery, exculpatory evidence, E11
Dual sovereignty doctrine, E12, M51
Governmental overreaching, E7, E9
Handwriting exemplars, M2
Instructions to jury, impropriety with respect to material issue of law, E11
Out-of-state counsel, representation by, M60
Shocking of conscience, M33

Eavesdropping
See Wiretapping and Eavesdropping

Effectiveness of representation, E6, E11, M47, M60

Eighth Amendment
See also Cruel and Unusual Punishment
Applicability to states, E3

Impeachment
Illegally seized evidence, use of, M48
Un-*Mirandized* statement, use of, E19,
M12, M89

Indigent persons
Bail and recognizance, E3
Counsel, right to, M62, M100

Inevitable discovery, search and seizure, E3, E4, E10, E18

Infants
See Children and Minors

Informants
Arrest warrant, issuance on basis of information obtained from, E19, M32
Counsel, right to, E10, E16, M36, M97
Search warrant, issuance on basis of information obtained from informants, E2, E4, E19, E21, M19
Self-incrimination, M86

Instructions to jury
Impropriety with respect to material issue of law, E11
Self-incrimination, instructions regarding failure to testify, M93

Intoxication of declarant, self-incrimination, E18

Inventory searches, E3, E10, E16, M21, M22, M24, M38, M40, M91

Jury trial
See also Grand Juries; Instructions to Jury
Juvenile delinquency proceedings, E15
Number of jurors, M61
Peremptory challenges, M15
Right to jury trial, M54

Juvenile delinquency proceedings
Jury trial, right to, E15
Self-incrimination, E15

Lineups, E16, M69

Metal detectors, search and seizure, E17

Minors
See Children and Minors

***Miranda* warnings**
See also Confessions; Self-incrimination
Generally, E1, E2, M70

Adequacy of warnings, E1
Crime unrelated to arrest, interrogation regarding, M43, M44
Custodial nature of interrogation, E2, E5, E7, E8, E11, E14, E17, E18, E21, M86
Disability affecting accused, effect on waiver, M44
Impeachment, use of statement for, E19, M12, M89
Interrogation, inquiry as, E1, E2, E5, E7, E9, E13, M34, M94, M95
Minor, waiver of rights by, M44
Motor vehicle stops, E5, E18
"Please," use of, E5
Private party, inquiry by, E19, M36, M95
Public safety inquiry, E2, E4, M45, M96
Standing to raise issue, E1, E9
Subsequent confession following un-*Mirandized* first confession, E13
Voluntariness of statement, E7, M45, M71, M94
Waiver of rights, E2, E9, M43, M44, M46, M52

Misplaced property, search and seizure, E9, E20, M88

Mistrial, effect on double jeopardy, E12

Mobile homes, searches of, M39

Motor vehicles
Arrest or detention, E5, E8, E17, E18, M13
Miranda warnings, E5, E18
Search and seizure, E3, E4, E8-E10, E17, E20, M14, M21-M23, M39, M81

Murder scene, search of, M24

Number of jurors, M61

Omnibus Crime Control and Safe Streets Act, wiretaps, M35

Out-of-state counsel, representation by, M60

Pen registers, search and seizure, M49

Peremptory challenges, M15

Permission
See Consent and Approval

Plain sound, search and seizure, E14

The Emanuel Law Outline Series

Each outline in the series is the work of Steven Emanuel.
Each is packed with features that take you from next-day
preparation to night-before-the-exam review. Outlines are
available for all major law school subjects and many are
revised annually. This year, Steve will prepare new editions
of Evidence, Constitutional Law, Torts, Criminal Procedure
and Property.

Available titles
Civil Procedure
Constitutional Law
Contracts
Corporations
Criminal Law
Criminal Procedure
Evidence
Property
Torts (General Edition)
Torts (Prosser Edition)

Law In A Flash Series

Flashcards add a dimension to law school study which
cannot be matched by any other study aid, and these
are the acknowledged leader in flashcards. They make
legal issues and answers stick to your mind like glue.
Each Law In a Flash card set contains 350-625 cards
arranged to give you black-letter principles first. Then
they teach you all the subtleties by taking you through a
series of hypotheticals filled with mnemonics and
checklists. Excellent for exam preparation.

Available titles
Civil Procedure 1
Civil Procedure 2
Constitutional Law
Contracts
Corporations
Criminal Law
Criminal Procedure
Evidence
Federal Income Taxation
Future Interests
Professional Responsibility
Real Property
Sales (UCC Article 2)
Torts
Wills & Trusts

Available at your local bookstore or from us directly at www.aspenpublishers.com